WASHINGTON REMEMBERS WORLD WAR II

PERSONAL ACCOUNTS FROM THE DEADLIEST CONFLICT IN WORLD HISTORY

all the best!

John C. Hughes & Trova Heffernan

Office of the Secretary of State
Legacy Washington

First Edition

Copyright © 2016
Legacy Washington
Office of the Secretary of State
All rights reserved.

ISBN 978-1-889320-37-3

Front cover photo: Bob Hart
Back cover photos: Fred Shiosaki, Arnold Samuels,
Clayton Pitre, Robert Graham, Joe Moser,
George Narozonick, Regina Tollfeldt and Stan Jones
Book Design by Lori Larson
Cover Design by Laura Mott

Printed in the United States of America
by Gorham Printing, Centralia, Washington

To the Washington veterans who served in the war, their families and thousands more who served on the homefront.

Legacy Washington is dedicated to preserving the
history of Washington and its continuing story.
www.sos.wa.gov/legacy

Where the Salmon Run: The Life and Legacy of **Billy Frank Jr.**
Nancy Evans, *First-Rate First Lady*
The Inimitable **Adele Ferguson**
Lillian Walker, *Washington State Civil Rights Pioneer*
Booth Who? A Biography of **Booth Gardner**
Slade Gorton, *a Half Century in Politics*
John Spellman: *Politics Never Broke His Heart*
A Woman First: The Impact of **Jennifer Dunn**
Across the Aisles: **Sid Snyder's** *Remarkable Life in Groceries & Government*
Pressing On: **Two Family-Owned Newspapers** *in the 21st Century*
An Election for the Ages: **Rossi vs. Gregoire**, *2004*
Krist Novoselic: *Of Grunge and Government*
Bonnie J. Dunbar, *PhD: An Adventurous Mind*
Charles Z. Smith: *Trailblazer*
Robert F. Utter: *Justice's Sailor*
Carolyn Dimmick: *A Judge for all Seasons*
The Rev. Dr. **Samuel B. McKinney**, *"We're not in Heaven yet"*
Duane French, *"Pity is just another form of abuse"*
Amy Alvarez-Wampfler and Victor Palencia, *new-generation winemakers*
JoAnn Kauffman, *Roots & Resilience*
Jolene Unsoeld, *"Un-sold"*
Rudy Lopez, *veterans' advocate*
Erik Larson, *our youngest-ever mayor*
Bill Ruckelshaus, *The Conscience of "Mr. Clean"*
Hank Adams, *Native American trailblazer*
Patsy Suhr O'Connell, *Asian American cultural leader*

Contents

Fred Shiosaki
     The Rescue of the Lost Battalion   1

Clayton Pitre
     The Invisible Marine   40

Regina Tollfeldt
     She Gave Them Wings   62

Les Amundson
     18 Months in Captivity   86

George Narozonick
     Sailor on the Longest Day   88

Bob Hart:
     The Odyssey of a "Battling Buzzard"   106

John Robert LaRiviere
     Gunner in the 94th   138

Joe Moser
     Missing in Buchenwald   140

Arnold Samuels
     Eyewitness to the Holocaust   156

Henry Friedman
     Jewish Boy in Hiding   192

Robert Graham
     Country Boy in the South Pacific   194

Stan Jones
     The Atomic Veteran   218

Bibliography   232
Source Notes   240
Index   254
About the Authors   264

A LONG OVERDUE REUNION FOR TWO OLD SOLDIERS. Bob Hart (left) and Fred Shiosaki fought in two of the most legendary battles in military history. In 1944 their paths crossed after weeks of savage combat in Italy. Hart's 517th Parachute Regimental Combat Team was relieved by the all-volunteer Japanese American 442nd Regimental Combat Team. Hart says the men of the 442nd were the sharpest troops he encountered during the war and a sight for sore eyes. Hart went on to fight in the Battle of the Bulge. Shiosaki is one of the few survivors of the rescue of the "Lost Battalion." *Ben Helle/Washington State Archives*

NO GREATER GIFT

I sometimes walk to the World War II monument on the campus of the Washington State Capitol. There, inscribed on granite tiles, are approximately 6,000 names of Washingtonians who gave their lives to defeat tyranny. Twenty-five were awarded the Medal of Honor. They're more than names on a wall; they are heroes of The Greatest Generation.

At this writing, on Veterans Day 2016, there are 24,000 living World War II veterans in Washington State—men and women mostly in their 90s. We are losing approximately 450 each day. This sad reality propelled this book.

Washington Remembers World War II is a tribute to veterans and citizens on the home front—some who represent little-known chapters of the war and others who lived through horrors most of us cannot imagine. Their stories can be difficult to hear, even shocking. Each is vitally important to understanding history's deadliest conflict and its far-reaching impact.

On behalf of the people of Washington, I humbly thank you, our veterans, for your service to this great country. To those featured in this book, I can think of no greater gift to the people of this state than the experiences you have bravely shared.

Kim Wyman

Washington's 15th Secretary of State

FRED SHIOSAKI

The rescue of the Lost Battalion

"Dogface GIs like us could sympathize with the German soldiers. They were living like animals, just like us. You dig a hole; you're wet all day, cold all night, then you get up and shoot some kid your own age."

—Staff Sgt. Fred Shiosaki, 442nd Regimental Combat Team

"You fought not only the enemy, but you fought prejudice and you've won," President Harry S. Truman told the 442nd Regimental Combat Team on July 15, 1946. By then, Fred Shiosaki and most of the other original members of the 442nd had been discharged from the Army. *National Archives*

Fred Shiosaki, a high school senior, was doing his homework and listening to the radio. It was December 7, 1941, a cold, gray Sunday in Spokane. Shortly before noon, an announcer broke in. "We interrupt this program to bring you a special news bulletin: The Japanese have attacked Pearl Harbor Hawaii by air, President Roosevelt has just announced."

Fred's father, who ran the laundry below their tiny apartment, was in the next room. "Hey, Pop," Fred said. "The Japanese have attacked Hawaii!"

Nearly 1,200 sailors and Marines died on the *USS Arizona* at Pearl Harbor on December 7, 1941. *National Archives*

Kisaburo Shiosaki was at first skeptical. Then, as more details came in, he predicted, "It's not going to last long." By supper time, however, with the Japanese reportedly advancing everywhere in the Pacific, Fred remembers that his parents were visibly shaken. Their firstborn, 24-year-old George, was attending college in Japan. What would happen to their family now? The five Shiosaki children were U.S. citizens, second-generation *Nisei* (nee-say). But Kisaburo and his wife Tori, were *Issei* (e-say)—immigrants who couldn't even own property. Now they all had the face of the enemy in a city that was 99.1 percent white.

Across the state at Grays Harbor, Natsu Saito, a widow who ran an Asian import shop, was getting ready for church. Her oldest son, Lincoln, was in Tokyo studying for the ministry. Two FBI agents in fedoras and trench coats soon took her into custody as a suspected spy. The captain of a Japanese ship docked at the port reportedly had asked her for maps. Mrs. Saito vehemently denied being disloyal. The agents insisted she had "patriotic ties to Japan," never mind that her sons bore the names of great Americans. Her No. 2 son, Perry, had to rush home from college at Pullman to care for his younger siblings. It was two frightening weeks before they learned their mother was being held in Seattle.

The Saitos and 120,000 other American Japanese were sent to concentration camps. "A Jap's a Jap," said the general heading the Western Defense Command. "It makes no difference whether he's an American citizen or not. I don't want any of them here."

The Shiosakis, by virtue of living east of the Cascades, were allowed to stay in Spokane, but they sent two sons into combat. Staff Sgt. Fred Akira Shiosaki, whose story this is, won a Bronze Star and Purple Heart with the U.S. Army's 442nd Regimental Combat Team. Comprised of Japanese American volunteers from Hawaii and the mainland, the "Go for Broke" 442nd is one of the most decorated units in American military history: twenty-one Medals of Honor and nearly 10,000 Purple Hearts. Its rescue of the "Lost Battalion," an infantry outfit surrounded by Germans in the long, cold winter of 1944, is legendary. And for good reason. Shiosaki's platoon pushed ahead through murderous machine-gun and artillery fire. "Chills went up our spines when we saw the Nisei soldiers," one grateful white GI said. Though their average height was only 5-3, "honestly, they looked like giants to us." Company K of the Third Battalion of the 442nd went into the Vosges mountains with 186 men and came out with 17. Miraculously, Shiosaki was only slightly wounded. "I looked around and said, 'Goddamn, this is all we have left?' Some of those guys had saved my skin and I'm pretty sure I saved some of theirs. So we were really blood brothers. How do you mourn when you lose five guys in your platoon? You're just numb. I cried inside."

It's said that war is hell. Shiosaki was there and back. At 92, Fred is a slightly stooped old infantryman with lovely manners, an infectious laugh and a good memory, though there are some things he'd like to forget. Fred shakes his head over the friends he lost and rails at the "stupid sonofabitch" generals on both sides who saw young men as expendable. "Dogface GIs like us could sympathize with the German soldiers. They were living like animals, just like us. You dig a hole; you're wet all day, cold all night, then you get up and shoot some kid your own age."

Have you ever heard it put better than that?

Fred Shiosaki is such a gentle, well-spoken man that when his jaws clench and profanity emerges like a hiss you know you're hearing the authentic voice of the GI's who were doing the dying. Listen carefully, too, because time is the enemy now.

IRONIES ABOUND in the stories of the Japanese Americans who fought the Nazis and Imperial Japan while back home, fathers, mothers, brothers and sisters were living in tarpaper huts at desolate camps ringed with barbed wire and guard towers.

Fred "Rosie" Shiosaki as a 19-year-old infantryman.
Fred Shiosaki collection

The "relocation center" plan was authorized by a president who in his 1941 State of the Union Address pledged "the preservation of civil liberties for all."

Only one cabinet member, Interior Secretary Harold Ickes, decried "these fancy-named concentration camps."

Earl Warren, the California attorney general who pushed for internment, went on to become chief justice of the U.S. Supreme Court that unanimously struck down state-sanctioned racism—segregated schools.

FBI Director J. Edgar Hoover, who operated with impunity, put out a nationwide dragnet for suspicious aliens—Germans, Italians and Japanese—but opposed wholesale incarceration of Japanese Americans.

Army Colonel Karl Bendetsen, the architect of Roosevelt's executive order, was a Jew from Grays Harbor who lied about his ethnicity to get ahead in college and the military.

In the South, where blacks were subjected to dehumanizing Jim Crow laws, the Japanese American soldiers who arrived for boot camp were told they were "honorary whites." Fred Shiosaki, though only a teenager, was dumbfounded. "Can you imagine coming out of a concentration camp and suddenly discovering that in Mississippi you're a white man? It was ridiculous and illogical." Pullman porters looked on in amazement as the cocky little soldiers piled out of the trains. Black GIs—with a few exceptions, notably the Tuskegee Airmen and Montford Point Marines—were relegated to menial jobs in the mess hall and ammunition dump.

Shiosaki, immune to prejudice because he'd lived it, knew one thing instinctively even before he arrived in the heart of darkness: When you're in combat "everybody's blood looks the same."

THERE WERE ONLY 276 JAPANESE in Spokane in 1941. Fifty-five percent were young American-born Nisei like Shiosaki, who was 17 when America entered World War II. Eighty-two percent of the state's 14,500 Japanese lived in King and Pierce counties along Puget Sound. Thousands of them tended immaculate truck farms on leased land. "Fully 90 percent of the vegetables sold in Seattle and Tacoma up to now have been raised by Japanese," the *Seattle Post-Intelligencer* reported in 1942.

The Issei immigrant elders had left behind a land of peasanthood and upheaval. Like immigrants of every nationality, they especially wanted something more for their children. "My father's story," Fred Shiosaki says, "is really an American saga."

Kisaburo Shiozaki—the "z" was changed to an "s" by mistake in America—left Japan in 1904 when he turned 21. "As the No. 3 son of a tenant farmer, my father stood no chance of inheriting anything," Fred says, "so he indentured himself to the Oriental Trading Company, which imported thousands of Japanese boys with strong backs and weak minds to lay railroad track in the Northwest, from British Columbia to Montana." Nearly 26,000 Japanese came to Washington State between 1899 and 1910.

Though his formal education ended with the equivalent of fourth grade, Kisaburo did not have a weak mind. And his ambition was even stronger than his back. Family lore has it that he jumped rail, so to speak, in Montana after meeting a family from his home town. Their relatives ran a restaurant in Spokane. Kisaburo became a short order cook, with an assortment of odd jobs on the side. When Spokane's grand Davenport Hotel opened in 1914, Kisaburo landed a fulltime job as a bus boy, setting tables and schlepping dirty dishes in a handsome uniform. With a steady job, what he needed now, at 31, was a wife. Kisaburo, a determined looking young man with a shock of coarse black hair, sailed home to Japan. "Find me a bride," he told his family. Soon, in a neighboring village, he was introduced to 18-year-old Tori Iwaii, a classic Japanese beauty.

Newlyweds Tori and Kisaburo Shiosaki in 1915. *Fred Shiosaki collection*

The newlyweds rented a tiny apartment in Hillyard, the blue-collar railyard town northeast of downtown Spokane. In 1915 when Shiosaki and two partners opened a hand laundry at 3108 East Olympic Avenue, a half-block from the Great Northern tracks, Hillyard had grown to some 4,000 residents. Many were immigrants, including clusters of Japanese, Italians and Germans. Hillyard had a lively business district and its own weekly newspaper.

Kisaburo shortly became sole proprietor of the Hillyard Laundry. He worked 16-hour days to make it thrive, adding new washing machines and steamers. Gallingly, he couldn't own the property or become a naturalized citizen. Strident exclusion laws targeting Asian immigrants—the "yellow peril" to white jobs and Anglo-Saxon nativist Americanism—saw to that.

THE FIRST THREE SHIOSAKI CHILDREN arrived in quick succession—George in 1917, Blanche in 1919 and Roy in 1920. Fred was born in 1924, the year Hillyard was annexed to Spokane, Floyd in 1927. Kisaburo proudly acquired a second-hand Maxwell automobile. He was now a business proprietor and family man.

In Hillyard everyone knew the Shiosakis. They starched shirts, laundered bedsheets, cleaned butcher shop aprons and somehow got the grease out of railroad work clothes. Kisaburo and Tori became "Kay" and "Mrs. Kay" to their customers. They were both about five feet tall, and their English was a long ways from fluent. Shy smiles and efficient service never got lost in translation. The kids helped out after school from an early age, doing homework between chopping wood for the boiler and learning how to shake out sheets. "You were to do well in school so you could go to college," Fred says emphatically. "That was the expectation. We all lived in the shadow of George, who was the family genius." Eighty years on, Fred and Floyd remember their big brother as bearing the weight of filial piety and scholastic pressure. "George set a bad example for the rest of us!" Floyd, a retired architect on Vashon Island, quips. As the only girl and second oldest, Blanche was also a role model. She did her best to help keep the younger boys in line. Roy, Fred and Floyd were bristling at old-school Japanese patriarchal norms.

"All our friends were Caucasian," Fred remembers. "Saturday was football and baseball and running the streets, but our parents insisted that we attend Japanese language school at the Methodist Japanese Mission in downtown Spokane. Honest to God, it was just a rebellion every Saturday. I felt sorry for my mother and dad. I can still hear them saying, 'You are not to talk English at the meal table. You will talk Japanese!' So it was absolutely silent. And they were furious with us. I knew *Dōmō Arigatō* (thank you very much) and some other everyday phrases. But that was the extent of it. There were no enlightening conversations at supper time!" Fred says, laughing at the memory of all those tight lips. "That's got to be so typical for immigrant families. You have kids in America and they grow up speaking English. They're Americanized. It's the way things work."

George Shiosaki, the salutatorian of the Class of 1935 at Spokane's Rogers High School, left that winter to study sciences at a prestigious Japanese university and become fluent in

Kisaburo and Tori Shiosaki with their five children in 1935. Fred, 11, is standing at right. The other children are Blanche, Roy, George, the eldest, and Floyd, between his parents. *Fred Shiosaki collection*

the language. Blanche dutifully went next, but was back home by 1940, working at the laundry. Roy, who graduated in 1938, insisted on staying home to attend Gonzaga. "He was as stubborn as his father," Fred remembers. "If the war hadn't started I think I would have said 'no' too. I didn't want to go to Japan."

Roy was a good student, studying engineering, but he left college in 1940 when his father bought him a laundry in Whitefish, Montana.

GLOOM DESCENDED on the Shiosaki apartment as the radio crackled with the news that Pearl Harbor was awash in oily death and destruction. Much of the U.S. Pacific Fleet had been caught napping by the Imperial Japanese Navy. In addition to the carnage on Battleship Row, 180 military aircraft had been destroyed on the ground.

Fred, Blanche and 14-year-old Floyd sat transfixed with their worried parents. Fred suddenly wished he'd paid closer attention to the escalating tension between Japan and the U.S. "I didn't know diddly about what was going on in the world beyond Spokane." His kid brother was even more confused. "I didn't really grasp" that the world had changed between breakfast and lunch, Floyd says. He would soon enough. All three of his big brothers were caught up in the maelstrom. George would suffer terrible deprivations before being forced to join the Japanese army.

The Hillyard Laundry Building. *Historic Preservation Office, City/County of Spokane*

"I didn't go to school that Monday," Fred remembers. "I just didn't want to go. My mother insisted that we return on Tuesday, and it was really uncomfortable—for me at least. I felt so conspicuous. My friends were still my friends. I was on the track team at Rogers and active in clubs, but some of my classmates were now standoffish. I don't think I suffered an overt act of any kind. No one beat me up or called me names. There was just this level of discomfort. I was an American but I suddenly felt more Japanese than ever before."

Fred's father arrived at the laundry at the crack of dawn, as usual. Business, as he had feared, was not as usual. By 8 it was obvious customers were staying away. One of Shiosaki's regular rounds was a house call. Spokane's postmaster was

Mr. and Mrs. Shiosaki at work in the Hillyard laundry. *Fred Shiosaki collection*

one of the most influential New Deal Democrats in the county. "Pop considered him a friend and mentor," Fred remembers. "Every Monday, Pop would drive up to his house, pick up his shirts and return them on Wednesday. On December 8, the fellow met him at the back door and said, 'Kay, look at this!' He had the Monday morning extra published by *The Spokesman-Review* with a big headline that said 'Japanese attack Hawaii.' Pop didn't know what to say. Finally he said something like it was a dumb move or it wouldn't last long. Then his old friend said, 'I'm sorry, Kay, but I can't do business with you anymore.' You've never seen a man so crestfallen as my father. They had been friends for 20 years, or so he thought.

"Well, business just about died. Then over the next month rail traffic ramped up with the onset of the war. Hillyard was buzzing. People also suddenly discovered that nobody else would do those dirty, greasy, heavy work clothes. So it got busier and busier until finally Pop said, 'Old customers, I'll take you. But new customers, no more.' He had to turn people away. Some of them said, 'You just wait 'til the war's over!' Then one day, his old friend showed up, saying he couldn't find anybody to do his shirts like our laundry. 'Sorry,' Pop said. 'I'm just too busy.' " Fred believes his father, a proud man, fought back the temptation to say, "By God, I don't need your business!" There's a Japanese word—*Gaman*—that sums up perseverance.

WITH SO FEW JAPANESE in Spokane County, there was no epidemic of fear and loathing, at least nothing to rival the front-page stories about "Seattle Japs Who Disobeyed Orders" and the wild rumors that gripped California. Air raids were imminent, authorities there warned, and "Jap spies" masquerading as ordinary shopkeepers were said to be transmitting coordinates for power plants and military installations. Print shops in California cranked out thousands of pseudo-official "Jap Hunting Licenses."

Chinese shopkeepers in downtown Spokane, worried that to whites "all Orientals look alike," as the old saw goes, wore buttons declaring "I am Chinese."

A handful of Spokane's Japanese elders "just disappeared that Monday," Fred remembers. FBI agents searched the Shiosakis' apartment. They confiscated a short-wave radio, Fred's camera, a pair of binoculars and a .22 rifle the boys plunked around with. That the Shiosakis had sent a son and daughter to study in Japan "put an extra stigma on us," Fred says. "We drove down to the FBI office in Pop's old Maxwell. I remember being terrified that my parents would never come out. They had to register as enemy aliens. From then on, we knew we had to tread lightly: 'Stay away from people you don't know,' my parents told us. The orders came down that all Japanese in Spokane County were banned from im-

An Uncle Sam propaganda poster.
National Archives

portant public buildings, power plants, airports and dams. Japanese couldn't withdraw more than $100 a month from their bank accounts. We couldn't travel more than 10 miles from home without a special pass and we had a 9 o'clock curfew."

The Spokesman-Review, Eastern Washington's largest newspaper, editorialized on Dec. 9, that the "great body" of U.S.-born Japanese likely would remain loyal Americans:

> But for the others, considering the perfidious example of their government to which they are fanatically devoted, it would be folly to trust them. As a precaution that should be a first essential, it would seem that all Japanese nationals on our islands and our mainland should be rounded up and placed in concentration camps for the duration of the war. That would not only prevent them from committing depredations, but would protect them from harm as outraged tempers rise in this country.

As tempers rose, the influential morning daily backed away from the "Jap" headlines that pockmarked most newspapers and on Dec. 11 warned:

> ...nothing could be more unjust or unbecoming loyal Americans than indiscriminately to suspect or persecute their fellow citizens of Japanese birth or descent. The patriotism of a citizen can not be distinguished by the color of his skin, and many a Japanese, both native born and naturalized, is just as devoted to America as any white American of Revolutionary stock. ...Let us not repeat the shameful cruelties of ostracism and persecution against these fellow citizens that was visited against so many loyal Americans of German birth or descent in the last world war.

During World War I, Germans were depicted as "Mad Brute" gorillas and drooling "Huns." Hamburgers became "liberty burgers," sauerkraut "liberty cabbage." Many German American merchants renamed their stores. At the outbreak of World War II, when the systemic evil of the Nazis' "final solution" to European Jewry had yet to be fully revealed, the most popular anti-German lapel pin was "To Hell with Hitler!" Relatively mild stuff compared to the tsunami of race hate generated by Pearl Harbor. The "dirty Japs" had enslaved Korea and raped and murdered tens of thousands in China, beheading civilians and bayoneting babies. Now they had killed 2,500 Americans in a sneak attack. There was no compunction about giving blatantly racist patriotic propaganda Uncle Sam's seal of approval. Superman was enlisted in Action Comics to vanquish Japanese soldiers caricatured as bespectacled bucktoothed rats. An office supply company in Hoquiam on the coast, where there were fears of an invasion, advertised that the job at hand was to kick "every dirty yellow tooth ... out of every repulsive Jap's mouth." In *Our Enemy: The Japanese*, a U.S. Office of War Information film shown in theaters around the nation, the narrator intoned that the Japanese "are as different from ourselves as any people on this planet. ...They are primitive, murderous and fanatical." In truth, 99.9 percent of Japanese Americans would prove to be just as devoted to America as, well, any white American of Revolutionary stock.

The FBI rounded up 11,000 German "enemy aliens"—some had been engaged in major espionage since 1939—together with approximately 2,000 Italians, yet there was no call for wholesale incarceration of either ethnic group. That would have been a taller order than incarcerating the Japanese: There were 1.2 million German-born Americans and nearly 700,000 Italian immigrants in the U.S. in 1942.* Nazis on the home front worried Roosevelt. He dismissed the Italians as "just a bunch of opera singers." And, like the Germans, they were white.

---

* By the same token, authorities deemed it impractical to incarcerate the 150,000 Japanese Americans living on the Hawaiian Islands. Nearly 90 percent of the 127,000 mainland Japanese were on the West Coast.

Fred, second from left, second row, with the Camera Club at Spokane's Rogers High School in 1941. Fred was vice-president of the club. *Rogers High School Treasure Chest yearbook*

A DARK SHADOW had descended over the last semester of Fred Shiosaki's senior year. He looked like the enemy.

After a motorist spotted him photographing the front of the high school, he was summoned to the principal's office. "An ominous looking" FBI agent wanted to know what he was up to. "I stammered that I was the snapshot editor for the school annual and we needed a photo of the exterior of the school. The agent warned me to cut it out—that I was not allowed to take pictures of buildings. It scared the hell out of me. I thought they were going to haul me off to jail. From then on someone else took the pictures because I just didn't need any more problems. You learn to keep your mouth shut. It was a painful experience. But when they rounded up the Japanese on the other side of the mountains and sent them to concentration camps with only what they could carry, I began to realize we were lucky. I was still angry, but if we had been sent away my father would have lost everything he'd worked for. On the west side, the property owners had the farmers by the short hairs. Just as soon as they had the chance, they took all that property. Japanese guys had worked the soil for years, made it very productive. And when the Caucasians took it back they couldn't raise the fruit and vegetables the way the Japanese had. Nobody wanted to work as hard as those Japanese immigrants."

ON FEBRUARY 19, 1942, a date Japanese Americans believe should live in infamy, Franklin D. Roosevelt signed Executive Order 9066. It authorized the Secretary of War and his designated commanders to create military areas "from which any or all persons may be excluded" and to provide transportation to new "accommodations" for those thus excluded. A month earlier, the Canadian government had set in motion the removal of 23,000 Japanese Canadians from British Columbia.

Besides being incensed by Pearl Harbor, Roosevelt had long harbored doubts about whether the Japanese were assimilable. As an exercise in executive power, his order was breathtaking in its scope. With the stroke of a pen, the president gave the military the power to incarcerate civilians without a declaration of martial law—never mind habeas corpus and the constitutional prerogatives of Congress. "More importantly," historian Greg Robinson notes in *By Order of the President*:

> Executive Order 9066 was unprecedented in the extent of its racially defined infringement of the basic rights of American citizens. The evacuation was not limited to the approximately 30 percent of the Japanese-American population that consisted of immigrant "enemy aliens." If it had been, it would still have been arbitrary, but it would clearly have fallen outside the guarantees of due process and equal protection of the laws granted to American citizens by the Constitution.

General John DeWitt, the military's West Coast commander, was a flighty character who disseminated incendiary rumors about air raids and Japanese espionage—"farcical and fantastic stuff," one disgusted peer told his diary. The "military necessity" rationale for incarceration was crafted by DeWitt's ambitious young legal aide, Karl Bendetsen. A Stanford Law School graduate, Bendetsen had advanced from captain to colonel in the space of a few months. It was Bendetsen who asserted that "a substantial majority of the Nisei bear allegiance to Japan, are well controlled and disciplined by the enemy, and at the proper time will engage in organized sabotage, particularly should a raid along the Pacific Coast be attempted by the Japanese." It's tempting to call this bald-faced chutzpah, except that Bendetsen was also busy inventing Danish ancestors. That he was suddenly no longer Jewish would come as a shock to the parishioners of Temple Beth Israel in Aberdeen, where he had grown up as the son of an observant haberdasher.

Michi Nishiura Weglyn, who was interned in Arizona as a teenager, wrote that "one of the gross absurdities of the evacuation was that a preponderance of those herded into wartime exile represented babes-in-arms, school-age children, youths not yet of voting age, and an exhausted army of elderly men and women hardly capable of rushing about carrying on subversion. The average age of the Nisei was 18. The Issei's average age hovered around 60."

Colonel Karl Bendetsen, architect of the exclusion order. *U.S. Army*

"Be as reasonable as you can," Roosevelt told aides.

When a Catholic priest in Los Angeles informed Bendetsen that the parish orphanage was home to children who were Japanese, half Japanese and "others one-fourth or less," the colonel declared, "I am determined that if they have one drop of Japanese blood in them, they must go to a camp."

U.S. Senator Mon Wallgren, a Democrat from Everett, was the de facto leader of a West Coast senatorial delegation united in its call for removal of Japanese Americans from the coast. Washington Governor Arthur B. Langlie, a strait-laced Republican reformer, backed internment. So did two up-and-coming congressmen, Democrats Warren Magnuson and Henry M. "Scoop" Jackson—Jackson with such vehemence that the episode would go down as one of the few blots on his illustrious political career. At the time, however, Magnuson's statements were no less bellicose: "I can't believe that any informed, right-thinking American wants any Japanese on this Pacific Coast for the duration of the war," Magnuson said, "and I might add that there are some of us who don't want them here even then." Tacoma Mayor Harry P. Cain's opposition to incarceration was a lonely profile in courage.

SOON AFTER THE PRESIDENT SIGNED the exclusion order, Fred Shiosaki remembers that hundreds of new Japanese families began arriving in Spokane.

In California, Nisei children wearing I.D. tags await a bus for a "relocation center." *National Archives*

Those living west of the Cascades had been urged to vacate the newly designated Military Areas. Spokane County Prosecutor Carl Quackenbush, a former Hillyard school teacher, assembled business and civic leaders to discuss what he saw as "plans to make Spokane a dumping ground of aliens." By March 27, when General DeWitt canceled voluntary relocation, some researchers estimate as many as 4,500 Japanese had moved to Spokane County. Shiosaki believes it was around half that. Most Japanese on the West Side hadn't enough money to just pick up and move, he says, and only a lucky few had friends or family to take them in. The influx worried some members of Spokane's longstanding Japanese community. "Are we drawing attention to ourselves?" Shiosaki remembers the elders thinking. "Are they going to move us *all* out of here?"

From Port Angeles to San Diego that spring, the exodus to 10 bleak concentration camps, and that's what Roosevelt himself often called them, was under way. Boats, cars, tractors, furniture, washing machines and pianos—prized possessions—had to be left behind as 110,000 people were uprooted from the West Coast. Some 13,000 were from Washington

Theodore Geisel, who would become "Dr. Seuss," drew this cartoon for the New York newspaper *PM* in 1942. *Mandeville Collection, University of California at San Diego*

State, 93,000 from California. They couldn't even take their pets, particularly heartbreaking for Nisei children. On Bainbridge Island, home to 271 Japanese, mostly strawberry farmers, one evacuee remembers men in trucks "rolling through his neighborhood" like packs of looters, shouting, "Hey, you Japs! You're going to get kicked out of here tomorrow. I'll give you ten bucks for that refrigerator." In Los Angeles, a hotel valued at $6,000 was sold for $300. Random acts of kindness—white neighbors who carefully stored household possessions, tended crops and placed the profits in savings accounts—would be long remembered too.

It may surprise many, particularly young Japanese Americans, that Shiosaki empathizes with Roosevelt. And some might suggest it's easier for Shiosaki to be charitable since his family was not incarcerated. "I'm not saying Roosevelt was right," Shiosaki emphasizes, "but there were enormous

A U.S. Army poster announces the internment of Japanese Americans. *Washington State Archives*

political pressures on him. I blame people like Earl Warren, who was politically ambitious and got himself elected governor of California [in 1943]. Practically every politician on the West Coast wanted the Japanese Americans interned. The public was inflamed—'Remember Pearl Harbor!'—and believed all those wild stories about Japanese Americans signaling submarines." Moreover, General DeWitt, Colonel Bendetsen and other military officials misled the president about the danger. "Deluged with problems, Roosevelt did the best he could with what he was being told," Shiosaki maintains. "It was a very, very difficult time. We were a tiny minority with no political support; 120,000 Japanese Americans didn't amount to a hill of beans. Hell, they could have taken us out and shot us and nobody would have done anything about it. There was this whole crew of Caucasian farmers who were out to get the Japanese Americans' property and eliminate the competition." An official with a California agricultural group made no bones about it. The Japanese could "undersell the white man" because they put their wives and children to work in the fields, he told the *Saturday Evening Post*. "We're charged with wanting to get rid of the Japanese for selfish reasons. We might as well be honest. We do."

FRED'S 21-YEAR-OLD BROTHER, Roy, was drafted in February before the military cut off induction of Japanese American citizens. No one had heard a word from George in Japan.

"After high school graduation that June, all of my Caucasian friends who were 18 started disappearing into the military," Fred remembers. "At the end of the summer when I turned 18 I went down to the draft board and discovered I was classified as '4-C'—an enemy alien. That was like a kick in the balls. I told them 'No I'm not! I was born in America. *I'm a citizen.*' 'Well,' they said, 'the State Department says you're an enemy alien, so you're an enemy alien. You are not eligible to enlist or be drafted.' I didn't have a friend left from high school, and I'm sure people wondered, 'What's the matter with him?' "

Shiosaki's parents insisted he enroll in college. Washington State College in Pullman was out because he was barred from traveling that far from home. "So it was either Whitworth or Gonzaga and I could ride the bus to Gonzaga. Gonzaga was an all-male school that had lost its student body. But it had landed the Navy V-12 officer training program, so those guys were hup-hup-hupping down the street in uniform and here I was 4-C, the enemy alien. You want to see someone who stuck out like a sore thumb? It was at best a very difficult situation. The military was recruiting translators. I looked the part, but beyond dinner table talk I couldn't speak, read or write Japanese. So that idea didn't get very far."

IN FEBRUARY OF 1943, Roosevelt and the Secretary of War—stung by Japanese propaganda about American concentration camps—announced that "loyal" Nisei would be allowed to volunteer for a segregated infantry regiment. Gung-ho former Hawaii National Guardsmen were already at Camp Shelby, Mississippi, undergoing rigorous combat training. The Hawaiians' 100th ("One Puka Puka") Infantry Battalion would keep that designation throughout the war as a salute to its roots and valor. In European combat, however, it would function as the first battalion of the 442nd Regimental Combat Team.

"By spring, I was flunking out of college. I don't think I passed anything. Can you imagine being 18 years old in the middle of a war where you looked like the enemy and didn't know what to do next? Then I heard about the new Japanese American infantry outfit." Without consulting his parents, Shiosaki volunteered for the 442nd, with induction deferred until the end of the school year. (Fred also surmises the FBI was doing a thorough background check.) A few weeks before he was to report to Fort Douglas, Utah, he broke the news to his folks. "They were in the kitchen. It was a terrible scene. Dad was the *paterfamilias*, and his expectation was that he would run my life until I got married. I thought he was going to hit me."

Fred Akira Shiosaki enlisted in the United States Army on August 14, 1943. He turned 19 nine days later. The next 24 months were the most tumultuous of a long, eventful life.

SHIOSAKI AND THE OTHER MAINLAND NISEI who joined the 442nd were in for a rude awakening when they arrived in Mississippi for basic training: The scrappy Hawaiians were already real soldiers. "They loved to drink beer, play cards, shoot dice and pick fights," Fred remembers. "It was clear from the get-go that they didn't like us. We actually looked different. The Hawaiians were darker from working on the plantations, and those whose parents were from Okinawa were shorter than us. We could not get along. The damn Hawaiians talka pidgin English alla time," Shiosaki says in a dead-on imitation of their plantation patois. "We couldn't understand them and they thought we talked funny. They resented the fact that we talked normal English, like white men—stuck-up *haoles*—or college boys. They'd say, 'Whatsa matter you?' They had a chip on their shoulder all the time. Some night when you'd be walking home from the PX about four guys would jump you. Hawaiians were famous for that. I had that happen to me once. Since we were outnumbered, I got to be a pretty good pidgin English talker!"

Shiosaki says too much has been made of the Hawaiians calling themselves "Buddhaheads" and the mainlanders "Kotonks"—the empty-head sound a coconut makes when it falls to the ground. "Don't let them kid you," he says. "Those were names that got thrown around, but all that got exaggerated after a movie about the 442nd came out after the war." The squabbling wasn't about name calling; it was about differences in culture, "like between people from the North and South," Shiosaki says. The tension began to ease when the Hawaiians learned that most of the mainland Japanese GIs had left concentration camps to volunteer for the 442nd, with the added insult of filling out loyalty questionnaires as a prerequisite for military service. "Once we got overseas and saw combat, we were all brothers—not Kotonks, Buddhaheads or anything else," Shiosaki says. "Just brothers. And we all felt like we had something to prove: We were Americans."

As for nicknames, Shiosaki quickly became "Rosie." "You had to know me when I was 18," he says, laughing and touching his cheeks. "I had these beautiful rosy cheeks like my mother and sister. The Hawaiians were all brown, and here's this Japanese American—an honorary 'white man' in Mississippi—with rosy cheeks."

WHILE THE 442ND was being toughened up with war games, the 100th Infantry Battalion arrived in Salerno for the real thing shortly after the Allied invasion of mainland Italy in September of 1943. Moving out from the ancient city 45 miles below Naples, the Hawaiians plunged into combat against crack German troops. Field Marshal Albert Kesselring defended the Gustav Line, beyond which lay Rome, a strategic, symbolic

Nisei soldiers herd a group of surrendered German troops in Italy. *National Archives and Go For Broke National Education Center*

prize, with everything at his command. The hilly terrain advantaged the defenders. The bloody stalemate continued through the winter. War correspondents dubbed the Nisei soldiers the "Purple Heart Battalion."

U.S. forces, meantime, were advancing in the Pacific, island by island, against a do-or-die enemy. On Wake, the atoll in the center of the Pacific, Japanese troops executed 96 American POWs. Meanwhile in Japan, George Mutsuo Shiosaki, Fred's 26-year-old brother, was in a terrible fix. The authorities had clamped down on Japanese American students, and native-born university students, previously exempt from conscription, were being drafted. Soon, boys as young as 15 would be inducted. George Shiosaki was reduced to bare-subsistence rations and threatened with being sent to an internment camp, where conditions were appalling. George went to the village office and had his name entered in his uncle's family registry, not realizing it would compromise his U.S. citizenship. Having gained Japanese citizenship past the age of 21, "I thought I would be exempt from military service [in the Japanese Army]," George would recall in a letter to his congressman a decade later. As the war entered its third year, his parents and siblings knew nothing of his situation.

Just before the remainder of the 442nd Regimental Combat Team shipped out for Europe, Fred visited his brother Roy. After months of mowing lawns and pulling KP in Kansas, the 23-year-old draftee had been sent to the University of Minnesota to study engineering through an Army Specialized Training Program. "What a deal!" Fred ribbed his brother. A year later, Roy would be an infantryman, too—the only Japanese American in a New York National Guard unit—though the brothers never crossed paths on the outskirts of the collapsing Third Reich. Two "Zags" were a long, long way from Spokane. In a window above the laundry their mother placed a banner with two blue stars.

THE MAINLAND NISEI GI's landed at Anzio just below Rome in the spring of 1944. Shiosaki was assigned to a weapons platoon. "I was a bazooka man for a while; later a gunner on a little 60 mm mortar. When you're in combat you pick up a weapon and sometimes that's it." Nearsighted like everyone else in his family, Fred nevertheless qualified as a marksman with the M1 rifle and .45 caliber pistol, squinting through his smudged glasses. "Being shot at in real combat gives you focus, especially the first time, which scares the hell out of you. In the beginning we were so dumb that we stuck our heads up too much. The Germans had some of the best snipers in the whole world. God, they were good shots! They'd put a bullet right in your forehead. *Pow!*"

In the dog days of that bloody Italian summer, the 442nd scampered from foxhole to foxhole, advancing yard by yard, cave by cave, hill by hill, "boldly facing murderous fire... from a numerically superior enemy," in the words of a Presidential Unit Citation. From Civitavecchia, the seaport city above Rome (" 'Sonofabitchia,' " Shiosaki quips), the reunited Nisei battalions fanned out. They seized strategic hillsides and decimated a battalion of Hitler's fanatical Waffen-SS. The Germans were now engaged in a desperate effort to hold the line. It became a rearguard action.

The final 40 miles to the Arno River crossing between Pisa and Florence extracted a terrible toll from the 442nd Combat Team: 1,016 wounded, 256 dead or missing. The enemy's losses, by consolation, were far heavier. One sobering fact italicizes the price paid by the Nisei soldiers: The team's combat strength, including artillery, engineers and medics, was around 3,800. By war's end, 14,000 men had served in the 442nd. "When you lose guys for the first time it's a shock. You never forget it," Shiosaki says. Nor can old infantrymen like Fred forget the drill to give comrades some semblance of dignity in death. "Usually, you'd pull his shirt over his head, pull his helmet down and stick his rifle in the ground so the graves registration people would see there was a dead GI. Then you had to keep moving. You don't have time to mourn." Replacements arrived, wide-eyed guys who'd never fired a shot in anger or seen someone die. Then they'd be dead too.

THE 442ND LANDED AT MARSEILLE in late September. The shell-shocked Mediterranean port had been liberated a month earlier in "the second D-Day" invasion of occupied France. From there, by troop truck and French cattle cars, the Nisei soldiers

Nisei soldiers board a truck as they advance north in France in 1944. *Seattle Nisei Veterans Committee*

advanced up the Rhone Valley to Alsace-Lorraine. The first objective was Bruyères, a crossroads town on the western edge of the Vosges Mountains. Just beyond Bruyères lay Saint-Dié, the gateway to three passes that led to the Rhine. Once across, the Allies would be in the Nazis' hallowed *Vaterland*.

In the Vosges—rhymes with "shows"— the 442nd Regimental Combat Team paid a heavy price for its legend. "Steep, wooded and nearly trackless, the mountains barricaded the German border so successfully that no invader had ever made it through them. There, Hitler had ordered what was left of two German armies to stand and fight," Geoffrey C. Ward writes in *The War*, a compelling book produced to accompany Ken Burns' World War II documentary.

"We took a lot of casualties in Italy," Shiosaki remembers, "but it was nothing like the Vosges. Sometimes it was almost hand-to-hand combat." Daniel Inouye, a Nisei platoon sergeant from Hawaii who would become a U.S. senator 20 years later, remembered being gripped by a sudden "sense of nightmare" the first time he saw the Vosges.

THE JAPANESE AMERICAN SOLDIERS were assigned to the 36th "Texas" Division of the U.S. Seventh Army. Their new commander, Major General John E. Dahlquist, was a big Swede from Minnesota. "Humorless, blunt, and given to brooding," he would win nothing but their undying enmity. The consensus of military historians is that Dahlquist was an exemplary "desk-jockey" general but in way over his head as a battlefield commander. That's being charitable, according to Shiosaki and countless other members of the 442nd, including front-line officers. They maintain that General Dahlquist—nearly fired for foot-dragging earlier in the campaign—"violated every principal of leadership and tactics." They say he sacrificed the Nisei soldiers to keep the brass off his back, satisfy his ego and rescue a battalion he had foolishly sent a ridge too far. "Dahlquist should have been court martialed," Shiosaki says, eyes glistening with anger, "and if we hadn't saved his ass he would have been!"

Major General John E. Dahlquist, who was loathed by the Nisei soldiers. *National Archives*

Ignoring reconnaissance reports to the contrary, the general insisted the Germans had largely abandoned four strategic hills. When a Nisei battalion radioed it was taking heavy fire as it advanced, Dahlquist sputtered that they were "a bunch of damn liars." Just get the lead out. "He kept insisting 'There are no Krauts up there!'" Shiosaki remembers.

So off they went, charging up slippery hills under withering interlocking fire in the icy October rain. Comrades crumpled right and left, crying out for medics and their mothers as artillery shells burst through the canopy of 60-foot evergreens; machine guns chattered, mortar shells whooshed down; shrapnel and pine-tree splinters as lethal as crossbow bolts slammed into soldiers. Darting from tree to tree, some men stepped on mines or had legs crushed by booby traps in the underbrush. It was a jungle in there, especially when eerie fog smothered the slopes. As the 442nd crested one hill, medics in tow, the Germans opened fire on wounded men on stretchers. The outraged Nisei resolved they would take no more prisoners that day.

Finally, after nine days of relentless combat, the general granted the Nisei a 10-day rest break. With numb brains and aching feet, the sleep-deprived soldiers slumped into trucks and lit a smoke. "You'd been wearing the same filthy, sweat-stained clothes day after day," Shiosaki remembers. The prospect of a hot shower and a decent meal was like heaven. Dry socks would be an incredible luxury. "The Quartermaster Corps had good heavy waterproofed boots, but they didn't get them to us. We were wearing leather combat boots" in foxholes and slit trenches calf-deep in freezing rainwater. "Your soaked socks made your feet swell even more. My feet still ache when I go out in the cold."

The rest break was canceled less than two days later. The general was in a jam.

DAHLQUIST HAD ONCE AGAIN ignored the advice of battle-savvy subordinates. He ordered the 1st Battalion of the Texans' 141st Infantry Regiment to advance deeper into the Vosges. The crafty Germans—the ones the general maintained weren't there—sprang a trap. They encircled a company of 275 soldiers on a narrow ridge, felling huge trees to block escape routes. A "gantlet of machine guns and anti-tank weapons" twice repelled rescuers from the 141st. Dahlquist called in the Nisei. Without them, "The Lost Battalion" might have met its Alamo in the primeval mountains along the French-German border. The Texans, who had been in combat for 70 consecutive days, were running low on food, water, plasma, ammunition and hope.

Shiosaki remembers being rousted out at 3 a.m. "Within the hour we

Nisei soldiers scramble up a hillside in the Vosges.
PBS, *The War*

Members of the 442nd prepare to move out from a command post near Saint-Dié, France, in the winter of 1944. *U.S. Signal Corps/National Archives, 442nd Regimental Combat Team Website*

were on the move. It was absolutely pitch dark—so dark that we hung onto the backpack of the guy in front, moving in single file." GI's in other platoons stuck strips of white toilet paper onto their backpacks. Company K—Fred's outfit—made its way "up a corduroy road that seemed interminable. When the road finally ended, the mud began. Someone would fall down up ahead and you'd hear them curse; then you'd stop a moment before moving on again, little by little. Finally when it broke light there was small arms fire. And then came the artillery!" The fog was so dense there was no hope of air support or supply drops; the roads were too narrow for tanks to traverse. "We'd move about a hundred yards, losing men with every yard. We did that for about four days. Every morning the general would come in and jab us. I'd see him up there arguing with our battalion commander, Lieutenant Colonel Pursall. He'd be yelling, 'There's a battalion about to die up there!' I thought it was going to end up in fisticuffs because our colonel was saying, 'We cannot move until you give us more artillery support!' "

Alfred Pursall, a blunt Midwesterner, stood 6-5 and weighed at least 250. The colonel had a pair of ivory-handled

.45's, à la General Patton, but he was no peacock. When the men of the 3rd Battalion say "our" colonel, it's a mark of respect. Pursall was a fighter. He revered his Nisei soldiers for their courage. When General Dahlquist gave him a ration of crap once too often, Pursall was having none of it. Company K, though outnumbered at least four to one, had just repulsed a German counterattack. Dahlquist nevertheless demanded to know why they hadn't rescued his Texans, still trapped some three miles to the east. "Order your men to fix bayonets and charge!" the general bellowed at Pursall when he discovered elements of the 3rd Battalion regrouping at a crossroads. "Those are my boys you're trying to kill!" the colonel shot back, grabbing the general by his lapels. "I won't let you kill my boys. If there's any orders to be given for my boys to attack, I'll give the orders personally and I'll lead them." A few minutes later, an alert Nisei battalion warned field artillery that a barrage ordered by the general would have landed right in the middle of the Lost Battalion.

Say this for the general: If his judgment was suspect, he was no coward. Awarded the Silver Star for leading an earlier

A Nisei soldier makes his way up a foreboding hillside in the Vosges as the 442nd sets out to rescue "The Lost Battalion." *National Archives and Go For Broke National Education Center*

"Go for Broke!" a painting in the collection of the Army Center of Military History, depicts the 442nd Regimental Combat Team assaulting German siege forces in the rescue of "The Lost Battalion." *U.S. Army Photo*

attack, Dahlquist traipsed the front lines, studying maps and barking orders.

On October 29, 1944, the third day of the Nisei rescue mission, the general visited a makeshift command post, his aide de camp in tow. The young lieutenant was Wells Lewis, son of the Nobel Prize-winning novelist, Sinclair Lewis. As Lewis stood to retrieve a map, a German machine gun nest picked him off. The general caught Lewis in his arms as he slumped dead. Shiosaki remembers Dahlquist walking past Company K, face ashen, one hand covered in blood. The general revealed his inner turmoil in a letter to his wife: "It astounds me how these men are able to stand the physical and mental strain under which they are constantly living. It is almost beyond comprehension that the human being can stand so much."*

Company K, together with two others, was now within a mile of the Texans. Some 700 Germans, armed with mortars

---

* Franz Steidl, author of *Lost Battalions*, is one historian who maintains that Dahlquist drove his Caucasian regiments no less hard than the Nisei.

and machine guns and buttressed by tanks, were dug in along a narrow, heavily mined ridge "with steep drop-offs on either side." As they advanced, the Nisei continued to absorb heavy casualties. Seventy-one years later, it's all still so vivid for Fred Shiosaki—the sights, sounds and smells of what came to be called "Suicide Hill."

During a momentary lull in the fighting, "Our colonel stood up. Here's this big white guy exhorting the little Buddha-heads. He's shouting, 'Come on you guys! Let's go! Let's go!' Waving his pistol. And I thought, 'You crazy bastard, they're going to shoot you!' But he didn't flinch.

"We were all charging up the ridge when all of sudden something hit me right in the ribs—like being hit by a baseball bat. I went down. Oh Jesus it hurt! They pulled up my shirt and here was a great big piece of shrapnel sitting on my ribs. Just broke the skin and cracked a rib." One of the medics stopped to look at the wound, which was barely bleeding. Shiosaki believes it was probably Jim Okubo from Bellingham. "He had more guts than a burglar," Shiosaki says, and often used his body to protect a wounded soldier. "All the medics in the 442nd were amazing."*

Shiosaki struggled to his feet and rejoined his wild-eyed platoon. "We didn't care anymore; we were like a bunch of savages," one of his comrades said. A painting at the Pentagon depicts their intrepidity. With "fearless courage and complete disregard for personal safety," the 3rd Battalion kept charging up the slope, "shouting at the enemy and firing from their hips, while the enemy fired point-blank into their ranks," U.S. Army historians wrote. "Completely unnerved by the vicious bayonet charge, the enemy fled in confusion after making a desperate stand."

Pursall was alongside his men all the way, Shiosaki says. "And as we pushed across off that hill I thought, 'God, colonel I'll kiss your hand!' I consider Colonel Pursall to be one of the real heroes of the war. He was a real soldier's soldier."

When the shooting suddenly stops, "it's so quiet it's a roar," Shiosaki remembers. "The silence is deafening." As he

---

* James K. Okubo, whose family was incarcerated back home, went on to become a dentist in Detroit, only to be killed in an auto accident in 1967. "He saved more lives than anybody else in that outfit," Shiosaki says. "A really good guy. We got together after the war. Then he gets killed in an auto accident. I couldn't believe it. Talk about irony!"

crested the hill, he heard someone crying. "There's this kid—a German kid, and he's wounded. Just a teenager. I thought, 'You sonofabitch!' I could easily have shot him, but I didn't. I just kept on going, even though I'd just lost most of my platoon. I hope he had a long life. I remember that so vividly. People ask what it's like to have to kill someone in combat. I had no self-doubts. It was either me or them. There was never any question when I drew a bead on somebody. It had to be one of us. Except that one time. That German kid looked like he was 14 years old—like my younger brother."

After the combat team's artillery chased away the last clump of Germans, the 442nd reached the Texans on the afternoon of October 30. "Patrol from 442nd here," they radioed. "Tell them that we love them!"

"It was the happiest day of my life," one of the rescued GI's said. When he spotted a Japanese soldier cresting the ridge, wearing a helmet that looked "several sizes too big," race no longer mattered. "Here was a brother of mine coming up to save my life." Another remarked: "It was really ironical that we were so glad to see Japanese, but, boy, they are real Americans." They shared a pack of real American cigarettes.

DURING A BRIEF REST BREAK, the 442nd finally got winter uniforms and better boots before setting off again in pursuit of the Germans. "I got my boots off and, jeeze, my feet were pretty," Fred remembers. "They were purple and red, but I couldn't stand on them. Then we were ordered out by General Dahlquist to pass in review so he could 'thank' us. I could hardly walk, my feet hurt so bad. But they made us show up. The general reprimanded the colonel: 'I said I wanted *everyone* to pass in review! Where are all your men?' There were only 17 of us from K Company out of the 186 guys we'd had at the beginning of the battle and eight from I Company. And the colonel says, 'Sir, these are all the men I have left!' That's all we had. Barely a battalion left out of the whole 442nd. We looked like we'd gone through a sieve." The chaplain said it was the first time he'd seen the colonel cry.

Eyes flashing, Shiosaki shakes his head: "Big old general! If I'd had a pistol I would have shot the son of a bitch! You talk about angry! When you think of all the friends we'd lost. Goddamn, I'm still mad about that!"

A day after the dress review, "Dahlquist called out the ravaged 2nd and 3rd Battalions for patrolling and reconnaissance duty, in case the enemy mounted a counterattack," wrote Lyn Crost, the war correspondent who covered the 442nd. "So the tired, tattered Nisei soldiers, still mourning their dead and wounded, trudged back onto the line."

The 442nd was finally relieved of duty in the Vosges in mid-November, happy to be transferred to another command. Shiosaki spent the remainder of the European war in the Maritime Alps between southern France and Italy. "It

Lt. Col. Pursall is swathed in leis at an event in Hawaii after the war. *University of Hawaii at Manoa Library*

was the so-called 'Champagne Campaign,' but don't let them BS you," Fred says. "It was cold and rainy—not the Riviera, but better than being shot at all the time."

In the 1950s at Fort Bragg, when Dahlquist was a four-star general, he bumped into the former commander of the Hawaiians' 100th Battalion. "Let bygones be bygones. It's all water under the bridge, isn't it?" the general said, offering his hand. The colonel saluted and stared straight ahead.

WHILE THE HEROISM OF THE 442ND had been featured in articles and newsreels, Japanese American soldiers returned home to indifference at best, outright hostility at worst; no confetti or keys to the city. The Spokane VFW post refused membership to a Nisei vet. When Fred Shiosaki took a pretty teenager named Lily Nakai to the skating rink on one of their first dates he was accosted by a drunk who hated "dirty rotten Japs." If the man had had an ounce of sober civility, he might have discovered that Fred was a decorated combat veteran who fully agreed with Harry Truman's decision to unleash history's first atomic bombs on Hiroshima and Nagasaki. "We did what was necessary to end the war," Fred says. "I wouldn't have wanted any more American boys to die going in there. In fact, I would have liked [the bomb] to have been used against Germany."

In Hood River, Oregon, a year earlier, the American Legion post had removed the names of 16 Nisei servicemen from its "roll of honor." All along the West Coast, as Japanese Americans straggled out of the camps, many found themselves with no place to go. They'd lost most of their worldly possessions; their farms and orchards—never really their own property—were being cultivated by the land owners or new tenants. Bucolic Hood River was far from the only place to publicly declare the Japanese would not be welcomed back. The postwar housing shortage forced many former internees into trailer parks, old barracks and "shoddy new government facilities." Thousands of younger Nisei moved elsewhere in America.

Through second-hand sources late in the war, the Shiosakis had learned George was alive, if not well, in Japan. When Floyd, the youngest of the four Shiosaki brothers, arrived there in 1946 as a member of General MacArthur's Army of Occupation, he heard George might be working at the same military depot. "It was quite a shock to all of a sudden see your brother for the first time in five years," Floyd remembers. He learned that George had been drafted into the Japanese Army late in the war. By then, however, he was so malnourished that he was hospitalized for months. Now an interpreter, George was conflicted about leaving Japan and worried about his U.S. citizenship.

UNDER THE GI BILL, Fred returned to Gonzaga. He was a chemistry major, mulling pre-med while also picking up credits for a teaching certificate. Living at home and working part time at the laundry was often tedious. He was a grown man now. For the first year, he found it hard to concentrate on his studies. In the middle of a lecture, memories about the war would pop into his head. Loud noises could startle him. The university had a slew of veterans, but still only a few Asians. One day in English Lit, the professor—a Jesuit priest no less—made an offhand crack about "a bunch of Japs." Fred remembers feeling "so rummy" that he just kept his head down. Sometimes in the middle of the night his mother would shake him awake, saying, "You were screaming again." Slowly things got better, though he still didn't want to talk about the war. When his brother Roy got back from Europe, he was that way too. Most of their buddies had the same baggage. "Today we can talk about it, even kid about it. But not back then," Fred says. "It was part of your psyche. After a while, I learned it was an exercise in futility to get in fights. I learned to recognize the source and just walk away."

"Can't ya read signs?"

Pulitzer Prize-winning cartoonist Bill Mauldin, whose cartoons made him a hero to dogface GIs, drew this one to satirize prejudice at war's end. *National Archives*

When *Go For Broke!*, a movie about the 442nd—starring Van Johnson as a Texan who lost his bigotry in the Vosges—opened in Spokane, Fred was invited to attend in his uniform. The movie was steeped in "Hollywood BS," Shiosaki says. But he didn't say so then.

Fred graduated from Gonzaga in 1949. His adviser urged him to pursue a master's degree in chemistry at the University of Washington. By then, however, he and Lily were serious. "I'm in Seattle; she's in Spokane. It was just an impossible situation. I couldn't study!" Ed Foubert, a mentor and friend from the biology department at Gonzaga, got him a job at Hollister-Stier Laboratories, a pharmaceutical company in Spokane. That was followed by a short stint at Kaiser Aluminum. Shiosaki finally landed a solid job as a chemist with the City of Spokane's Health Department.

MGM Archives

In 1952, when first-generation Japanese immigrants were finally allowed to apply for naturalized citizenship, Fred and Roy began coaching their parents for the tests. "My mother was just hilarious," Fred remembered in a 2006 interview with Tom Ikeda, executive director of Densho, the rich repository of Japanese American experiences during World War II. The boys would ask their mom, "Where was the Constitution signed?" Unfortunately, nothing in the Japanese language approximates "Philadelphia." Mrs. Shiosaki would say something like "Hooloodaupiya" as her sons practically rolled on the floor. Kisaburo and Tori Shiosaki passed the tests and proudly became official Americans. Fred felt then, and even more so now, that what the Nisei soldiers proved in combat played an important role in changing the law. "By god, Fred," he said to himself, "you had a piece of this one."

FRED AND LILY GOT MARRIED. Having inherited some of their Issei parents' conservatism, they had waited until he had a steady job. His duties with the city were expanding to assist the police and fire departments. He was involved in clubs and other civic activities. All this made his father proud, yet there was a hole in Kisaburo Shiosaki's heart.

In 1958, the patriarch was dying of cancer. He desperately wanted to see his firstborn son. George Shiosaki, now 41, had married a lovely Japanese girl. He was working as a proofreader for an English-language newspaper in Tokyo. The pay was paltry, and the couple now had a child. His sister Blanche was active in the Japanese American Citizens League, which helped him secure an emergency visa. He came home with his wife and daughter and desperately wanted to stay to help run the laundry. "I have always felt that America is my country," George wrote to Congressman Walt Horan, an energetic Republican from Wenatchee. George explained how he had been coerced into the Japanese Army. Horan introduced a resolution to overturn Shiosaki's expatriation. George's attorneys filed a parallel action in federal district court. Two months after his father's death, the State Department reversed itself and affirmed George Shiosaki's U.S. citizenship.

FRED AND LILY BECAME PARENTS in 1959. First came Nancy, then Michael, two years later. In 1967, Fred became the founding director of the Spokane Air Pollution Control Authority. He soon emerged as a regional pacesetter in the growing environmental movement. More opportunities came his way.

During the xenophobic 1930s, Washington Water Power Company "felt it necessary to assure its customers it employed no Japanese workers." Now it wanted the son of an immigrant laundryman to become one of its top managers. WWP made several runs at Shiosaki. In 1978, he finally agreed to oversee its environmental program. "They were building a new coal-fired plant. I think they hired me because I was harassing the hell out of them!" Fred says, laughing. Shiosaki went on to serve as chairman of the Washington State Ecological Commission for seven years. Rogers High School named him to its Walk of Fame.

Governor Gary Locke appointed Shiosaki, a passionate fly-fisherman, to the Washington Fish and Wildlife Commission in 1999. "In some of those high-pressure jobs I had, I'd go home at night and spend an hour down in the basement tying flies. That would kind of smooth things down." As a commissioner, Shiosaki rubbed some lawmakers and user groups the wrong way. Never a table-pounder, he nevertheless spoke his

Michael Shiosaki with his parents at their Seattle apartment. *Wells Fargo Stories*

mind. "In all of the jobs I had over the years, I always felt that you gotta rile somebody or you're probably not facing up to the tough decisions." During his eight years on the commission, Shiosaki championed youth programs. "Many kids today have never been fishing in their lives, especially underprivileged kids. Our 'Fishing Kids' program is one of the highlights of all the stuff I've been involved with." He was also instrumental in securing funding for a new Fish and Wildlife Department regional headquarters in Spokane Valley, including a $1.9 million laboratory. The facility was renamed to honor Shiosaki.

AMERICA WAS NOW RIGHTING half a century of wrongs against Japanese Americans. In 1988, President Ronald Reagan signed legislation formally apologizing for the wartime concentration camps and allocating redress. Each surviving victim was to receive $20,000; in all, 82,219 victims were compensated.

Twenty combat decorations awarded to Nisei soldiers during World War II were upgraded to Medals of Honor in 2000 during a White House ceremony. Senator Inouye, who lost his right arm fighting fascism and gave his heart to seeking justice for his comrades, received the Medal of Honor. So did the fearless medic, Jim Okubo—posthumously, 56 years late. "Rarely has a nation been so well served by a people it has so ill-treated," said President Bill Clinton. "They risked their lives, above and beyond the call of duty. And in so doing, they did more than defend America; in the face of painful prejudice, they helped to define America at its best."

In 2011, Fred Shiosaki and other Nisei World War II veterans from around the nation were awarded the Congressional Gold Medal, one of America's highest civilian honors. By then, however, the majority of the 19,000 one-time "enemy aliens" who served their country with such valor were gone. At least not forgotten.

Staff Sergeant Shiosaki, who somehow survived one of the bloodiest battles in U.S. Army history, is now 92. His cheeks are still rosy; his sense of whimsy is intact. Daughter Nancy is teaching English in Japan; son Michael is the director of planning and development for Seattle Parks and Recreation. Michael is also married to the mayor—and "bossy," Fred deadpans. A couple of years ago, Michael moved his aging parents to a comfortable senior-citizen apartment complex in Seattle. Lily, the love of Fred's life, died on the Fourth of July in 2016. Self-effacing and modest, she also possessed great resilience and was devoted to Fred and their children. He misses her. And Spokane too. It's a good thing every Gonzaga Bulldog basketball game is on TV.

Fred proudly wears his World War II tunic during a Gonzaga event saluting veterans. *Gonzaga University*

It's hard to fathom, but Fred says some stupid geezer actually called him a "Jap" the other day. He shrugged it off. More worrisome, Fred says, is that even after all the apologies, belated medals, books and documentaries, "a lot of people—especially young people—don't know enough about what happened to Japanese Americans during the war. People forget what democracy is all about—that the least of us are supposed to be protected. But it doesn't always happen. It's a lesson of history that bears repeating."

Otherwise, it might happen again.

John C. Hughes

CLAYTON PITRE

The Invisible Marine

"This is not just black history or Marine Corps history. This is American history. The world needs to understand the history of the Montford Point Marines."
—Dr. James T. Averhart Jr., president,
National Montford Point Marine Association

C layton Pitre, a Creole person of color from Bayou Country, is hung up on justice, not race. The longtime Seattleite fought two wars in the spring of 1945—prejudice on the home front and tyranny abroad. He acquired the grit of a U.S. Marine in a country that labeled him inferior, and then dodged enemy fire on an island subjected to suicide warfare.

Pitre's love of country isn't overshadowed by America's dark history—even the mind-bending truths that surround his ancestors and his own life. Pitre has long refused to let racism get under his skin, and he's lived discrimination like any African American from the segregated Deep South. Pitre has been ordered to the back of the bus. He's been intellectually underestimated. And he's been called a Negro, a term he abhors. A descendant of enslaved ancestors and slave owners, the wrongs against Pire's family run centuries deep. Still, he's over the mistreatment. It's the historical record that matters to him now.

At 92, Clayton Pitre is among the only surviving World War II Montford Point Marines in the Pacific Northwest. *Lori Larson*

Pitre and 20,000 African Americans broke the color barrier in World War II when they trained at a segregated base in Jacksonville, North Carolina, and joined one of the most elite military organizations in the world. No black man had enlisted in the United States Marines Corps since a known slave from Delaware fought in the Revolutionary War with a handful of other African American Continental Marines. The World War II milestone generated little recognition for decades. In 2012, the Montford Point Marines were finally awarded the Congressional Gold Medal.

Pitre has outlived most of the men now. At 92, he is charming and sharp. Pitre emerges from downstairs in his Seattle home with a book on the men who made history. A picture of them, the Montford Point Marines, appears in a frame on the hearth of his fireplace. Over the years, Pitre has flown off to gatherings of the Montford Point Marines, hoping to connect and do his part to preserve their legacy. The goal is becoming more difficult to achieve. Pitre is among a dwindling number of WWII Montford Point Marines who can tell their story. There are approximately 400 still living in the country. Pitre is believed to be one of the only survivors in the Pacific Northwest.

IT WAS PRESIDENT ROOSEVELT who helped the Montford Point Marines break the color barrier. His Executive Order 8802

Some 20,000 African Americans trained at a segregated base in North Carolina during World War II. "They had to fight for the right to fight. They wanted to serve. They wanted to prove that they were brave," says James Averhart Jr., president of the Montford Point Marine Association. *U.S. Marine Corps*

EXECUTIVE ORDER

REAFFIRMING POLICY OF FULL PARTICIPATION IN
THE DEFENSE PROGRAM BY ALL PERSONS, REGARDLESS
OF RACE, CREED, COLOR, OR NATIONAL ORIGIN, AND
DIRECTING CERTAIN ACTION IN FURTHERANCE OF
SAID POLICY.

WHEREAS it is the policy of the United States to encourage full participation in the national defense program by all citizens of the United States, regardless of race, creed, color, or national origin, in the firm belief that the democratic way of life within the Nation can be defended successfully only with the help and support of all groups within its borders; and

WHEREAS there is evidence that available and needed workers have been barred from employment in industries engaged in defense production solely because of considerations of race, creed, color, or national origin, to the detriment of workers' morale and of national unity:

NOW, THEREFORE, by virtue of the authority vested in me by the Constitution and the statutes, and as a prerequisite to the successful conduct of our national defense production effort, I do hereby reaffirm the policy of the United States that there shall be no discrimination in the employment of workers in defense industries or government because of race, creed, color, or national origin, and I do hereby declare that it is the duty of employers and of labor organizations, in furtherance of said policy and of this order, to provide for the full and equitable participation of all workers in defense industries, without discrimination because of race, creed color, or national origin;

Executive Order 8802 is considered one of the 100 "Milestone Documents" by the National Archives. The order banned discrimination in the defense industry. *National Archives* opened the ranks of the U.S. Marine Corps in the spring of 1941, as Hitler conspired to invade the Soviet Union. Racial tension mounted with the competition for home front war-industry jobs. Construction soon began at Montford Point, a segregated depot known for its infestation of poisonous snakes as much as its rigorous instruction.

Total acceptance of African Americans remained elusive on and off the military base. "There would be a definite loss of efficiency in the Marine Corps if we have to take Negroes," warned Major General Thomas Holcomb, the Commandant. During a boxing match at the segregated boot camp, a one-star general declared to hundreds of black recruits: "They've made many changes since I was stateside. They've added the woman ... And when I came into this camp and saw you people wearing our globe and anchor, I knew there was a war on."

Authorities who'd never seen a black Marine reputedly arrested Montford Pointers on liberty in their distinctive dress blues. One was R.J. Wood in Cleveland. They took him into custody and accused him of impersonating a Marine.

Major General Thomas Holcomb resisted the notion of opening up the U.S. Marine Corps to African Americans. "There would be a definite loss of efficiency," he said. *U.S. Army*

It took more than 160 years to break the color barrier, but acceptance would require still more time. "They had to fight for the right to fight," says James Averhart Jr., president of the Montford Point Marine Association. "They wanted to serve. They wanted to prove that they were brave."

Despite their sacrifices at various battles—they killed the enemy in Guam, risked their lives in the vicious fighting at Iwo Jima and suffered injury at Peleliu—thumb through most World War II chronologies and the Montford Point Ma-

The Montford Point Marines engaged in landings throughout the war in the Pacific. Seventeen of the Marines were wounded in the Battle of Peleliu.
National Archives

rines are nowhere to be found. "Your history was not credited to you," Pitre explains. "Therefore, it was easy to show him [an African American] as lesser than the other because he hadn't done anything. Some people say, 'You ain't got no history.' "

"If you bring up the history, you have to bring up the bad part," suggests Joe Geeter, a past national president of the Montford Point Marine Association. "People don't want to hear it. But African Americans today need to understand where their legacy started."

THE DEEP ROOTS OF CLAYTON PITRE unfold against a backdrop of lush green pastures and low-lying swamps. His hometown of Opelousas, Louisiana—the state's third oldest city—became the temporary Confederate capital during the Civil War and the scene of a deadly race riot in the Reconstruction Era that followed. Pitre's ancestors—black, white, mulatto, slaves and slave owners—began a legacy in farming that afforded them more dignity than enslaved blacks of the 18th century. Nearly 100 years before America abolished slavery, his white ancestor, Francois Lemelle, professed the value of justice and equality.

Pitre's great-great-great maternal grandmother, Marie-Jeanne Davion, was an African American slave who bore the children of Francois Lemelle, a prominent grower in Southwest Louisiana. Marie won her freedom on December 5, 1772, nearly a century before the country abolished slavery with the 13th Amendment. Marie eventually took Francois' last name.

Francois Lemelle died in 1789. In his will, he recognized his relationship with his onetime black slave and the children they shared. Lemelle left part of his estate to Marie and his household goods—beds, mattresses, pillows and blankets—because "of the care and pain which the said Marie-Jeanne took of him for many years and for which he had not given her any salary." Francois' children and his Caucasian wife, Charlotte Labbe, agreed with his wishes.

Opelousas is one of Louisiana's oldest cities and Pitre's hometown. During the Civil War, it was temporarily named the Confederate capital. *Library of Congress*

"They renounce all claims to her servitude, even if the law would have been in their favor. They do so because of the intentions of their deceased mother, Dame Lemelle, whom they remember stating many times that she desired that Marie-Jeanne enjoy freedom. They also do so because of the act of freedom passed by the said Francois Lemelle stating that he wanted and intended that Marie-Jeanne and all her children, without distinction, enjoy the rights, privileges and prerogatives held by free people."

Marie Lemelle settled near Opelousas in St. Landry Parish after Francois' death. There she acquired more than 800 acres along the Bayou Courtableau, in South Central Louisiana. Marie, her sons and 15 slaves made something of the land, and so be-

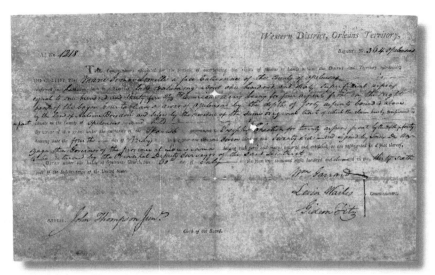

A certificate of land ownership for Marie Lemelle, Clayton's great-great-great grandmother who bore children with a prominent Caucasian grower. *The Historic New Orleans Collection—Williams Research Center*

gan the family's long history in farming. The land and home gave the family a sense of pride and respect. "In southwest Louisiana, there were all of these small farms—60 acres, 40 acres, 20 acres, 80 acres," Pitre says. "There is a difference of that ownership of a small section of land and the type of citizen you have who can profess ownership of something. He has a certain kind of dignity for himself. In the south, a man's home is his castle."

Clayton's paternal ancestors, Acadians, were banished from Nova Scotia for refusing loyalty to the Protestant King of England. Many of the French Catholics made their way to the bayous of Louisiana.

Pitre came along on June 30, 1924—the fourth child of seven and a Creole of color in Jim Crow America. Slavery had long been abolished, but discrimination became the life he knew. "You go downtown to the courthouse to pay the taxes. There are two water fountains—one is white and one way down the way is black. There is one restroom for white and one for colored. When you go in there most of the time it hadn't been cleaned, you know? As a child you grow up with that. Sometimes you ask your folks, 'Why?' And they say, 'Shut up.'

Pitre's parents, Eugenie and Gilbert. Clayton's father taught him the psychology behind a strong work ethic. He considers the long hours out on the farm among the greatest lessons of his childhood *Clayton Pitre collection*

"We always got the short end of the stick. Our parents had used logic with us knowing that you weren't going to win. If you're not going to win, why would you alone take up that battle?" Clayton never let it get to him.

Pitre has fond memories of a childhood filled with influential role models. His maternal grandmother Victoria, who was slow afoot and knew little English, taught him French. His father Gilbert, a stern taskmaster, taught him how to work—the great lesson of his earliest years. "He just insisted. You have to do it. And it came from the survival of the family first. That's what it was. You work as a unit in your home. You had to do your task. If you didn't, something went wrong." His mother Eugenie, wise and educated by a Belgian tutor, demonstrated the power of prayer—a ritual he carried with him to the Pacific. "I did come from a Roman Catholic family and my mom was a praying woman. She said her Rosary in French in the morning and at night." The Pitres had seven children—Gilda, Emmett, John, Willie, Clayton, Wilfred and Edgar. Their sons served their country. Their daughter became a nun.

Clayton was the son of a yam and cotton farmer, and he worked long, hard days in the country. At first light, he'd quiet the animals—chickens, cows, hogs and horses. He remembers his father ginning the cotton. "And they would factor it, and grade it and things like that. And he would go from one person to another and whoever would give him a better deal, that's where he sold it. Oh, they had a marketing strategy." When the droughts came, Pitre watched the corn dry up like sunbaked cigars on a stalk.

Even in tough times, the Pitres proudly never depended on welfare. They learned to reap the most of the farming life. "You put some tomato plants in, some cucumbers, string beans, okra and you're on your way. My mom always knew how to can. Rather than having all this dry stuff, you can open up a jar and have almost fresh tomatoes."

Pitre was a self-described odd-ball kid who read voraciously to escape to places he could only imagine. "Reading did make a difference for me—like if I got something on New York and they would talk about the subway. Opelousas still doesn't have a public transportation system, mind you, but here I was reading about people using a subway or train, or an elevated train in Chicago. So, it was telling me about a world that existed in my time, but I'm nowhere around to use it."

He was around Opelousas when the Depression hit and still remembers the looting and empty wallets. But World War

Gilbert and Eugenie Pitre raised six boys and one daughter. All six young men served their country, but only Clayton trained as a Montford Point Marine. Clayton appears in the background, holding a child. *Clayton Pitre collection*

II spurred a recovery: "They started building at Camp Polk, Louisiana, and in Alexandria, Camp Beauregard. They began to build those places up. And they started an airfield down in Lake Charles, Louisiana. In Texas, they started running a pipeline across the country to the east coast."

Pitre was 17 when the Japanese attacked Pearl Harbor and 19 when he was drafted into the U.S. Navy. He chose to enlist in the U.S. Marines instead. His papers were stamped "Colored." Then he boarded a bus bearing a sign that ordered him to the back row. He was bound for a segregated base in North Carolina. Like his five brothers and his father, who escorted POWs during World War I, he would serve his country.

CLAYTON PITRE ARRIVED at Jacksonville in August 1943, amid stifling humidity, swarms of mosquitoes and terrain crawling

New recruits prepare for rigorous training at Montford Point, a segregated military base in Jacksonville, North Carolina. *U.S. Marine Corps*

Pitre arrived in North Carolina in August 1943, after Montford Point had been operating about a year. He was assigned to Platoon 126. *Clayton Pitre collection*

with poisonous snakes. Like the other African American Marines, he slept in a pre-fabricated hut made of pressed cardboard, not the barracks the white recruits lived in at nearby Camp Lejeune. He was banned from crossing the railroad tracks or from entering Camp Lejeune without a white escort. He could wear the globe and anchor, but he couldn't advance up the ranks like his white counterparts and wear the gold bars of a second lieutenant. "What happened in the Marine Corps that was strange for a whole period of time was they limited the black servicemen to not becoming officers. They could become master sergeants, any kind of non-commissioned rank you could get it, but when it comes to wearing a gold bar, no. You find that person with the same education— he's the officer. We protested in various ways and let them know we didn't like it."

Pitre was assigned to Platoon 126 and he began proving himself on day one. "When I was drafted into the Marine Corps, those guys from Chicago and New York, they expected me to be a dummy. They really did. But it wasn't so," Pitre says.

The attitudes were familiar to Clayton, who'd grown up in the segregated Deep South. "As far as I was concerned, it was old hat for me. I came from Louisiana—out there in the tulies you might say—and this was a way of life, you know?"

Black Marines who'd grown up north of the Mason-Dixon Line found themselves in another world. According to the Montford Point Marine Association, the men were treated as an experiment initially, doubted for their intellect and performance. Many Montford Pointers reported weeks of discrimination—name-calling and other verbal abuse, extra physical activity and physical abuse. Says Joe Geeter, a past president of the Montford Point Marine Association, "What they did was make them better Marines."

Soon, Montford Point Marines broke gunnery and anti-artillery records and prepared for some of the bloodiest battles of the Pacific Theater.

PITRE'S UNCOMPROMISING TRAINING began as early as 5:00 a.m. "You couldn't hardly see the guy and he's calling off—telling you what's going to happen that day. And then you would march back to your tent and you would fix your bunk and you would clean the floor and everything else." His schedule matched the whites': weapons and field training, physical conditioning, marksmanship training and a week of live firing at a rifle range. To this day, Pitre holds the utmost respect for the U.S. Marine Corps for the discipline he learned at Montford Point. All things considered, Pitre believes he was treated fairly.

The Montford Point Marine was assigned to the First Marine Ammunition

African American drill instructors were tough on their recruits. "What they did was make them better Marines," says Joseph Geeter, past president, Montford Point Marine Association. *National Archives*

Company with eight officers, 251 enlisted men and a fleet of trucks, jeeps and trailers for carting ammunition. There were 12 ammunition companies established in the war in total, and they were crucial in accommodating hundreds of thousands of fighting Marines in the Pacific. The Corps depended on a better system to load and offload ships and trucks, and to haul supplies to men on the frontlines. The laborers who would support those in hand-to-hand combat would learn all there is to know about handling ammunition, fuses and detonators. Then they'd haul the explosives to the heart of battle.

Like 13,000 Montford Pointers, Pitre was assigned to the Pacific Theater. After 21 days zigzagging through the Panama Canal, he arrived at the ruins of Pearl Harbor on New Year's Day 1944. "When we pulled in and I saw those ships on that side in the harbor—they hadn't cleared them out—then I really knew what the Japanese had done to us. There was no question about the fact that we were into something."

Pitre left Hawaii. He was sent to Kwajalein, Saipan and back to Hawaii before making his way toward Okinawa.

KAMIKAZE SUICIDE BOMBERS swarmed like bees over the Ryukyus Islands. It was Easter Sunday, 1945. Clayton Pitre watched from aboard the USS Bladen as his ship neared the rugged mountains and deep ravines of Okinawa—the chain's largest island. This was the scene of the last major battle of the Pacific War. The massive amphibious assault demanded control of Okinawan air bases that would allow the Allies to launch pivotal bombing raids against Japan, more than 300 miles away. The Allies were dominating Imperial Japan, but the savage fighting on Okinawa would make history as the bloodiest battle of the Pacific.

Launched in May 1944, the USS Bladen carried Pitre to Okinawa. The ship received two battle stars for her service in World War II.

Pitre prepared for his role as a decoy. "Oh my God. We went into the bay on the north part of the island, in Nago. There were these kamikazes that wanted to dive into those ships and the sky was just messed up with antiaircraft."

He climbed down the nets and into landing craft in a feint attack at the northern part of the island. "We got into those barges and we went within so many yards of the island and then turned around. A whole fleet of us went back to the ship to pull the Japanese north. Meanwhile, our Spitfires were just shelling the beach. They were just firing along the beach. They landed in the south end of the island, a whole bunch of fighters."

Pitre, one of 2,000 black Marines who fought on Okinawa, lived the working conditions of the Pacific War for nearly three months. He slept in a pup tent, dodged enemy fire and shook off the constant hum of Japanese warplanes flying overhead.

Pitre and the men in his company carried heavy explosives in driving rains and through deep mud. There was no cover. "You think that you may lose it but you've gone this far. You just hope that it won't happen. I can't describe it. What happens with people is there is something in you. I prayed. I prayed to myself. I prayed that I'd make it. But I saw others

U.S. Marines land in Okinawa. Their 82-day campaign in 1945 would prove to be the bloodiest battle of the Pacific War. *National Archives*

who broke. I saw others who broke and they just had to send them back."

Some of the Montford Point Marines carried the wounded on stretchers. Others found themselves in hand-to-hand combat. "Okinawa was a long, hard run, really. And it was the last one because President Truman—after he found out we had the atomic bomb— he wasn't for landing on Japan. We had radios by then on Okinawa, and if you heard what those Japanese were saying. They told us, 'You don't know us! We will fight you to the last man!' And they didn't stop after one bomb was dropped. So that tells you the effort we were up against."

The Japanese, ferocious defenders of the island, used the setting to their advantage—surfacing from tombs, caves and tunnels to lob explosives at the enemy. Suicide warriors plunged from the skies and targeted warships. Psychological warfare occurred day in and day out. The constant threat of a Japanese pilot became unbearable. "He would come by just about the time you were trying to get yourself together, about 6:00 in the morning. He would fly over you and the guys would be shooting at him. But they wouldn't get him. You would have to take cover while he's flying all over your head. And then come 12 o'clock, by the time you're getting ready to eat, he'd come back. The psychological thing—it broke some people."

National Archives

Pitre witnessed the breakdown of Floyd Hayes, a fellow Marine, en route to San Diego after the war. "Floyd started walking through the chow hall and he started preaching—something about being saved. He was not coherent to me. Someone came and got him and gave him a shot. I didn't see him anymore. They kept him sedated.

"Well, I was down at Third and Union in Seattle to take

a bus one day and here's Floyd. And he said, 'Man, they've got some good doctors in San Diego.' He said what happened to him. After a while he got a vision that his father had died while he was on the ship. But he said really, he couldn't sleep. His insomnia kicked in until finally he broke."

Beyond the psychological warfare and arduous labor, monsoons swept across the island. "One of them came through and we were in this tent," Pitre remembers. "We were in each corner holding down this pole. I'd never seen anything like it. I didn't know what they meant when they said monsoon season. That wind is something else! And it comes from the southwest. I said to someone, 'Why do you always have hedges on the southwest part of your yard?' They said, 'When the evil spirit comes, he comes straight. He does not know how to come around.' "

Pitre avoided disaster another day, when he climbed into a foxhole in the middle of a vegetable farm during heavy rains. He dug trenches to drain the water away from the fox-

The Battle of Okinawa produced a sea of mud and debris, leveled the island and resulted in a staggering death toll. *National Archives*

hole where he'd take cover from the kamikazes. He found two old doors and rested them on top of gallon cans nearby. Then he spread his canvas out. He'd sleep there on his dry makeshift bed.

"Why don't you come on?" a buddy asked. "We're going to stay in that old building tonight."

"I'm not going over there." Pitre could make out the old farmhouse with the coral tile roof—beaten and battered by monsoon winds and a mortar shell. The men were huddled south of Yontan Airfield on the Okinawan coast.

Pitre's fears were realized when the building collapsed overnight, breaking one man's hips. "If we had gone in there, that would have been a bad deal," Pitre says.

Montford Point Marines rest during the Japanese retreat on Okinawa. *National Archives*

All told, the very worst of the Pacific War was not the fierce winds or backbreaking labor, but the loss of life everywhere. It's the image he's never forgotten. "I saw men stacked up like cordwood–dead, moving bodies like five high. That was about the saddest thing I saw. That makes you cognizant of what you're into when you see a lot of dead bodies that way. That's the price of war.

"It appears to me we've still got people who don't really realize what the heck war is all about. As a president tries to bring these guys back home and somebody gets mad. There's a limit to how many lives you're going to sacrifice over there."

In the throes of battle, a non-commissioned black officer once openly challenged the positioning of black Marines during Pitre's service on Okinawa. "We were in a lower part of a valley," Pitre remembers. "If you interfere with coral, when the water comes that coral is going to shift. One time something like that happened. Water that had been draining lost its course. It just came down upon us in the valley. I grabbed my shoes, both of them, and it just washed stuff away. Then, we're all out in the water. We blacks are down here and the whites were in high ground. Not that they intended that, but this guy protested."

The 82-day campaign to seize Okinawa ended in favor of the Allies, but the price was steep all around. Across the landscape, you could see bombed-out buildings, bloodstained caves and farm fields in ruins. The death toll was staggering—14,000 Allies, 77,000 Japanese soldiers and 100,000 civilians or more. Japanese commanders and soldiers killed themselves rather than surrender. Civilians jumped from rocky cliffs to take their own lives. "It was a scene straight out of hell," remembers Higa Tomiko, then 7. "There is no other way to describe it."

The gruesome battle for Okinawa set the stage for the atomic bombs dropped in August on Hiroshima and Nagasaki that ushered in the end of World War II.

PITRE'S FIRST MARINE AMMUNITION COMPANY was soon assigned to North China. The men would repatriate the Japanese and stand guard on trains vulnerable to attack. Black Marines who traveled there remembered the Chinese touching their faces as if to determine "if the color would run off on the fingers." But eventually the reception was warm.

Pitre has never forgotten standing guard himself on a freight train bound for Tientsin: "We were going to deliver to some Marines there who would see that it would get to where it should be. But until I delivered it to them, I had to stay with it. So the train would stop different places. Attendants to the train—they could talk the language of the people around. And people would come toward this train. The trainman had no business to get into a fight with another civilian there. But anyway, it happened. This man from the community—he picked up an instrument and hit the trainman on the side of the head.

And it was a bad, bad hit. So here I have this guy come crying to me and bleeding. And I just looked all around to see where I was. And then I saw a building with the American flag on it. It looked like it could be military. I scribbled in longhand that this man was traveling with us as we were moving this food. *Please give him some medical aid.* And I wrote my name and rank and serial number. And he went over to that building and we moved. The CIA got involved."

It remains Pitre's fondest memory of World War II.

EXCEPT TO VISIT, Clayton never returned to Bayou Country after the war. He considered the family farm there a dead-end and followed his brother to Washington instead, chasing a possible job with the U.S. Navy. Pitre started working for Todd Shipyard when he overheard recent high school graduates talking about their prom. The conversation led to his enrollment at Broadway-Edison Tech, a school for GIs, which awarded Pitre his high school diploma. A college degree at Seattle University

Clayton and Gloria, flanked by family in Washington D.C. in 2012. Pitre and 400 Montford Point Marines finally received the Congressional Gold Medal. *Clayton Pitre collection*

followed. He met his wife Gloria. They married and had three sons. Pitre eventually became Chief Housing Developer for the Central Area Motivation Program, a group that provides housing to families earning low or moderate incomes.

Looking back, Pitre is grateful for the GI bill that afforded him his education and the clear objective of his service in World War II. "We had a true mission. You knew what Hitler was doing and what he had done. You knew what the Japanese were doing and what they had done. But we find ourselves sometimes getting into skirmishes. This mission is not as clear for these youngsters today."

Clayton Pitre stands topside on the *USNS Montford Point* in Everett. The ship is a tribute to African American Marine Corps recruits. *Mass Communication Specialist 2nd Class Jeffry Willadsen/U.S. Navy*

He's proud to be called an African American and considers America "halfway there" on its long road to equality. "The fact is that when all is equal you have gained. The military no longer has to worry about that problem. They have fine people from all races who've done well for their country."

Over the last dozen years or so, Pitre has belonged to a Northwest support group for U.S. Marines. Every year around November 10th, the birthday of the United States Marine Corps, members get together. The first slice of cake is presented to the oldest veteran who, in turn, passes the slice on to the youngest. Clayton Pitre, at 92, is always the oldest Marine in the room. Sizing up the new generation in an integrated Corps, Pitre smiles. "I know we'll be in good shape. We've got what we need."

Trova Heffernan

REGINA TOLLFELDT

She Gave Them Wings

All the day long whether rain or shine,
She's a part of the assembly line.
She's making history,
working for victory,
Rosie the riveter!
Keeps a sharp lookout for sabotage,
Sitting up there on the fuselage.
That little frail can do more than a
male can do,
Rosie the riveter!

—"Rosie the Riveter," lyric and music by Redd Evans and John Jacob Loeb, 1942

The cover girl for the May 29, 1943, issue of *The Saturday Evening Post*, was no leggy starlet. "Rosie the Riveter" was a beefy redhead, muscular arms bulging from the rolled-up sleeves of her work shirt—certainly not the "little frail" working girl of the popular song. Norman Rockwell's Rosie was taking a brief lunch break on the assembly line, ham sandwich in hand, rivet gun on her lap, one penny loafer resting on a copy of Hitler's *Mein Kampf*.

Rosie came in all sizes and colors. She became an icon, symbolizing the six million American women mobilized for home-front factories during World War II. Four million were young, unmarried defense plant workers like 19-year-old Regina Sawina. With her girlish face and boyish figure—she weighed 97 pounds—Regina could have passed for 14. More like Rosie's coltish kid sister.

Now 93, Regina Sawina Tollfeldt of Olympia is one of the last of the some 15,000 women who worked in Boeing's Seattle factories during the war. Regina literally gave wings to the American airmen pounding the fascists from 27,000 feet. Eight hours a day, seven days a week at the apex of the war, she wriggled through the wing jigs for the gleaming B-17s leaving Plant No. 2 at the rate of a dozen a day.

Regina's job was to drill the holes for the rivets that fastened the bomber's aluminum skin to its ribs.

Regina Sawina as a teenager. *Regina Tollfeldt collection*

Today, she calls herself a "peace-afist." Practically every Friday night during the second Gulf War, Regina stood silent witness against militarism with the Olympia chapter of an international group known as Women in Black.

In 1942, however, she had no compunctions about building a lethal warplane. Regina sees no contradiction. The dictators were threatening to extinguish democracy. Hitler and Mussolini had savaged Poland and Slovenia, the homelands of her parents; Imperial Japan had attacked America and subjugated much of the Pacific Rim. "The thing I hate is hate," Regina says. "That's never changed."

Another thing that's never changed is Regina's resilience and appetite for knowledge. She grew up in logging camps and small towns during the Depression and never had the chance to go to college.

When you learn more about her eventful life it won't surprise you that she became an ace stenographer and typist, a talented artist and a respected counselor with the Washington State Division of Vocational Rehabilitation. She is marvelously self-educated, with shelves full of books and a fine collection of classical records. She loves opera. She writes letters to the editor and helped circulate a petition to the U.S. attorney general to "Throw the Wall Street crooks in jail!"

"My mother always said I was nosy. I didn't think I was nosy. I was just curious!" Regina says, laughing at the memory.

Mother was a stubborn Slovenian, father an industrious Pole. Their countries had been shuttlecocked among princes and potentates for centuries. The assassination of Archduke Franz Ferdinand, an heir to the Austro-Hungarian Empire, in the summer of 1914 at Sarajevo lit the short fuse that ignited the First World War. Woodrow Wilson called it "a war to end all wars." That was tragically unprophetic. The war that broke out only 25 years later—the one Regina Sawina helped fight from the home front—soon enveloped the globe. Sixty million people perished, including 40 million civilians. The death toll included 5½ million Poles and a million Yugoslavians. One of Regina's uncles had joined a special Polish American regiment to fight the Nazis before the U.S. entered the war. John Sawina lived to tell about it, but many of Regina's relatives in the old country disappeared in the fog of war. Two who miraculously survived were an educated young Polish couple—a geologist and a nurse. The Nazis tattooed numbers on their forearms and shipped them to an armament factory to toil as slave laborers. They were liberated at war's end and came to America.

Regina's father joined the U.S. Army in 1917. To his disappointment, he never made it overseas. *Regina Tollfeldt collection*

REGINA'S LIFE STORY begins in the third wave of immigration that swept America at the beginning of the 20th century. Her father, Valentine Sawina, left Poland for America at the age of 18 in 1907.

Fifteen percent of the U.S. population and 24 percent of the labor force was now foreign-born. Sawina worked his way across the continent to Grays Harbor on the coast of Washington State before backtracking to Libby, Montana. Fourteen years later, fleeing the chaos that followed World War I, Regina's 21-year-old mother, Gizela Stor, arrived from Slovenia and ended up in the same timber town.

Valentine ("Val-in-teen"), a proud naturalized citizen, had joined the U.S. Army when America entered the war. He was bitterly disappointed not to make it overseas before the armistice. Gizela saw the carnage and it seared her soul. More than 30,000 Slovenian men conscripted into the Austro-Hungarian Army were killed in combat during World War I; thousands of refugees died in squalid camps. "Mother didn't do a lot of talking about her life in the old country," Regina says, "and Daddy was just glad he got out. He loved this country. To him, this country could do no wrong."

Regina's future husband, Roy Tollfeldt, who saw heavy combat as an American infantryman in Europe during World War II, was the handsome son of a Swedish father and Norwegian mother. You will not be surprised, then, to know that Regina Sawina Tollfeldt knows her world history. There's another thing: She'd like you to pronounce her names correctly: It's "Reg-eena Sah-Veena Toll-felt," with a strong "g" and "v" and a silent "d."

Roy Tollfeldt of Aberdeen as an infantryman in Europe during World War II. He saw heavy combat. *Regina Tollfeldt collection*

"Sawina" in Poland is pronounced "Sah-Veena," Regina explains. "That was a problem for me growing up because people wanted to pronounce it 'Sah-Weena.' When I worked at the National Bank of Commerce in Aberdeen right after the war, the manager was Tony Savina. His father had changed the 'w' to a 'v.' Sawina with a 'w' is very unusual in America. My Uncle Frank changed his

Regina's parents, Walenty Sawina and Gizela Stor, on their wedding day in 1922. *Regina Tollfeldt collection*

name to 'Savina' when he came to Aberdeen to avoid a lot confusion. But I'm stubborn. For Heaven sakes! If my name is Sawina and pronounced 'Sah-Veena' I'm not going to change it."

Valentine Sawina was one of four brothers drawn to Grays Harbor by the promise of steady work in the logging camps, lumber mills and canneries. Though they weren't as numerous as the ubiquitous Finns, hundreds of other Poles were already there along the muddy banks of the Wishkah, Chehalis and Hoquiam rivers—the Kalinowskis, Malinowskis and Zelaskos, to name a few. "The older brother came first," Regina says. "He worked hard and earned money to send for the next one. Then they worked together to earn the money to bring over the next." Valentine found a job at a whale-rendering plant, but couldn't stand the smell and soon set out for Montana.

Valentine changed his often-mispronounced first name to Walenty and homesteaded near Libby. He was working at a lumber mill when Regina's mother arrived to live with an uncle. Walenty was 14 years her senior. His English was better than hers. She spoke Slovene and passable German, which was all Greek to him. For Walenty nevertheless it was love at first sight. For Gizela it was, all things considered, a proposal based on slim alternatives. The work available amounted to being a maid in a boarding house or a cook at some roadside greasy spoon. "It was hard for a woman to make a living," Regina says. "I always used to think she should have been born a man because she loved traveling. Wanted to go places. She finally gave in and married Daddy. She didn't want to be a homemaker, but that's what she ended up being."

REGINA JEANNE SAWINA, the first of Walenty and Gizela's three daughters, was born in Libby in the spring of 1923. The following year, encouraged by relatives in the Midwest, Walenty packed up his family and moved to Detroit where he landed a job on Ford Motor Company's new Lincoln assembly line. Henry Ford had created a sensation in 1914 when he doubled his workers' pay to $5 a day and shortened the workday from nine hours to eight. His goal was to reduce turnover. It worked. The bonus was that more workers could afford to buy his cars.

Regina, right, with her mother and sisters around 1927 in Detroit. *Regina Tollfeldt collection*

Walenty always told his friends and kids it was the best job he ever had. Then he got sick. Very sick. "The doctors didn't know what was wrong with him," Regina says. "But they concluded he needed to have a job outdoors so he could breathe clean air."

Walenty found a new job with his former employer, the J. Neils Lumber Company, in a place about as different and far from Detroit as one could imagine.

"When I was 5, we moved to the Gifford Pinchot National Forest along the Columbia River just south of Mount Adams," Regina fondly remembers. "Every winter we had six to seven feet of snow. For a while we lived at Camp 5 at Glenwood, just a little dot on the map in Klickitat County. The nearest town was White Salmon. My first job was when I was 12. I worked for the teacher at Camp 5. When she was on vacation, she needed someone to watch over her cottage and water her flowers. I earned 10 whole dollars a month that went

The school kids at Camp 5 in Klickitat County around 1930. Regina is fourth from left in the middle row. *Regina Tollfeldt collection*

to my parents. Mamma and I worked for a farmer, delivering milk to 32 families every morning; then we got our milk for free. We kids—there were now three girls—helped Mamma. That's how we learned to cook. We worked hard. Daddy always said, 'Don't be ashamed of anything you have to do to earn a living. Just do it.'

"Life in a little logging camp was wonderful. The cottages were built on skids so they could be moved by rail. Daddy was at Camp 5 first, then at Camp 7. We played outside. All the kids, all the time. When it was Halloween, we built big bonfires; during the winter we had skis someone made for the kids. I don't envy children nowadays. They don't have the kind of life I had growing up, even during those hard times." J. Neils Lumber Company was good to its workers, continuing operations at Klickitat during the depths of the Depression despite steep losses.

Concerned that the logging camp school wasn't accredited for high school courses, Regina's parents moved the family to White Salmon in 1938 after her freshman year. "Daddy stayed in camp during the week. Then in the summer months we girls would take turns going up to camp and

Regina, left, and her sister Viola along the Columbia Gorge around 1940.
Regina Tollfeldt collection

cooking for him." Regina remembers how diligently her parents kept up with her schoolwork. "It started when I was in First Grade. When we brought our schoolwork home, they did it with us. That's how they learned the language. My father was very loving, and a more fervent Catholic than my mother. When we lived at Camp 5, he's the one who taught us the catechism, the Way of the Cross. We would kneel at the edge of the bed every Sunday and he would teach us our prayers. We learned manners, too. We were never allowed to call our neighbors by their first names. It was always 'Mr.' or 'Mrs.' And Daddy always said 'Eat what's on your plate. Don't take more than you can eat. You can always take seconds.' He was very strict about waste."

Regina Sawina was a bookish, practical girl who rejected her mother's attempts to make her frilly. Regina loved history and geography. Two of the 34 students in the Class of 1941 at Columbia Union High School at White Salmon were Japanese. "They were my friends. When their families were interned in Idaho during the war I couldn't understand why."
  Regina's Uncle Frank, who had a good job at Rayonier's pulp and paper mill in Hoquiam, had been prodding her father to move back to Grays Harbor. "I think they purposely waited until I could graduate, then they loaded up the car—a '36 Plymouth—with what they could, leaving everything else behind, and drove to Aberdeen."

Regina found part-time jobs at five-and-dimes and was contemplating business college when the Japanese attacked Pearl Harbor. The five Sawinas were living in a tiny house along the street that funneled traffic to the ocean beaches. A nighttime blackout was immediately ordered along the coast. "Everyone was told to pull their blinds at night," Regina remembers, "because there was the fear that the Japanese might start their invasion of the West Coast by coming ashore along the beaches on either side of Grays Harbor. And we were just a few miles inland. Someone said Japanese submarines could come right up the harbor. One night a few days after the attack, here came the Army in their camouflaged trucks, moving through the night with blue headlights. We were scared to death, peeking out the windows." The Army set up an anti-aircraft installation near Westport and manned the beaches at Pacific Beach and present-day Ocean Shores. The airfield under construction on an island off Hoquiam was hurriedly completed. "I think what scared me the worst was that I had lived such a peaceful life, and to think that we were going to go to war against these terrible people with their massive militaries, I was frightened."

Walenty Sawina, newly employed by a lumber merchant, was turned away at the enlistment office. He was 59 years old. His wife and oldest daughters were hired by Boeing, which established a training facility in Aberdeen a few months into the war. It was a precursor to eight Boeing subassembly factories in Western Washington, including plants at Aberdeen, Hoquiam, Chehalis, South Tacoma, Everett and Bellingham. Regina and Viola were soon learning how to use power tools. *The Girl Mechanic's Manual* "emphasized the importance of safety around heavy equipment to prevent losing an arm, 'for after all, arms are nice things to have—both on and around you.'"

Imagine their excitement when they moved to Seattle that summer to start work at Boeing's mammoth B-17 factory near Boeing Field along the east bank of the Duwamish Waterway.

WHEN THE PROTOTYPE FOR THE B-17 was rolled out in 1935, its "elegance and impression of power caused a media sensation." Surveying its four big engines and array of machine guns,

Boeing's subassembly plant in Aberdeen receives a production award in 1944. The plant employed 750 workers in two shifts. *John Hughes collection*

Seattle Times reporter Richard Williams dubbed it the "Flying Fortress." Fourteen were delivered to the U.S. Army Air Corps in 1937. For the next two years, War Department bureaucracy, inter-service rivalry and isolationism limited its production. The Navy jealously maintained "that it was its task, and its task alone, to counter any seaborne threat." Boeing had to haggle to get past the break-even point on the plane. After deleting some features, the company reduced its rock-bottom price by $2,500 to $202,500, but the War Department was still bullheadedly demanding a $199,000 airplane. (One B-2 stealth bomber costs the Pentagon about $2 billion.) The inertia was a major blow to Boeing. It had used its own funds to build the prototype "in anticipation of large orders for the production aircraft." Then with war clouds gathering and the big bomber setting speed and altitude records, Boeing received orders for nearly 80 more. By comparison, Hitler's armament factories produced 700 bombers and nearly 2,000 military aircraft all told in 1939. Charles Lindbergh, America's famed "Lone Eagle" aviator, toured the Third Reich's warplane plants, piloted a new Nazi bomber and pronounced the Luftwaffe unbeatable. That summer, when Roosevelt named General George C. Marshall

Army chief of staff, the U.S. Army was the world's 19th largest, "behind Portugal and only slightly ahead of Bulgaria."

In September of 1939, Germany and the Soviet Union, in a devil's pact that would boomerang on Stalin, crushed Walenty Sawina's homeland. They divvied up Poland, perpetrated mass atrocities and touched off six years of slaughter. Great Britain and France declared war. Nine months later, France surrendered. The Brits bravely hunkered down, facing the juggernaut alone. In his year-end Fireside Chat on December 29, 1940, FDR declared that America would become "the great arsenal of democracy." Boeing had 8,400 workers. A month later it was 10,500. A year later, when America entered the war, it was nearly 29,000. Polly Reed Myers, a scholar who analyzed Boeing's World War II manpower campaign, writes that the company's Seattle employment peaked at 31,750 in 1945.

> As the labor shortage intensified nationwide after the attack on Pearl Harbor, women began to fill jobs traditionally done by men. The defense industry and government agencies such as the War Manpower Commission intensified their efforts to recruit women workers in 1942, when it became clear that the number of men leaving jobs for the military was outweighing the number of women entering the work force. ...Boeing managers had long resisted the idea of hiring women for the production lines. ... Amidst the growth, Boeing's supply of men ran out.

In January of 1943, when Regina Sawina was drilling holes inside the wing jigs and her sister Viola was working on a plane so secret she couldn't breathe a word (it was the B-29 "Superfortress") there were 14,874 other women on the production lines at Seattle and Renton—44 percent of Boeing's workforce. And it needed more. "WOMEN!" a help-wanted ad declared, "Even if you've never done anything except housework there's almost certainly a job for you here at Boeing—a clean and pleasant one—and you can take pride in being a Boeing

Boeing camouflaged Plant 2 to make it appear a suburban neighborhood from the air in the event enemy planes made it past the coast. *Washington State Archives*

worker. Your husband—your son—your brother or boyfriend will be proud that you are doing your part in building the axis-blasting Flying Fortresses."

The ad didn't mention that to help blast the Axis you had to buy your own tools—in Regina's case a power drill and an assortment of bits. "But we didn't have to pay up front. We paid them back out of our wages—72 cents an hour when I started in the summer of 1942."

The Sawina sisters went house-hunting and scored a find, a rental on Queen Anne Hill. "It was a *house*, not an apartment," Regina remembers, still marveling at their luck. "The fellow who owned it was in the service. There were five of us girls—all working for Boeing: Viola and me, another girl from Aberdeen and two others. All we did was work, eat and sleep. In the beginning, I worked the graveyard shift, which started at 11:30 p.m. Viola was working swing shift and the other girls were on the day shift, so we were always coming and going. The house came complete with a player piano, which was our entertainment whenever we were all together.

We got a big kick out of that. It was all innocent fun— not going out drinking and taking drugs like today. We were innocents, really."

They all rode the bus. "From Queen Anne I had to transfer at the Pike Place Market to catch the bus to South Seattle. It was dark when I went to work and dark when I came home, which was scary to a kid who had never lived in a big city. Coming home, the bus stop was three blocks from the house. I walked down the middle of the street. But it was exciting, too. Seattle was working around the clock. Later, when I worked the swing shift, we'd stay downtown after we got off work and eat and go to a movie. We'd take any breaks we could because we worked seven days a week for a long time, putting out plane after plane after plane."

Viola and Regina heading off to work at Boeing on a snowy day in Seattle. *Regina Tollfeldt collection*

While defense plant workers all along Puget Sound cheered the U.S. Navy's headway in the Pacific, the specter of a Japanese attack on the mainland prompted Boeing to camouflage Plant 2 by creating a three-dimensional faux suburban neighborhood over its roof tops. "Grass" grew over burlap and chicken-wire; make-believe houses were fashioned from plywood. "We had a real scare one day when all the sirens went off and we thought we were going to be bombed. We ran down into a tunnel. When we got the all-clear, it turned out there were two unidentified planes in the vicinity. Relieved, we got back to work."

HER UNIFORM WAS COVERALLS—a one-piece blue jumpsuit— and a hard hat that wasn't all that hard over a bandana. Here's what she was doing:

A Rosie works inside a B-17 wing. *Boeing Images*

"When you build a B-17 wing, there's the tubular ribs called trusses; there's the corrugation over the ribs and there's the aluminum skin. Each process requires that the person who goes through first marks where the holes should be drilled. Little X's. I would lie down and wriggle in. We used spring-loaded fasteners called 'clekos' that held the corrugation to the ribs after we drilled the holes. It was a temporary rivet. I'd go through first and do all that; then come back when the corrugation was on. Next came the skin. You got through one level, then there were two more. So you were going up and down, up and down, back and forth. It's funny I don't dream about that! I think I can still feel the heat if I close my eyes and think about it. It got so terrifically hot in the plant during the summer months, even with the doors wide open. One day I wasn't wearing my hard hat because it was so hot. There I was, inside the wing tip, wriggling my way through the ribs. A worker on the next level dropped her bucking bar—the tool used to form the head of the rivet—and it hit me on the head. I've got a scar." She points to her head. "I had to go to the nurse's station and get patched up. I learned a lesson! Wear your hat!

At the peak of production, Boeing Plant 2 in Seattle produced sixteen B-17G's a day. *Boeing Images*

"The riveters followed us, and the noise rattled your head: rata-tat-tat! They never told us to wear earplugs, so I have a hearing loss. They were more concerned about us getting dehydrated, so we had to suck on these salt balls the size of a gumball." She makes a face that tells you they tasted awful.

"Sometimes I would be drilling on one side of the wing and somebody would be drilling on the other side of the wing. I almost got jabbed in the butt once. When I felt my coveralls being twisted by the drill bit, I yelled 'Stop it!' Luckily they did. If I hadn't yelled, the drill bit would have gone right into my bottom." She laughs. "But that was only two incidents out of three years, so that's not bad. I did the same work on the wings all those years. I was small and that's what they needed—someone small. It was monotonous, but we all knew it was important work." The B-17's wings carried 2,700 gallons of fuel and four engines.

Nevertheless, Regina and other Rosies recall the

chauvinism they encountered at Boeing. "Women were considered too stupid to know how to do anything," one said. Another, who finally quit in disgust and frustration, said, "I had to work with a man who had never had a woman helper before. ...He hated me."

"The guys were pulling things on you all the time," Regina remembers, "like sending you off to fetch some tool when there was no such thing. But I worked with one young man who was great. He told me, 'Regina, just tell me what they're asking you for before you go. They're pulling your leg.' Then he got drafted. We were sorry to see him go. Mostly, they were guys just being superior. Not all men are that way, but there were a lot of them at Boeing who resented that they were there working with women instead of fighting the war. But the thing is, we were all fighting the war, and the women helped immensely. Some women even flew the bombers across the country." (They piloted practically every military aircraft, including experimental jets; 38 died in accidents.)

Local 751 of the Aeronautical Mechanics Union, an affiliate of the International Association of Machinists, also obstructed the hiring of racial minorities for as long as it could, with Boeing management claiming it had no jurisdiction over union eligibility issues. The unions "finally lifted the ban on African American union membership in April 1942," but their "system of work permits underscored the temporary nature of employment for white women and African Americans at Boeing and across the defense industry," Polly Reed Myers notes, adding:

> Although racial tensions at Boeing ran high, the number of African American workers there was low. In July 1943, Boeing employed 44 African American men and 285 African American women out of a total work force of 29,393. Even those few workers experienced discrimination. [That month] managers reported "continuing racial problems surrounding the use of negroes in present facilities" at Boeing.

Workers pose with "Five Grand," the 5,000th Boeing-built Flying Fortress, on May 13, 1944. Regina signed her name on the fuselage, and she's in there somewhere. *Boeing Images*

For Regina, it was disconcerting and confusing. "I was colorblind. But until I started work at Boeing, I'd never really been around a black person. One time there was a furor in my area of the plant. I looked over and there was a black woman and a white woman facing off. I turned away because I didn't want to see what was going on. I heard later that the white woman said something she took objection to. She pulled a knife on her, so it must have been something awful. A lot of Southern blacks came up here to work in war production plants. They weren't being treated decently down there, but some ran into prejudice up here, too. There are racists everywhere."

My parents had impressed on us that racism is wrong—that all people are human beings. You have to be taught to hate." Ironically, when comedian Jack Benny visited the plant it was his hilarious black "valet," Eddie "Rochester" Anderson, who made the biggest hit, Regina remembers.

BOEING PRODUCED 6,981 B-17s. There were thousands of upgrades—a new tail, more firepower, better armor, improved propellers, a chin turret—but the basic design never changed. "The wing, in fact, was exactly the same on every model," Edward Jablonski writes in his history of the Flying Fortress. Small-town boys from Aberdeen, Olympia, Klickitat, Walla Walla and Wenatchee—many barely out of their teens—were flying Regina Sawina's wings. Had they known about her handiwork they might have added her name to one of their planes. The famous "nose art" of World War II saluted sweethearts and taunted the enemy—and fate. Given the appalling losses aircrews were experiencing, the brass in the 8th Air Force figured anything that boosted morale couldn't be bad, even bare breasts and double entendres. There was *Our Gal Sal, Piccadilly Lilly, Alice from Dallas, Bastard's Bungalow, BigAss Bird, Phartzac* (GI slang for sleeping bag) and the all-encompassing *Horny*. When the censors cracked down, as they did periodically after a racy B-17 appeared in *Life* magazine, the 100th Bomb Group's talented artists added diaphanous negligées to their mascots.

"The fighters are our salvation," Winston Churchill said in 1940, "but the bombers alone provide the means of victory." The Royal Air Force early on flew Boeing B-17s but claimed supremacy for its Lancaster bomber, which took the fight to the Third Reich while the Yanks were amassing airpower. The blunt-nosed RAF machine—like Consolidated Aircraft's slab-sided B-24 "Liberator"—was a fine airship, but a plain Jane compared to the graceful B-17. With its aluminum fuselage, gun turrets and pinup girls, the star of *Twelve O'Clock High* and *Memphis Belle* is the all-time classic bomber. "It came with a high tingle factor: Just looking at it could prickle a man's scalp," Geoffrey Perret writes in *Winged Victory*. Brigadier General Ira Eaker, who headed the U.S. Army Air Force's VIII Bomber Command during some of

On May 10, 1945, Boeing employees in Seattle celebrate the Allies' victory in Europe by rolling out a B-29 bomber carrying an "On to Toyko" sign. Viola Sawina, Regina's sister, is somewhere in that crowd. She was a Rosie on the B-29 production line. *Boeing Images*

the bloodiest missions of the war, believed the B-17 was "the best combat airplane ever built. It combined in perfect balance, the right engine, the right wing and the right control surfaces. The B-17 was a bit more rugged than the B-24. It could ditch better because of the low wing and it could sustain more battle damage. You wouldn't believe they could stay in the air."

"No enemy bomber can reach the Ruhr," Reichsminister Hermann Göring boasted in 1939. "If one reaches the Ruhr, my name is not Göring. You can call me Meyer!" When Allied bombers began pounding the Ruhr's synthetic oil refineries in 1943, Germans sarcastically referred to the air raid sirens as "Meyer's trumpets." A B-17 dubbed *Rosie's Riveters* was helping make Göring's name mud with Hitler. It was piloted by Lieutenant Robert "Rosie" Rosenthal, a Jewish kid from Brooklyn.

By the fall of 1943, America's factories were producing a new military aircraft every five minutes. The brave men who flew them suffered appalling losses. "Of the 416,800 American battle deaths in World War II, 79,265 were airmen," historian A.J. Baime writes in *The Arsenal of Democracy.*

May 13, 1944, was a proud day for Regina and her co-workers. Before it was rolled out, they all signed their names on a B-17G, serial number 43-437716. It was the 5,000th to leave Plant 2. Regina's scrapbook contains a photo of the christening of "5 Grand." She's there somewhere in the sea of happy faces. "We were all in it together. We were gonna win this war!"

And they did. A year later, Germany surrendered, and on August 15, 1945, Japan gave up, too. The high-altitude B-29 Superfortresses Regina's sister helped build had decimated two cities with atomic bombs. Regina remembers being simultaneously happy it was over and frightened at what man hath wrought. "The propaganda was that the A-bomb saved the lives of hundreds of thousands of American GI's," she says. "And it probably did, but look at the lives that were lost—innocent civilians, and the way they had to suffer. The thing that bothers me now is that we don't want anyone else to have nuclear weapons. But we've got 'em. We need to get rid of all of them!"

With the war won, "naturally we were all fired by Boeing," Regina says with a wistful shrug. "Contracts were cancelled and the men returning from overseas would want their jobs back. But women had done all kinds of work during the war, and I think ultimately that's what opened the eyes of a lot of women and changed society. The thing is, a woman has got to consider the future, too. I survived my husband. My income was crucial."

REGINA INVESTED HER LAST CHECK from Boeing in four months' of business school. She worked at the bank for $91 a month, met a handsome young carpenter just home from the war and landed a new job as secretary to the director of the State Board for Vocational Education in Olympia. "I took shorthand at 80 words a minute and typed at 140 words per minute," she recalls. "I had a heavy touch, maybe from drilling all those holes, so no one could type a stencil like I could. Regina got all the stencils! Which was OK with me. I was a workhorse. I think my success had a lot to do with the fact that I was ready to do anything they gave me."

Regina Sawina and Roy Tollfeldt didn't rush into things. In 1955, they were watching *My Sister Eileen* at the D&R Theater in Aberdeen when he slipped an engagement ring on her finger. It wasn't happily ever after. Roy was haunted by things he'd seen during the war. They lost an infant to a miscarriage and planned to adopt. Then Roy developed Crohn's Disease. But he built them a cozy home, and worked too hard too long. They both loved music. Roy sang with the Choir of the West at Pacific Lutheran University. Regina was a mainstay at the vocational rehabilitation office in Aberdeen until her retirement in 1978. "In all, I worked for the state for 32 years. I loved vocational rehabilitation. We were one of the departments that spent money on people, found them jobs and kept them as productive taxpayers. We had to find them jobs, and that's where I really excelled because I love people. All they had to do was come in one time. I'd write their names down and then I knew them. I treated them like an equal—the way everyone should be treated."

Newlyweds Regina and Roy Tollfeldt on November 11, 1955. Fittingly, it was Veterans Day. *Regina Tollfeldt collection*

Regina and Roy moved to Olympia in 1980. Regina had been a caregiver to her mother, father and father-in-law. In 1999, Roy was gone, too. And in 2009, her sister Viola—the other Rosie—died of leukemia.

Regina Sawina Tollfeldt is resilient and of good cheer. She has her record albums, her books, her paintings, blue ribbons from the county fair, good friends, caring neighbors and a delicious sense of humor.

What's the secret to her longevity?

"I have no idea," she says, eyes twinkling. "Why should I be the one to live this long when I was the skinny kid?"

The one who helped win a war.

John C. Hughes

Regina's painting of her husband Roy using his helmet as a wash basin during World War II. *Regina Tollfeldt collection*

LES AMUNDSON

IN FOCUS
18 MONTHS
IN CAPTIVITY

" We had periods of starvation. You'd chew [one stale slice of black bread] with your front teeth like a chipmunk, and with your saliva you could build up a kind of slurry. You'd swallow that. Then you'd do that with another little piece. You'd try and make that last. "

– 2d Lt. Les Amundson, U.S. Army Air Forces

Amundson in his official portrait for the U.S. Army Air Forces, and as a POW. Conditions were grueling at his compound, Stalag Luft I, north of Berlin. At roll call each morning, a guard verified to see that no prisoner had escaped or died overnight. *Les Amundson collection*

Amundson (top left), and his 10-man crew train on the B-17 in Walla Walla in 1943. *Les Amundson collection*

Les Amundson's doomed B-17 bomber sped toward a turnip field in The Netherlands. A woman on the family farm watched openmouthed as the Flying Fortress skidded the length of a football field before groaning to a halt. It was November 26, 1943, the day of Amundson's first and last bombing mission.

The Dutch Resistance led the pilot to a hayloft. Traveling with the Underground in Holland for a month, he eluded capture. But the Gestapo finally caught up to Amundson in Amsterdam. He was taken to Stalag Luft 1, a POW camp 100 miles north of Berlin.

Amundson survived 18 months in captivity before Operation Revival evacuated him and 9,000 other prisoners. He returned to his home in Sunnyside, Washington.

GEORGE NAROZONICK

Sailor on the Longest Day

*"You could feel the effect and smell the real thing, gunpower.
D-Day was the day it was for real.
It wasn't a maneuver anymore.
It was not an exercise.
Either you knew how to pray or you learned how to pray "*

—Shipfitter, 3rd Class, George Narozonick, U.S. Navy

No one had ever witnessed anything like it when they came by sea and by air. A massive armada as far as any bystander could see crossed the English Channel. Aircraft rumbled up and down the French coastline. The blustery storm had softened by then, but dawn still broke in a gray fog with heavy winds gusting from the Northwest. And four-foot waves still rose.

George Narozonick, an 18-year-old shipfitter from central New Jersey, stood topside on a ship longer than a football field. He peered out at the coastline. Years of logistical and intelligence planning approached a daring end. "You could feel the effect and smell the real thing, gunpowder," he remembered. "D-Day was the day it was for real. It wasn't a maneuver anymore. It was not an exercise. Either you knew how to pray or you learned how to pray."

One of the largest amphibious assaults in world history, D-Day turned the tide in World War II and lives on in survivors like Narozonick. *National Archives*

This American flag, a gift presented to Narozonick years ago, once flew over the beaches of Normandy. It was one of his most treasured possessions. *Laura Mott*

Narozonick watched the men climb down cargo nets to landing craft swaying and pitching in the water below. He'd see their faces the next 70 years, heroes with dreams like his drifting away to a fate unknown.

Seventy years on in 2015, Narozonick, 89, remembered the heavy price of freedom, the unlucky and lucky of history's Longest Day. Photos and scrapbooks were scattered across his dining room table in Olympia, Wash. He glanced at a model of his famous ship. Outside his living room window was a symbol of his sacrifice: An American flag that once flew over the very coastline of one of the largest amphibious assaults in world history. Here he could easily flash back to his small mattress and the large mess hall. He could feel the fatigue that could lull him to sleep anyplace and the seasickness on the high seas of the North Atlantic. But mostly, he remembered those men he'd last seen in the churning surf. He never forgot them. The GIs gallantly waded through the water. It was miserably cold. They stormed Utah Beach—wide open, sandy and pocked with dunes—and amid howling chaos, helped liberate France.

GEORGE NAROZONICK took his first breath 50 miles from Manhat-

Narozonick, born on a farm in Manalapan, New Jersey, was raised in a large Catholic family. Shown here with his sister Jenny on the day of their First Communion. George *Narozonick collection*

tan. His hometown, Manalapan, New Jersey, proudly holds a place in history as the site of the Battle of Monmouth in the Revolutionary War. (With great fanfare, re-enactments of the 1778 battle still take place in Manalapan every June.) Narozonick arrived in 1925, the year Adolf Hitler released his hate-filled manifesto, *Mein Kampf*. He could have been any farm boy around—racing through the fields, milking Bessie and watching over the garden with his siblings. They grew all the food they could ever need on the 102-acre farm and they raised their own animals. His attractive mother Alice had emigrated in 1906 while the Poles rebelled against their Russian rulers. Alice left the upheaval in Poland and went to work in an American tobacco mill. His father Stanley, a native New Jerseyan, had chauffeured the owner.

Narozonick remembered the skies darkening when a marvel as long as three city blocks flew overhead to nearby Lakehurst. The luxury airship *Hindenburg* was the fastest way across the Atlantic. He was 11 when the monster airship blew apart in that New Jersey town and erupted into a ball of flames. "Oh, the

As long as three city blocks, the *Hindenburg* burst into a ball of flames near Narozonick's hometown in 1937.

Narozonick as a young boy in New Jersey. *George Narozonick collection*

humanity! All the passengers! I don't believe it!" a reporter had said. The explosion, likely the result of a hydrogen leak, rattled the windows in homes below and took the lives of 36 people.

Hard times had fallen upon the country by then. The American economy had collapsed in 1929, putting millions out of work. The kids never understood they were living in a Great Depression, but it uprooted their lives just the same. Farmers the country over struggled with falling agricultural prices and mounting debt. And George's father Stanley lost his farm in Manalapan. The Narozonicks packed up their family of 10 and moved to nearby Freehold. Stanley found a steady job as a lineman for the Jersey Central Power Company.

Years passed in the small community. Narozonick graduated from Lakewood High School and promptly enlisted in the U.S. Navy—a decision sealed by his love for his country and the Navy's sharp uniforms. (He'd tried to enlist the year before, at 16, but his mother had refused to sign the papers.) It was the summer of 1943. World War II had raged in Europe for nearly four years by then, and engaged the U.S. for two. The month Narozonick enlisted, the Allies toppled Benito Mussolini from power and the Nazis liquidated Jewish ghettos in Belorussia and the Baltic states. Narozonick would join the war effort in a matter of months.

The young recruit first acquired the grit of a sailor at Sampson Naval Training Station in Seneca, New York, where more than 400,000 "boots" trained during World War II. The military installation, built in nine months, spread across 2,600 acres of former farmlands and vineyards. "You walk into this big camp and there's 50,000 recruits in there," he remembered. "People from all walks of life—probably gangsters and criminals and medical people, who knows? We had some pret-

Narozonick, one of 400,000 recruits trained in Seneca, New York, during the war, said boot camp taught him how a teenager should behave. "They kept us up day and night—in the rain, in the sun." *George Narozonick collection*

ty wild kids. They rebelled against authority. They were rough and tough. And they didn't like discipline. You glob that many people into one big camp, it takes a lot of discipline to keep that place running. Otherwise, the boots would take over the camp.

"They kept us up day and night—in the rain, in the sun. The transition from a civilian life to military life is not easy. It took its toll on a lot of people. And I would say about a half-dozen in our company got out ... They didn't like authority." Narozonick met the challenge. He was bound for war.

THE NEW SAILOR FOUND HER IN INDIANA. Looking at her—328 feet long, rugged, and homely—you could see why they called her a low, slow target or a sea sled or a floating barge. Or why they likened her to a large, empty self-propelled box. Some even labeled her a nautical monstrosity. Winston Churchill once quipped to General Eisenhower that "The destinies of two great empires seemed to be tied up in some goddamn things called LSTs." The *USS LST-501*, the only name she'd ever been given, was a Landing Ship, Tank or LST. Built 600 miles from the Atlantic Seaboard—in one of those cornfield shipyards—she was a vessel historians would call the linchpin of the seaborne assault that turned the tide in World War II.

She was conceptualized by the British after the Battle of Dunkirk—a staggering maritime evacuation Churchill described as a "miracle of deliverance." The Germans had stormed into Belgium, Luxemburg and ultimately France. They dominated the Allies in the spring of 1940, trapping British, French and Belgian troops on three sides, near the Port of Dunkirk. The flotilla sent to save them from German capture included 900 naval and civilian craft—the result of a public plea for personal craft. Rescuers lifted nearly 340,000 men from the beaches and waters of Dunkirk in only 10 days. Whenever weather permitted, the Luftwaffe attacked. The lives of 5,000 people and tons of heavy equipment were lost.

The need for a large vessel that could make shore-to-shore deliveries with men, vehicles and artilleries was abundantly clear. Shipbuilders made LSTs at a fever pitch in the coming years—more than 1,000 to be used in World War II. You might find the seafaring LST swinging open her enormous bow doors and disgorging Sherman tanks and landing

Historians called Narozonick's ship the linchpin of D-Day. Longer than an American football field, the vessel could make shore-to-shore deliveries of men and machines. *Navsource.org/Paulo Soukup*

The LST could swing open her enormous bow doors to disgorge Sherman tanks directly onto a sloped beach. *National Archives*

craft directly onto enemy turf. All she needed was a gradually sloped beach. Sometimes, she hauled as many as 15 Sherman tanks and 14 craft in a single crossing. Sailors could wait out the tide and pull the vessel back off the shore. Narozonick became engrossed in the mechanics of the LST. He proudly displayed models of the ship and had a collection of books detailing her crucial role: "You go in late in the afternoon. You get

More than 1,000 landing ship, tanks (LSTs) were built for use in World War II. The seagoing vessels traveled around the globe.

your stern anchor out and your bow anchor out," he explained, eyes lighting up. "When the tide goes out, you're left high and dry—without a drop of water beneath the ship. It's all flat-bottom, like a tabletop."

He boarded his vessel, becoming one of 16 million service members to serve in the conflict. There were no cameras or radios allowed and limited technology. "We didn't know how many men Hitler had behind the lines marching toward us or who was going ahead. We didn't have any idea. At that time, there was no radar. There wasn't any equipment to let us know how far anybody was away. You couldn't even determine what kind of weather it was the next day."

OUT ON THE NORTH ATLANTIC, in the winter of 1944, storms battered the *USS LST-501* more than the enemy, tossing her about on violent, high seas. The big vessel lived up to her reputation as a sea sled every time she slammed down onto waves as high as 15 or 25 feet. She'd departed the major convoy port in Halifax, Nova Scotia, for England with 60 ships and Canadian corvettes as escort. No mighty convoy could guard against the brutal crossing. The sea-lanes delivered men and materiel to

Europe, but crossed an open ocean of relentless winds, chilling cold and rough seas. The seasickness was debilitating.

A shipmate of Narozonick's, Eddie Cochran, manned the engines in the bowels of the 501 as they crossed the North Atlantic. "Sometimes you were sitting on top of two waves and there was no water under the middle of you. You'd flop off of one and down on another. You're underneath the water and you come up. You get the next one—head on. Or, you land flat on it. It vibrates the whole ship." Another Navy sailor explains, "LSTs go through all of the usual rocking motions that ships go through on the sea. But in addition to those, because the front end is so shallow, it smacks the waves and sets up a rolling vibration throughout the ship."

"We had a British converter carrier," Narozonick added. "It [the water] was so rough he could not land the plane or take off from the carrier for 18 days. It was the North Atlantic. The weather was 18 days of the wilds of the ocean. The North Atlantic is notorious for the winter months. I don't think there was anybody who didn't get seasick. Some guys had chronic seasickness and they finally had to let them go."

Eddie Cochran, a machinist from Ohio, crossed the North Atlantic and hit the beaches on The Longest Day with Narozonick. The two survivors always hoped to correspond. *Eddie Cochran collection*

Every morning and every evening, destroyers dropped depth charges, explosives designed to detonate enemy subs. Narozonick, in charge of a 40mm anti-aircraft gun, took his post in four-hour stints, day and night. "We had a pointer on the left side and a trainer on the other side. And then if we heard from the convoy boss, if he suspected anything, or if it was close to us, we'd solicit depth charges. Seventeen years old!"

After years of meticulous planning, the Allies ready to cross the English Channel, a formidable military barrier. *U.S. Coast Guard*

Narozonick and the *USS LST 501* arrived in Torquay, England, in one piece after nearly three weeks at sea. For more than four months, and in practiced maneuvers, the crew darted into ports along the English coast—landing, offloading and retreating. "We hit about every port in southern England," Narozonick said. "We had some close calls, but nothing like 'Tiger'—which was when four or five of our LSTs were damaged or sunk, along with hundreds of troops. This was pre-invasion maneuvers, which went on for months before the big one. There were so many troops and equipment on the British Isles everywhere, and everywhere and everywhere. They were waiting for the word to invade."

THE WORD CAME. The Normandy Invasion made history before a single paratrooper dropped from the skies. No invading army had braved the English Channel since the 17th century. Nearly 100 miles wide, it was a formidable military barrier. The assault demanded a spring tide and moonlight for paratroopers and bombardiers, limiting possible launch dates to a scant few. But Invasion Day came again in June 1944—despite fears of bad weather that resulted in a 24-hour delay.

The top-secret plan was code-named Operation Neptune.

Landing ship, tanks unload vehicles onto Omaha Beach. Of their crucial role in World War II, Winston Churchill once quipped to General Eisenhower: "The destinies of two great empires seemed to be tied up in some goddamn things called LSTs." *National Archives*

It would carry hundreds of thousands of Allies—millions of tons of weapons—across the English Channel and into Fortress Europe.

The assault began when more than 21,000 paratroopers of the 82nd and 101st Airborne Divisions began descending in darkness—to land behind enemy lines, to seize positions, to eliminate defenses and to capture causeway bridges.

Some 5,000 ships had traveled across the Channel, encountering five- and six-foot waves, and strong wind gusts. But somehow, they'd approached the French coast undetected "without a murmur from the enemy" and stopped miles from the Normandy coast. Grappling with a 75-pound radio device, George Hicks, aboard the *USS Ancon*, observed the ships lying in all directions, "just like black shadows on the grey sky." Narozonick's ship had dropped anchor a few miles from Utah Beach, the Allies' westernmost target on the east coast of the Cotentin Peninsula.

Bombs thundered across the coastline, clearing the way for troops. Aircraft hovered overhead. From the engine room of Narozonick's ship, Cochran, the machinist, poked his head through the escape hatch. "It sounded like a bunch of bees—bombers going straight over the top of us," he recalls.

"It was noisy. It was confusing. We had the rest of the U.S. Navy with us... battleships, cruisers, all pounding away on the beaches trying to get our troops ashore," Narozonick said.

The first wave of troops, some 600 men, plunged into the water, headed for the beach, but missed targets. Allied Forces captured the Port of Cherbourg, as planned, after the initial confusion. Of some 20,000 men who landed on Utah Beach, the Allies suffered only 200 casualties, the best casualty record of any D-Day Invasion beach.

That first night on Utah Beach Narozonick sat with fellow sailors on dry land when the Germans dropped flares on the beach, landing between the men and a British Air Ministry ship. "We did not have any air protection. That's when the Germans snuck in and bombed us. Scared the hell out of us. Here we were high and dry. No water around us. Oh yeah, it missed. But it rolls you out of the sack."

By nightfall, the wounded and dead Allies on all five, code-named beaches of Operation Overlord numbered 9,000. The bloodiest warfare took place on Omaha Beach where strong currents pushed landing craft east of their targets and troops landed ashore disoriented. Tanks were swamped and overcast skies made gunfire less precise.

Back in the states, an exhausted President Roosevelt addressed the American people in prayer: "Almighty God: Our sons, pride of our Nation, this day have set upon a mighty endeavor, a struggle to preserve our Republic, our religion, and our civilization, and to set free a suffering humanity.

"Lead them straight and true; give strength to their arms, stoutness to their hearts, steadfastness in their faith.

"They will need Thy blessings. Their road will be long and hard. For the enemy is strong. He may hurl back our forces. Success may not come with rushing speed, but we shall return again and again; and we know that by Thy grace, and by the righteousness of our cause, our sons will triumph."

TRIUMPH CAME AT A COST. With the next tide, Narozonick prepared for the grim job of hauling hundreds of prisoners and the dead, both German and American, back to England. Troops led the wounded and German POWs away—their hands clasped behind their heads—and collected the dead. "They took them all off the frontlines," he said. "All off the beaches. Take them back to England. Put them in a prisoner-of-war camp or a hospital. That was the only way to clean the beach up. We had a shipload going back the first day. There was nowhere else for them to go. There wasn't enough room on the beach to hold them all. The first load we took back—I think that when they came aboard the ship, they were afraid we were going to take them out to sea and sink them. That wasn't the case."

Men prepare to ferry the wounded and prisoners of war across the English Channel. "The first load we took back—I think that when they came aboard the ship, they were afraid we were going to take them out to sea and sink them. That wasn't the case," Narozonick said. *National Archives*

The LST doubled as a makeshift hospital. During her second cross-Channel return to England, the *USS LST-501* carried a striking 16-year-old German girl who suffered from chest wounds. As Cochran overheard her talking with the attending physician, he'd learned she'd trained as a sniper for four years. Her hatred for the enemy was also made clear. "She picked up one of these scalpels on the table by him and stuck it in his back and just missed his kidney."

All told, Narozonick's LST made more than a dozen crossings in the ensuing weeks of D-Day. The Allies secured a foothold by the end of June. The tide had turned, but the war kept on.

YOU NEVER HEAR MUCH about the forgotten Invasion of southern France. Originally code-named Anvil, Operation Dragoon depended on the might of 450,000 troops and more than 800 warships. For Narozonick, it brought the most frightening moments of the conflict. "With Normandy secured, the amphibious forces were available. And the battlewagons that had pounded Normandy. The goal was to secure the ports of Marseille and the Toulon because Cherbourg had been scuttled by the Germans," he remembered.

Preparations are underway at Nisida, Italy for Operation Dragoon. The code-named invasion of southern France depended on some 800 warships. Narozonick's LST again carried men and vehicles to the beaches. *National Archives*

Narozonick and the crew headed to the Mediterranean, supporting the Invasion of southern France from August 15 to September 25. The assault won the critical ports of Marseille and Toulon.

But at twilight one day, a bomb missile struck the ship next to Narozonick's, the *USS LST-282*, only 500 feet away. He ducked for cover under a gun tub and watched in horror. "This German bomber up 25,000 feet, he dropped a radio-controlled bomb. We didn't know what the hell it was. Well, this bomb came down and hit the ship next to us. It hit with a terrific explosion. The fully loaded ship was being torn apart with all the ammo gas that the Army had on board. We could see the bomber that dropped the bomb, and we fired back in vain. It was much out of our reach with our 20 and 40mm guns. Everybody was hiding. We had shells and everything else coming over the ship. It was a disaster."

Operation Dragoon was a victory for the Allies. For Narozonick, its end meant a new landing ship tank and a new theater of war. He participated in the three-month campaign for Okinawa Gunto, one of the bloodiest battles in the Pacific. While the Allies won control of the island, the U.S. lost approximately 12,000 soldiers and sailors. The Japanese lost 100,000. The landing ship tank fulfilled much the same mission. "The only scares we got there was when they started using the kamikaze bombers. They would level off at about 30 or 40 feet and we'd make smoke in order to detour them not knowing where we were. And they would fly along at that height until they hit somebody."

NAROZONICK LEFT THE PERILOUS FLIGHT of the kamikaze bombers to his memories alone after he was discharged from the Navy. He rarely mentioned the conflict at all. "What I went through in that war was like a nightmare and nightmares you don't talk about," he said. "I could say a lot of things that fill your imagination. I wish I had all my mementoes and a Bible."

Life took a much different course after the war. Narozonick spent his modest allowances from the Navy courting a pretty young ice skater named Vila Hanaford. The dark-haired girl with delicate features had taken a spill on a frozen lake, attempting to show off. They fell in love. He followed her to Washington so she could care for her ailing mother. They married in the fall of 1947 at St. Michael's Church in Olympia. Nearly 68 years later, they were still together. Their two daughters are now grandmothers.

Time brought a change of heart for George. In recent years, he opened up about his war experiences. As he looked way back, he counted himself among the lucky of the Longest Day. "If you had a company of infantrymen and you go through training, and you're together, you're real buddies. And then pretty soon, in one attack, 10 or 15 of them may be killed. They're good friends and they're dying in front of you."

He most appreciated the sense of camaraderie he found in the Navy. "Number one is probably the comfort that you get around men who are there for the same reason, same purpose. And the majority of them are too young to realize what danger they were in or realize what their objective was.

"Being just 18 years old, I didn't realize the major importance of the invasion at the time. It's really important that people do remember. With the passing years, some of the memories from D-Day are starting to fade, but the importance of what we did is still with me."

Narozonick returned to Normandy several times and was awarded the French Legion of Honor at Napoleon's tomb. He met movie stars and presidents. His attentive wife took meticulous notes of their journeys, stowing them in folders with his scrapbooks and photo albums.

At 89, George was the lone survivor of his large family. Memories of war and life itself tempered

George and Vila Narozonick stand with Elizabeth Dole, former senator, in 2009, marking the 65th anniversary of D-Day. Narozonick is awarded the French Legion of Honor, the country's highest award. *U.S. Department of Veterans Affairs*

Kim Wyman, Secretary of State, relived D-Day with Narozonick at his home in Olympia, Wash., in 2015. "Veterans like George are humble, but they are true heroes," Wyman says. "To learn from their stories is a gift." *Laura Mott*

him. "As he's grown older, I've seen more of a softening in his emotional reactions with people," daughter Barbara said in 2015. "He's gotten down to the basics of life. You don't know how much longer you're going to have."

Narozonick remained deeply proud of the seafaring LST that ferried men and machines to Africa, the South Pacific, Italy and the coastline of northern France during the war. He was especially proud, as a longtime Washingtonian, of the state's military heritage. "I think it's a great thing to have Fort Lewis and McChord up here. It's better than a concentration camp."

George and his wife Vila were seated in the living room by a window that overlooks Budd Inlet, the southernmost arm of Puget Sound. Narozonick's gaze returned to the American flag. "You see that flag out there?"

His wife Vila answered. "Sometimes, I think it should be in a case. But no, let it fly. I love having it there. To me, it just says, 'Hey, we're America and we're free.'"

George Narozonick died a few months later on October 1, 2015.

Trova Heffernan

BOB HART

The odyssey of a "Battling Buzzard"

> "Anything worth dying for ...
> is certainly worth living for."
>
> —Joseph Heller, *Catch-22*

It was August 15, 1944, D-Day for Dragoon, the Allied invasion of southern France. Fifteen-hundred feet above a drop zone shrouded in fog, the wind buffeted Bob Hart's helmet the instant before he plunged into the unknown at 4:35 a.m.

"As soon as you got to the doorway all you saw was white. Most of us figured we were jumping over the Mediterranean. And for a split second all you could think was 'I got 120 pounds of gear on me. What's going to happen when I land?'"

But now he was falling.

"A thousand and one," Hart said to himself as another paratrooper sprang from the doorway of the lumbering C-47.

"A thousand and two.

"A thousand and..."

Hart's body harness jerked taut reassuringly as the primary parachute billowed. Had he got past "three" he would have yanked the ripcord for the reserve chute bundled on his chest. The business about paratroopers yelling "Geronimo!" was mostly bravado that got old in a hurry after jump school.

Paratroopers prepare for a practice jump from a C-47. *Bob Hart collection*

Descending in the eerie whiteness, the 20-year-old machine gunner from Tacoma fleetingly remembered how he and a buddy had signed up for the paratroopers 16 months earlier at Fort Lewis, reasoning they wouldn't have to do much walking. Fat chance.

After Hart landed hard in a farmer's field in the foothills above the Côte d'Azur, he ended up tramping 50 miles through hostile countryside on an aching foot that turned out to be broken. The parachute bundle containing his machine gun was never found, and one of the battalion's officers was rendered *hors de combat* on landing, sustaining a stake up his butt. Only about 20 percent of the U.S. Army's 517th Parachute Regimental Combat Team landed within two miles of the drop zone. And the platoon's radio man didn't bring the battery.

Bob in 1945. *Bob Hart collection*

Good morning, World War Two!

For days like that, the GI's invented an acronym that became part of the American lexicon: SNAFU (Situation Normal All F***** Up. Or, in polite company, "All Fouled Up").

"Luckily, we were over dry land after all, but the parachute's coming down over my head because there wasn't much wind, and I'm trying to assemble the two pieces of my M-1." Hart chuckles as he pantomimes struggling with his rifle while draped in 28 feet of nylon. When he emerged into what was literally the fog of war, he heard someone nearby. "I said the first part of our password—'Liberty' or something like that. You were supposed to answer with 'France.' And very shakily I heard the right answer. It was Lt. Carl Starkey, the toughest guy in the outfit. Of all the people in the world, he was the guy I'd rather be with in this situation. And he was just as jittery as I was. We spent the next hour looking for my machine gun bundle. Finally, I said to myself, 'Well, I don't have to carry that goddamn machine gun any more!' Thirty pounds of dead weight.

"It took us three hours to find my assistant gunner and the ammo bearer. We trudged down the road leading to the crossroads village of Les Arcs and discovered that the gunner from the Second Squad has broken his back. His machine gun is there beside him in the ditch. So now I have a machine gun again."

He'd need it. Though the last large-scale night jump of World War II was off to a bumpy start, the "Battling Buzzards" of the 517th—some of the fittest, most resourceful soldiers in the annals of warfare—did what they were trained to do: regroup, improvise as needed and engage the enemy. They proceeded to throw the Germans "into a state of chaos," repulsed a counterattack and dug in as artillery duels "echoed through the valleys of the Maritime Alps," their proud colonel wrote afterward.

"There's not many of us left who remember that," Hart says, leafing through a souvenir booklet marked "Passed by censors for mailing home."

HART'S WISE AND WITTY WIFE of 69 years, Kathleen ("Kath"), asked the historian if he'd like a toasted cheese sandwich, noting, "Bob likes baloney on his." Bob shoots her a wink. Here's something important you should know about Bob: There's mischief but not much baloney in his war stories. In 1944, he was the quintessential American GI, a genuinely brave, blue-eyed kid striving to stay sane—and alive—in a world gone horrifically mad. Bob tells the sort of war stories you seldom hear. Some are hilarious, such as the perils of second-hand sleeping bags and the card-shark priest who dispensed communion before emptying your wallet. Many are heartbreaking: A crumpled glider filled with dead GI's; a squad of buddies killed by Friendly Fire. "You see stuff like that and you wonder how you can go on," Hart says, shaking his head. "You felt bad, but there wouldn't have been an Army in Europe if you didn't think 'It's not going to be me.' That's why they like 18-year-olds as soldiers. You get up to 25 and you start thinking, 'Hey, they're trying to kill me!' "

They were definitely trying to kill him when the 517th made it to Belgium in the dead of winter, 1944-45. Feet frozen, Hart was evacuated during the horrific Battle of the Bulge, Hitler's last-gasp gamble to repulse the advancing Allies. Hart was awarded a Purple Heart for his broken foot and the Bronze Star for his role in the combat team's assorted acts of heroism. Nearly 70 years later, he received a handsome medal—the Legion of Honor—from a grateful France. "It's for not doing anything special other than surviving World War II in France," Bob shrugs, handing over the impressive decoration. "It's the only medal I've ever seen that's the same on both sides. Pretty neat. Napoleon designed it. I like the French. Kath went to Europe two years ago on a cruise. I almost went back twice, but then De Gaulle made me mad twice. So I wouldn't go."

You should have a clear picture of Bob Hart by now. He lives at serene Lake Limerick a few miles from Shelton in Mason County and has many friends and admirers, especially at the Saints' Pantry Food Bank where he was for years a dedicated volunteer. Bob, unfortunately, is also a member of a club with dwindling membership. What he said when the historian called—"You'd better hurry"—sums up the urgency of compiling the oral histories of World War II veterans. Bob, happily, was overstating things. He has rebounded from a couple of nasty falls. The VA has finally agreed to pay for an acupuncturist for his aching back. He also developed arthritis around the bone he broke in his left foot. Bob buys Bengay in bulk. At 93, he regrets that his freewheeling motorcycling days are over. The flip side, he observes, is that most people his age "are either dead or a lot worse off." Hart has out-lived all but a handful of his fellow paratroopers. "You're also lucky that you have all your marbles," the historian said. "No," Bob said mischievously. "I've lost *three*.

But I still have the aggie"—his shooter. "That was always my lousiest game—marbles." Then the grin receded. "The kid who always beat me all through grade school was wounded at the battle of Anzio. I wrote a letter to him while he was in the hospital. I was on the Bulge when I received it back marked 'deceased.' "

Here's the rest of the story, including how Bob got to the Bulge, the largest battle in the history of the U.S. Army, and lived to tell about it:

THREE OF THE FOUR BRANCHES of his family tree are Germanic. His father's parents and his mother's father arrived in America during the first half of the 19th Century, together with nearly a million other Germans. That Bob Hart's job during World War II was "to kill Krauts," as he puts it, doesn't strike him as ironic because it boiled down to democracy vs. dictatorships, not the German people.

When you plug a 93-year-old into Ancestry.com, it's a time machine to a rustic world fraught with hard knocks. Bob's dad, William Hart, had a falling out with his stoic farmer folks in Wisconsin and left home when he was 13. Bill bounced around the West, tending bar and working for the Northern Pacific railroad. Around 1900 he landed in Billings, Montana, and met Inez Barkdoll, an industrious young woman whose girlhood was spent near the Custer battlefield at the Little Bighorn. Bob grew up hearing that Calamity Jane, the celebrated frontierswoman, was a frequent Barkdoll houseguest, though her personal hygiene left a lot to be desired.

The Harts lost their first child, a daughter named Frances, to mastoiditis in 1919 when she was 9. Before the advent of antibiotics, the agonizing middle ear infection was one of the leading causes of childhood deaths. "Can you imagine the pain?" Bob says of the sister he never knew. The grief-stricken parents moved from Montana to Midland near Puyallup in rural Pierce County the following year. Bill became a carpenter for the railroad.

ROBERT DARRELL HART was born in the summer of 1924, three years after Bill Jr. When the Depression hit, the Harts nearly lost their home. Bob's dad finally found a job through the New

Deal's Works Progress Administration. Bob's mom, with help from her boys, "peddled eggs door to door in South Tacoma. She had a regular route. She'd go all the way out to Yelm in her Model T Ford. You really had to crank that damn thing!" Bob says, cussing under his breath at the memory. "Somehow they managed to make house payments all through the Depression. It was a tough deal. With thousands of chickens, we never went hungry but we all worked hard. My dad would get up at 4 in the morning and stoke the brooder to keep the baby chicks warm. Then he'd catch a ride with another guy to go to work in South Tacoma. He worked hard, and I can't remember my mother not doing something, too. Every Friday night and every Tuesday night I'd wash eggs, then she'd deliver them. Midland was about eight miles out of town, so it was a long haul."

Bob was a handsome, wiry kid, 5-11, 150 lbs. He missed out on sports and socializing at Lincoln High School in Tacoma because he was always working—delivering papers, washing eggs, greasing pans at a bakery every night after school; cleaning turkey houses for two-bits an hour on Saturdays. He still made a lot of friends, including three Japanese boys he met in the machine-shop class overseen by an old Scot who was a fine machinist. That was Bob's goal. He liked history, too, and figured Stalin was a fool to think Hitler wouldn't turn on Russia when the

Hart's prized possession as an industrious teenager in Tacoma: A second-hand 1936 Oldsmobile with fender skirts and spotlights. *Bob Hart collection*

time was ripe. If he had any free time, Bob went to King Roller Rink where the kids skated to the strains of a Wurlitzer organ. He gave most of his earnings to his folks, but saved enough to buy a 1936 Oldsmobile with fender skirts and twin spotlights. All the girls thought he was cute. "That's possibly because I had the only car in the neighborhood," Bob suggests.

The attack on Pearl Harbor came midway in Bob's senior year at Lincoln. He was heading for the rink when the news came over the car radio. "It started out as a normal Sunday. But from then on, nothing was normal," he remembers.

Hart was troubled that spring when the West Coast's Japanese residents were sent to internment camps. "It was terrible. I also don't know what would have happened if they hadn't. There might have been killings because so many people panicked and believed the Japanese were all spies. One of my classmates' dads owned a hotel in Tacoma. He lost it when the family was sent off to a camp. The Japanese farmers in Fife who had developed beautiful farms were really screwed over. Just a rip-off! They had hundred-year leases, and that [the outbreak of war] was the way the property owners could break the leases. That was a terrible way to treat people. When I was fighting in Italy, we saw action with Japanese-American soldiers from the 442nd Regimental Combat Team and the 100th Infantry Battalion—guys whose families were being interned back home. The 442nd relieved us during one battle, and the next day they were ambushed by the Germans. They were fine troops and one of the most decorated outfits in the history of the U.S. Army."

Bob's brother joined the Army Air Forces and became a B-17 flight engineer. Bob signed on as a sheet metal worker at Todd Pacific Shipyards in Tacoma, helping build warships. The workforce soon topped 20,000. They kept giving him promotions. "It was essential war work, and I could have stayed there, but I finally told the boss, 'I'm going in.' Everyone wanted to kill Germans or Japs and get it over with."

Bob and Elmer Shipton, a guy he'd known since first grade, were inducted into the Army in the spring of 1943. "On the second or third day of orientation at Fort Lewis they marched us over to a big building and gave us a lecture on the importance of GI insurance. Then an officer walked in and asked the sergeant if he could make an announcement about the paratroopers. It sounded as if all you did was ride around in airplanes and wear those neat jump boots. Elmer nudged me and whispered, 'We won't have to walk!' When they asked for volunteers, two guys stuck up their hands out of the 200 or 300 in the room. Elmer and me. So what the hell! We never heard the rest of the lecture. They drug us out of there so fast you couldn't believe it. They gave us another series of shots. Elmer passed out cold, even though we'd already taken a bunch in both arms. I carried him back to the barracks. They rejected him and took me!"

Pfc. Robert D. Hart in the fall of 1943 after he won his jump wings. *Bob Hart collection*

As the prospective paratroopers arrived by the trainload at Camp Toccoa, Georgia, the weeding out intensified. Each group of 50 to 150 men "was met at the station and trucked to the parade ground where a 34-foot-tall parachute 'mock tower' had been erected." When you climbed to the top and donned the harness, "they'd tap you on the rump, and you'd better jump," Hart remembers. "Anyone who hesitated was washed out right then and there. I had no fear of heights, so I passed that test. Then they gave us another physical. We were all

standing around butt naked. The guy who'd been put in charge of our trainload on the way to Georgia had tattoos all over his body—even his penis. When the doctor saw that, the guy goes, 'Pretty good, huh?' And the doctor goes whoosh, 'You're out of here!' "

To be a paratrooper you needed intelligence to match your bravado. Those who'd signed up because of the "jump pay"—an extra 50 bucks a month—were also soon back on the train. Yet a former juvenile delinquent who could box his heart out and the wise-ass Italian kid who could do a hundred one-arm pushups became superb parachute soldiers. "Every guy who went to the 517th was interviewed as to his aptitude for the paratroops," Hart says. When he was being considered for a spot as a machine gunner in the Second Battalion, Hart had to pass muster with its commander, a lieutenant colonel.

Hart at basic training at Camp Toccoa, Georgia, in the summer of 1943. *Bob Hart collection*

At the apex of World War II, becoming a paratrooper meant surviving what still ranks as some of the most rigorous training in U.S. military history: Six-mile runs, an obstacle course, night marches in full field packs, relentless calisthenics, mock hand-to-hand combat, bayonet drills and exacting marksmanship practice. For Hart, "the hardest thing in Georgia was Mount Currahee." At 1,700 feet, it was a molehill compared to the majestic peaks he'd grown up with. It was, nevertheless, three miles to the top. "You got up at 5 o'clock and, no matter how cold it was, you ran up that mountain. Then you ran back down. I was in good shape, but I hated running. I had never run in my life. *Jesus!* And then in

Paratrooper recruits pose after a three-mile run at Camp Toccoa, Georgia, in the summer of 1943. Hart is third from left in the back row. The muscular GI at the end of the row, Charles McDade, died in the Battle of the Bulge around Christmas 1944. *Bob Hart collection*

the beginning you did it again practically every afternoon. Our officers—some of them not much older than the rest of us—did everything they expected us to be able to do. Lt. Starkey—probably the toughest man I ever met in my life—was also a nice guy. Just no hanky-panky. He was leading the platoon on my first day up the mountain. He hated to see anybody ahead of him, so he stepped it up. By this time I'm gasping. And I fell out. That was no-no. I just laid down in the dirt next to the road. A corporal told me to get with the program. Starkey saw what was happening. He fell out and declared, 'Get back in that goddamn formation!' And I said, 'Screw you!' I was just a dumb recruit who didn't realize you couldn't talk that way to an officer." Starkey glowered, turned on his heel and sprinted back to the front of the formation. Angry and energized, Hart dusted himself off and rejoined the runners. He made it back to the barracks with the rest of the platoon and was surprised when nothing more was said of the incident. "After four or five days I could run the mountain as well as anybody. You got used to it. You felt like you could do anything. There was *esprit*." Decades later at a 517th reunion at Palm Springs, Hart visited with Starkey.

Three new paratroopers in combat gear before shipping out for Italy in the spring of 1944. From left, Hart, Edward Meingasner and John Bonner. Looking on from the window is Corporal Charles Twibell, "who was wounded three times and evacuated to Paris, only to be run over by a truck," Hart remembers. *Bob Hart collection*

"I says, 'Lieutenant, why didn't you kick me out of the outfit?' And he said, 'You got up and got back, didn't you?' "

WHEN THE SURVIVING RECRUITS moved 200 miles south to Fort Benning, the sprawling home of the Army Infantry, a general observing their arrival was amazed and impressed. Instead of barking orders, their officers and NCOs "used whistles to form them up and marched them to the barracks without a single verbal command."

They graduated to 40-foot training towers, then to the 250-footers. They learned to pack their own chutes. Now came the litmus test: five jumps from a transport plane, the workhorse C-47 that a year later would drop 50,000 paratroops during the Normandy invasion.

"Jumping didn't scare me," Hart says. "Landings were what I worried about." They were taught how to approach the ground with feet spread and tumble on impact. Easier said than done. "We were one of the first groups that went through training wearing steel infantry helmets, instead of the old football-style leather helmets. On my third or fourth jump I came in swinging backwards. My heels caught and I hit hard. I could see stars and my head was ringing inside the helmet. The next thing I knew, a medic was standing over me saying, 'You all right?' And I went 'wawawawa!' I could barely talk. That was the only bad one.

Hart works out with a 90-pound barbell at Camp Mackall, North Carolina, in the fall of 1943. *Bob Hart collection*

"Everyone passed, which was unheard of. That told you what kind of outfit we had become. They gave us our silver jump wings and we got to 'blouse' our pants—tuck them into our jump boots, which were beautiful brown spit-shined leather. That was the day everyone was looking forward to. Getting your wings and boots was the most important thing in your life. *You'd made it.* There were maybe 30 guys in my platoon. Real fast, you become attached to two or three or four. There was lots of camaraderie. You had the confidence that everyone was as ready as he could be. These were guys you'd risk your life with. You had to feel that way or you wouldn't have gone into combat. You always had somebody at your back. And a machine gunner especially counted on that because the whole outfit was built around the machine gunners and the mortar men. I had the best score in the regiment with a machine gun."

The .30-caliber, air-cooled Browning machine gun—a

mainstay of World War II, Korea and Vietnam—weighed 31 pounds. It became Bob's burdensome baby; also a lifesaver. The gunner carried its tripod; the assistant gunner was supposed to carry the gun, while the ammo bearer toted the cartridge boxes. "Unfortunately my assistant gunner, Mickelson, weighed about 30 pounds less than I did. The ammo bearer, Duggan, was about the same size I was. His arms got longer and longer as the war progressed. I carried the gun probably 70 percent of the time.

"In basic training, the practice targets were only one inch square. You had a row of five. You set your sights on that first square. The idea was that if you got good enough you could close your eyes and still pop off an accurate shot. It was almost automatic once you got in the rhythm." Things were different when someone was shooting back. "When we got into combat, I had Mickelson there next to me with the binoculars. He'd go, 'Up one click. Down one click,' etc. The adrenalin was flowing but you needed to stay steady."

Next stop was the Army's new Camp Mackall, 40 miles east of Fort Bragg, North Carolina. While the training was no less intense, the needling diminished. They were real soldiers now. They ran hard, passing every test, physical and mental, with the highest scores the Army's inspectors had ever recorded. And they played hard every chance they got, lieutenants and privates alike. The risks they took to blow off steam were part of their cheeky self-confidence. Several paratroopers snuck away from a map-reading exercise, detoured to a nearby golf course, "stuffed their M-1s in the golf bags and played a spirited nine holes." When Hart returned a day late from a furlough, some martinet tossed him in the stockade. "But two guys I knew were guards. The next day they left and gave me a gun to guard the others. So it was a short stay."

March of 1944 found the 517th "shivering and knee-deep

in mud" in the woods of Tennessee for full-scale war games staged by the Second Army. "Everyone was tired of pushups and playing war," Hart remembers. "We were well-trained and in terrific shape—a bunch of young guys who felt they were immortal. We were anxious about how we'd do in real combat—anyone who tells you otherwise is lying—but after a year of getting ready we wanted to get on with it."

MOST OF THE 517TH PARACHUTE INFANTRY arrived at Naples on the last day of May on a former luxury liner. It seemed like an incongruous way to go to war, but no one was complaining.

They cooled their heels and trained some more in the crater of a dormant volcano awaiting the combat team's artillery. "Naples was pathetic," Hart remembers. "The Germans had sunk everything afloat and the harbor was clogged. It was a wide open city. You could do anything you wanted. People were desperate. Some kid would tug your sleeve and say, 'Follow me Joe, I've got a girl for you.' They were selling 12-year-old girls—sometimes their sisters—for a couple of cigarettes. Hungry kids—some of them only 2 or 3 years old—were everywhere. It broke your heart. They'd wait at the end of the chow line where guys dumped off what they hadn't eaten. A lot of us would give the kids anything we could. I hated Naples. It was the garbage can of the world."

Hart and some pals in Naples in May of 1944. Standing from left, Edward Meingasner, Hart and John Bonner; kneeling, Frank Wayda. *Bob Hart collection*

Rome was liberated on June 5,

517th paratroopers on the day before their first combat jump into the South of France. *Bob Hart collection*

the day before D-Day. While some American soldiers were being hugged, kissed and showered with flowers and Chianti, others, including the 82nd and 101st Airborne, were poised to enter savage combat at Normandy.

On June 18, 1944, a bright Sunday morning, the 517th finally got its chance. From Civitavecchia, a battered port city 45 miles north of Rome, the paratroopers began pursuit of the Germans, who were conducting a tenacious if disorganized rearguard action. Hart's outfit, the Second Battalion, outflanked the enemy and made a series of surgical thrusts, inflicting heavy casualties and collecting dozens of hollow-eyed prisoners. Every valley, wheat field and hill looked alike, Hart remembers, but the 517th captured higher ground, dug in at a strategic hilltop village and held it "despite desperate attempts by the enemy to dislodge the troopers by artillery fire."

Hart's battalion emerged from its first week of combat with light casualties and a ton of confidence. "Axis Sally," one of the turncoat American women whose radio broadcasts were calculated to undermine GI morale, acknowledged that the green paratroopers had done well. "You men of 517 are much better than we anticipated," she purred. "But you are foolhardy. ...You will lose men!"

Hart traces the combat team's movements on a map in his memorabilia-filled den. "At the end of June '44, we were pulled back to Frascati just outside Rome to get ready for the worst kept secret of the war—the invasion of Southern France."

HITLER KNEW IT WAS COMING, just not when. Early planning had envisioned simultaneous Allied amphibious landings at Normandy and along the Mediterranean. Eisenhower coveted the port cities of Marseille and Toulon. An intractable Churchill wanted to seize the oil-rich Balkans. Ike prevailed, with the unwavering support of his mentor, George C. Marshall, the U.S. Army's chief of staff. The invasion along the Côte d'Azur— code-named Dragoon—was postponed for 10 weeks because there weren't enough landing craft for both operations. "So we trained half the time and played the rest," Hart says, smiling. "If we hadn't all been so young" interspersing mortal combat with R&R would have seemed more surreal.

The paratroopers descended on Rome and sampled everything it had to offer. "The people were glad to see us— and really fed up with Mussolini," Hart remembers. Two of his buddies were Catholics, so he went with them to see the Vatican. A devout few managed an audience with the pope. Most went sightseeing, gawking at the Colosseum and Pantheon before hitting the cafes and bars. Any unattended jeep was fair game. "If they had a key in 'em they were gone," Hart says. "The British wised up and finally started putting a chain on the steering wheel, so you could turn it only so far. Sometimes you'd go one block, then turn again, then turn again. Maybe you'd end up in a total circle. So you'd abandon that jeep and steal another one. Our officers loved it when we would return with a requisitioned jeep. When we left Frascati, which had been the German headquarters in Italy, that hillside was like a used car lot!"

ON AUGUST 14, 1944, Frascati was abuzz with last-minute preparations for the first combat jump by the 517th Parachute Regimental Combat Team. It also would be their last. "None of us imagined that at the time," Hart remembers. "We figured we'd be jumping all the way to Berlin."
 A scale-model of the drop zone had been created in a closely-guarded tent. The paratroopers visited it in clumps. Then they donned their battle gear, pretending to be nonchalant, checked their chutes and received "escape kits" that included French currency and waterproof maps. At 1 a.m.—0100 hours— nearly 400 twin-engine C-47's loaded with paratroopers began to lift off from dirt runways and drone off into the darkness toward the French Riviera. The 1st Airborne Task Force assembled for Dragoon consisted of some 6,000 paratroopers, including the British 2nd Parachute Brigade and 2,500 men from the 517th. The paratroopers' mission was to bottle up the German units beyond the beaches so no reinforcements could get through to repulse the Allied landings.
 Dragoon got off to a ragged start. In the pre-dawn skies above the foggy hills and vineyards beyond the coast, some C-47s got lost. Several pathfinder units were dropped too soon or too late and couldn't set up their radio beacons and lights in time to assist the pilots. The 517th pathfinders landed in the woods 3½ miles from the drop zone and came under immediate enemy fire. Much of Hart's battalion, unable to see the ground, landed haphazardly. Some paratroopers were "scattered as far as 44 kilometers from their objective."
 As luck would have it, the amphibious assault and glider landings later that morning met with scant resistance from a ragtag German army group. "Instead of a bitter battle of attrition akin to Anzio or Normandy, Dragoon quickly turned

into a headlong retreat by German forces up the Rhone Valley, with American and French troops in hot pursuit," Steven J. Zaloga writes in his 2009 book about France's often overlooked "other D-Day." By day's end the Allies controlled the beaches. The Airborne's casualties were light—382 Americans and 52 British dead.

But when Bob Hart untangled himself from his parachute and put weight on his left foot, it hurt like hell. "I thought it was just sprained, so when Lt. Starkey and I hooked up, adrenalin flowing, we soldiered on, looking for our other guys." All three battalions soon regrouped. Buttressed by 80 British paratroopers, they ambushed a large German convoy racing toward the coast. They held the strategic village of Les Arcs, despite being badly outnumbered, and seized the offensive. The Germans fell back to the medieval town of Sospel, nestled in a valley along the French-Italian border.

"We went up, down and around," Hart remembers. "The Germans were retreating to the Italian border, but we had to fight for every town. Somewhere above Grasse, the perfume capital of the world, I couldn't walk any more. And Duggan, my ammo bearer, had boils all over his body. French water might have been good for Frenchmen but we weren't adapted to it. They called it the 'Champagne Campaign.' We would have been a lot better off drinking it instead of the water."

Hart and Duggan were evacuated to an aid station at the beachhead. An X-ray revealed a broken bone. Hart was lucky it wasn't worse after all that walking. He was taken to former German military hospital at Marseille and spent the next three weeks

In December of 1944, the 517th and thousands of other GI's lurched north by rail in French boxcars—the stubby "40 et 8's" designed to carry 40 men or eight horses. *Regina Tollfeldt Collection*

with his foot in a cast. "All I could think of was that I had joined the paratroops because I wouldn't have to walk."

Hart rejoined D Company in the Maritime Alps about a month later. Deprived of supplies, Sospel finally fell at the end of October after a 51-day siege. "With the Germans captured or gone, they billeted our platoon in a chateau. Then we went into Nice on a pass. When we arrived back around 4 a.m. the chateau next to ours was rubble. The Germans had left a time bomb. Seven of our guys were killed, and a buddy of mine lost a leg. We slept outside our chateau that night."

The 517th lurched north by rail in French boxcars—the stubby "40 et 8's" designed to carry 40 men or eight horses. "They'd been shot up so much they were full of holes; the floor was strewn with straw and it rained all the way—500 miles," Bob remembers with a shiver. "It took us three days to get up to Soissons, which was as far as the Germans got in World War I." Holding the line in 1918 had cost the Allies 32,000 soldiers during four terrible days. The Germans lost nearly 57,000. History was about to repeat itself on the Western Front.

The paratroopers arrived at Soissons, an ancient town northeast of Paris, on December 12, 1944. They were happy to

A member of the 517th struggles with a frozen machine gun at the Bulge. *National Archives*

learn they'd be quartered in barracks. One wag observed that there were "only 12 shopping days 'til Christmas."

HITLER, WHO WAS 55, looked 70. His hands trembled, his shoulders sagged; he couldn't sleep. "Yet he was still capable of sizing up his foes and sensing their weaknesses, as he demonstrated by recognizing that Allied forces in France and the Low Countries were overextended and vulnerable to a counterattack," Neil Kagan and Stephen G. Hyslop write in their fine book, *Eyewitness to World War II*.

"I have just made a momentous decision," Hitler informed his top commanders. "I shall go over to the counterattack!" Pointing on a map to Germany's border with Belgium and Luxembourg, he added: "Here, out of the Ardennes, with the objective—Antwerp!" ... Since taking Paris, Allied troops had advanced northward into Belgium and seized the vital port, but it remained closed to shipping because the Scheldt Estuary between Antwerp and the North Sea was mined and menaced by big German naval guns. Once the Allies secured that estuary, they could use Antwerp to supply troops preparing to invade northern Germany. Until then, supplies unloaded at more distant ports like Cherbourg and Marseille moved slowly along roads that were heavily congested because the French rail network had been shattered by Allied bombers. ...Hitler planned to exploit this situation by massing armor and infantry in the Ardennes and sending his forces barreling across Belgium to Antwerp."

To the dismay of his generals, Hitler demanded that they throw 10 Panzer and 14 infantry divisions at the Allies' weak center in the forested Ardennes plateau in the dead of winter. Heels clicked to a resigned chorus of "Jawohl, mein Führer!"

"General Eisenhower suspected something was afoot," Winston Churchill remembered in his stately prose, "though its scope and violence came as a surprise." A year earlier, Ike had bet Field Marshal Montgomery £5 that the war with Germany would be over before Christmas of 1944.

On the cold, foggy morning of December 16, "We were getting ready to go on R&R in Paris when all hell broke loose," Hart remembers. Two-thousand artillery pieces opened fire as hundreds of tanks and 250,000 German soldiers swept through the Allied lines. The "bulge" quickly grew 60 miles deep and 40 miles wide. At Bastogne, a vital crossroads, the 101st Airborne Division found itself encircled and heavily outnumbered. Cold-to-the-bone in the frozen snow, the paratroopers were low on ammo, short of food and medical supplies and facing possible annihilation one way or the other. (The Waffen SS had massacred 84 prisoners up the road at Malmedy.) Their commander's laconic American response to a German surrender demand, "Nuts!"—shorthand for "Go to hell!"—is now legendary. Hart has one word of his own for the stand by the 101st at Bastogne: "incredible."

It was slow going at the Bulge in the winter of 1944-45. *United States Army Center of Military History*

Eisenhower mustered all his reserves and ordered Patton's Third Army to attack the Bulge's left flank and relieve Bastogne. The 517th sped north to secure and hold at all costs other crossroads towns. "We tossed all our gear, including machine guns and mortars, on open semi-trucks and hit the road. At least we had overcoats," Hart says, "which was more than the guys in the 101st had."

They'd gain some ground, taking whatever cover they could find as artillery shells rained down. So fluid was the battlefront that some of the fire was "friendly," an occupational hazard. As the 517th moved into a crossroads village, hoping to seize a bridge, a popular sergeant died in a mortar blast. "He was killed right across the street from me. Things like that never leave your mind," Hart says.

Under fire, clumps of GI's would burrow into the snow, hide behind trees or hole up in hastily abandoned buildings. "Far more often than any commander would like to accept, the Battle of the Bulge broke down into an every man for himself," says military historian Gerald Astor. Before it was over, nearly 20,000 Americans had been killed, 47,000 wounded and 23,000 captured or MIA. The 101st sustained 2,000 casualties at Bastogne.

By Christmas Day the Bulge was shrinking. The weather had cleared and Allied aircraft were dropping supplies and bombs. "It was the first day in weeks that we'd seen sunlight," Hart remembers. "The sky suddenly was filled with bombers, thousands of them. It was horrifying when a B-17 got hit and spiraled out of control. You'd look for chutes. That poor tail gunner, he had to try to get out the side. And the belly gunner! How the hell would you get out from there? That day I and a lot of other guys said, 'Damn I'm glad I'm in the paratroops and not up there!' The losses they were taking in those B-17 squadrons were the highest of any branch of service. It was terrible!" It didn't occur to him just then that his brother Bill, a flight engineer with the 8th Air Force, might be up there. They didn't talk about it until after the war.

Bastogne was relieved on December 26-27. Bolstered by their mastery of the skies, the Allies were on the offensive by New Year's Day, 1945, though it was still bitterly cold and the snow knee deep. Poorly trained Nazi conscripts, some as young as 15, some old enough to be their grandfathers, had been mobilized for the Bulge. Still, the Germans clung fanatically to any higher ground and dug in around farm buildings. The German artillery fire seemed relentless. Hart's platoon cleared part of the strategic village of Trois-Ponts house by house. That night, Hart crept out of what had been a butcher shop to answer the call of nature. He was walking along a riverbank on numb feet in a jumble of discarded weapons when he encountered a German soldier "frozen solid as a statue. That's how cold it was. And the trench shoes they gave us weren't much. We had one blanket. No sleeping bags. Just a blanket in zero-degree conditions."

When another platoon pushed ahead, it was caught in the open by heavy machine gun fire and overrun. Lt. Starkey, their much-admired company commander, and a dozen other Buzzards were wounded.

D Company regrouped. Pfc. Robert D. Hart's war all but ended a few days later. It's a lousy pun, but it really was the agony of the feet.

Winter boots were in short supply. The 517th had none. "I'd taken my shoes off maybe once or twice in two weeks. I was on guard duty at midnight the night we finally got our sleeping bags. So instead of leaving my shoes on I just wrapped the sleeping bag around my feet and stood watch. The next morning when I tried to put my shoes on, my feet were way bigger than my shoes. They called it 'frozen feet.' No feeling whatsoever."

He was lucky he could be evacuated—and that his feet were not in worse shape. "The only time I saw Paris during World War II was out the back window of an ambulance. There

GI's with frozen feet doing an elevation exercise in a military hospital in England under the watchful eye of a nurse. *U.S. Army*

went the Arc de Triomphe!"

From Cherbourg, Hart and thousands of other Allied casualties were taken by hospital ship to England. The ghastly wounds he saw made him feel fortunate. "My frozen feet may have saved my life. I was damn lucky to have survived the Battle of the Bulge when so many guys died or were crippled for life.

"Unless your feet were in really bad shape from frostbite, the treatment was to keep them uncovered and cool. Sometimes it looked comical, with row after row of guys with their bare feet up in the air. But some guys were losing toes that turned black." And some guys were losing feet. That "amputation was preferable to dying of gangrene," as one doctor told a young rifleman, was scant consolation for most.

"There were so many guys with frozen feet that they ended up putting some of us in the Section 8 ward with the mental cases," Hart remembers. "That was crazy in more ways than one. I concluded that about a third of the mental cases were muckin' (faking) to get out and go home."

AFTER ABOUT A MONTH in the hospital, Hart was able to rejoin

Hart, center, and four other GI's pose for a photo after being discharged from a military hospital in England in February of 1945. *Bob Hart collection*

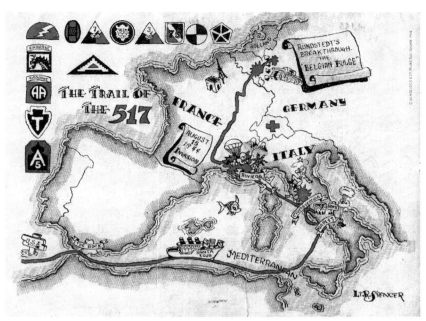

From a 517th souvenir booklet issued at war's end.

the 517th, which was mopping up. "Once in a while you'd hit one town with a group of Nazi defenders who would fight to the last man. And in the next town they'd all surrender," Hart remembers. "There were thousands of POWs—some barely into their teens—and hungry people, most of them glad to see us."

Hitler's delusional gamble had cost him 100,000 soldiers and vital materiel. Abandoned tanks and artillery were everywhere. With the Russians advancing from the East, his malignant "thousand-year Reich" was being squeezed down to its last three months. Five million German soldiers, at least a million civilians and six million European Jews had perished.

"Patton was moving so fast that we never had the chance to make another combat jump," Hart remembers with mixed emotions. "We had brand-new airplanes, too."

May brought victory in Europe. Hart opted to join the Army of occupation in Berlin. After months of combat and two stints in hospitals, that struck him as preferable to heading to the South Pacific after a 30-day leave.

He was detailed to help guard a prison housing suspected

war criminals—all civilians, including municipal officials, wives of Nazi leaders and American-born Nazi collaborators. "The wives of Nazi bigshots were indignant they were being held," Hart says. "If they wanted to go the bathroom they'd take a tin cup and rake it across the bars. Then we'd have to go over and let them out one at a time. It was embarrassing to them. We weren't too sympathetic. And when we took the male prisoners outside to police up the area (clean the grounds), we always put bayonets on our rifles because if we saw them trying to grab a cigarette butt they'd get stuck!"

Hart was amazed at how quickly Berliners, including thousands of women—many shoeless and in rags—set about efficiently clearing the rubble. "At Naples nobody had done much to clean up after the bombing. But German women, despite having been raped half a dozen times by the Russians, were cleaning every brick and stacking them in neat piles.

"When I got to Berlin the subways were still filled with water up to the street level and bodies were floating by. People were so hungry you couldn't believe it. They'd do anything for a candy bar, and the Black Market was thriving. I sold my wristwatch to a Russian underneath the Brandenburg Gate for a thousand bucks—and it was a lousy watch!"* American GI's could get a hundred dollars for a pack of Lucky Strike cigarettes. "At first, we could go over into the Russian zone any time we wanted. But within two weeks the Russians had restricted railroad traffic. We were allowed one train a day for our supplies. You could smell the cold war coming."

HART ARRIVED BACK in the U.S. on an aged Liberty ship in January of 1946, flew home from New Jersey and was discharged from the Army at Fort Lewis where his paratrooper odyssey began.

---

* In an article on the Black Market in postwar Berlin, historian Kevin Conley Ruffner notes: "Russians loved watches for a number of reasons. They always have been associated in the Muscovite mind with affluence and an established, even exalted, position in life. Peasants never owned watches. ... Watches soon became a universal commodity because troops had no confidence in Russian currency. Also, a soldier could send a watch home and his wife could barter it for a cow. ... Some Russian soldiers wore a half dozen watches. A Mickey Mouse watch was worth more than a jewel-studded trinket from Cartier."

The Harts on their wedding day, January 29, 1948, at the Tacoma home of Kathleen's parents. And today. *Bob Hart collection*

    Kathleen Williams, Bob's future wife, was dating a teenage sailor from Minnesota when Bob and two dashing paratrooper pals "came stumbling into a Tacoma bowling alley," having toasted their civilian-hood at several earlier stops. "He was cute, and I admired his shiny boots and all of his medals. A couple of days later, his friend called and wanted to know if I would like to go skiing with them. So our first date was skiing. And the following week I sent my boyfriend back to Minnesota."

    The GI Bill helped pay for Bob's degree in light-aircraft engine maintenance from Clover Park Vocational-Technical Institute. He lived with his folks and unloaded grain boxcars at Sperry Flour Company in Tacoma. He and Kath were married on January 29, 1948. Their first home was in Everett, where Bob bluffed his way into a job with Alaska Airlines at Paine Field, overhauling engines for 95 cents an hour. "I'd never worked on a big airliner engine, so I was lucky they didn't ask more specific questions. They were flying on a wing and prayer in those days." He and a partner wrangled a loan and built a service station that expanded into a fuel delivery business in Snohomish County. By 1953, the Hart family included two sons. The lure of aviation

Hart is congratulated by Jack Cowan, the honorary consul, at the French Consular Agency in Seattle in 2013 after receiving the Legion of Honor. *Bob Hart collection*

prompted Bob to acquire a private pilot's license. He became a flight line mechanic with Pacific Northern Airlines, then the largest carrier on the Alaska route. The Harts moved to Browns Point at Tacoma and added a third son. Bob ended his career with Western Airlines, retiring in 1984.

As their kids were growing up, the Harts were active in Indian Guides and Little League. Bob became a volunteer firefighter, donated blood for 40 years and volunteered at the American Lake Veterans Hospital near Tacoma. He was a stalwart at the Saints' Pantry Food Bank in Shelton until he took that nasty fall in the garage in 2013. Getting old is doubly frustrating for Bob because he was always such an active guy—flying his plane, riding motorcycles, working out at the gym. "We've had a good life," Bob says, smiling at Kath. Yet there was a tragedy, too. They lost their middle son, Karl, in a car crash in 1974. "His love for life will always be remembered by his parents and bothers," Kath says.

Their eyes glisten. You're not supposed to outlive your kids.

"Time," Dick Cavett once observed, "is the star of every reunion." Hart remembers the 517th get-togethers when all of a sudden no one was young any more. There was always catching up to do—wives, kids, jobs. Invariably the talk turned to what happened when they were young—the dimwit with the tattoo on his penis; Mount Currahee at the crack of dawn; their first jump; the day they rounded a bend north of Rome and first heard "the snap of hot lead as it passed over their heads"; the day when their sergeant got killed at Trois-Ponts.

Mickelson, Meingasner and McDade; Duggan, Bonner, Hill and Gallucci—the push-up king of the 517th. When Hart

Hart at the Saints' Pantry Food Bank in Shelton where he was a longtime volunteer. *Mason County Journal/Gordon Weeks.*

says their names he still sees them the way they were in 1943 when they arrived in Georgia from all over America. The average Joes who had grown up washing eggs, pumping gas and picking berries during the Depression turned out to have the smarts and courage to win World War II. Afterward, some got rich as lawyers and land developers; Terry Sanford was elected governor of North Carolina and ran for president. A disconcerting number—carrying too much baggage from the Bulge or unwilling to surrender to declining health—took their own lives. That strikes Bob as especially sad. In any case, "they're practically all gone now. Except me." He says it not so much wistfully as matter of fact.

Hart is proud to be one of the 517th. Once a paratrooper, always a paratrooper. They were—still are—elite soldiers. He made the grade and helped defeat fascism. "We did what we had to do." That said, he believes "the Greatest Generation" moniker is over-reaching. "Let's talk about those guys in Vietnam," he says, leaning forward. "I can't image what they went through: the terrain, the jungles, the heat, the insects, the snakes—everything I hated! And when they got home they were disrespected. Vietnam was a terrible war! Why we got into that I have no idea. Why we thought we could do something the French Foreign Legion couldn't do."

Bob's on a roll now: "And look at what's happening today. These guys fighting in the Gulf are amazing soldiers. How they can have the attitude they have, knowing that when they come home to their wife and kids—if they've got 'em—that they're going to go right back again after a few months ...one tour of duty right after another. That's courage. All the while, we have so many young punks sitting around drinking, doing drugs, getting fat and getting tattoos. I just read that the military plans to relax the enlistment standards to attract more volunteers. So I imagine if you weigh 280 pounds from all the junk you're eating then that's going to be OK. I think they should bring back the draft. It's a crying shame that these young guys are having to go over four, five, six times. I give to the Wounded Warriors. It's the least I can do. But I can't understand why [charity programs like that] are necessary. If you're killed or crippled while fighting for your country or tormented by PTSD, your country ought to take care of you and your family."

His back hurts but there's fight left in the old Battling Buzzard. And his sense of humor has never failed him. Time for a toasted cheese sandwich. With a little baloney.

John C. Hughes

IN FOCUS
GUNNER IN THE 94TH

JOHN ROBERT LARIVIERE

"The noise and the rumbling of the ground sent us to our knees. We prayed together, out loud, asking God to protect us. We had no other recourse. We could not leave the pit and the shells seemed to be getting closer and closer."

– Cpl. John Robert LaRiviere, U.S. Army

LaRiviere's souvenir booklet from 1945 tells the extraordinary story of the U.S. Army's 94th Division, "Patton's Golden Nugget."
John Robert LaRiviere collection

Company H, 301st Regiment, 94th Division, in front of St. Vitus Cathedral in Prague, September 1945. *John Robert LaRiviere collection*

John Robert LaRiviere, a mortar gunner in the U.S. Army, helped bottle up enemy forces guarding German submarine pens at Normandy; spent the frigid winter of 1945 in a miserable foxhole during the Battle of the Bulge; and dodged heavy shell fire as Allies attacked the Siegfried Line, a daunting maze of barbed wire and anti-tank ditches along the western border of Germany.

Conditions were brutal for LaRiviere, who lost close friends during the war. His unit is credited with 281 days of continuous fighting—many spent in frozen clothing and soggy boots.

LaRiviere described the awful conditions in a letter he sent home to Seattle: "Haven't been able to write for a while, but am still fine and dandy ... This is a sloppy looking letter but all my paper is wet and almost ruined. Only lately could we tell where we are now. Was debating whether to tell you or not—after what you said about worrying. Your guess was right Mom—but we are in Germany now—with Patton's 3rd Army."

– John Robert LaRiviere, February 13, 1945

Cpl. LaRiviere documents his World War II experience in *V-Mail Letters Home from World War II*.

There in the skies, 3,200 feet over north-central France, Joe Moser dangled beneath a twin-engine fighter. All around his aircraft fire raged, slowly consuming pieces of a boyhood dream. A window shattered. A gaping hole cut across the plane's left engine. The pilot hung upside down. The plane flew in terrifying form—inverted and damaged, barely resembling the marvel he'd once admired in a magazine. Moser locked his eyes on the twin-boom tail where plenty of pilots had met their fate. Danger never left his mind. By August 13, 1944, the day of this 44th mission, he had lost nearly a quarter of his buddies in the 429th Fighter Squadron, 9th Air Force. Approaching Dreux, France, man and aircraft continued to plunge.

Some 70 years later, Joe Moser steadied his model P-38 in his hands. He narrowed his dark eyes and pointed to the tail. "When you bail out, you have to contend with that tail," he said with a grin. Then he recalled the months that followed his precarious flight. He still had letters from anxious neighbors and the telegram that announced he was missing in action. He had his identification card as a prisoner of war. But the family photo

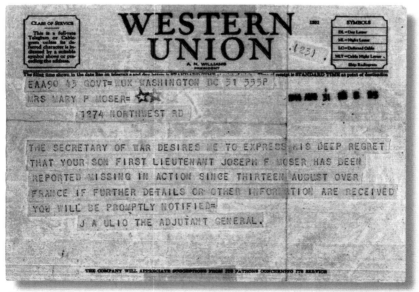

By way of Western Union, Mary Moser officially learns of her son's disappearance. The telegram marks the beginning of more than eight months in captivity. *Joe Moser collection*

albums capture a life long before the war. Here you will find the first evidence of his strength of character.

Joe Moser was just a kid on a farm in Ferndale when he began persevering in life and defying the odds. He used to split his time hunting for eggs or milking his twin cows. Sometimes, after a good rain, he'd follow the meandering Nooksack River for a mile to his grandparents' home and stomp in the waterholes. Out there on the farm, at a very young age, Joe Moser acquired the grit to fork hay and the resilience to overcome sorrow.

The Moser family on the dairy farm in Ferndale, Washington. "It was a good life, really," Moser said of his upbringing on the land he loved. *Joe Moser collection*

He was only 6 in 1927 when his younger sister Josephine toddled over to a trough with apples and drowned. Unexpected tragedy returned in the summer of 1936. Joe's father contracted pneumonia and his body quit fighting after a week. Joe never forgot watching him struggle the day he died, as Joseph Moser Sr. walked from the house to the barn. The elder Moser, a sturdy man with a bushy mustache and a briar pipe, emigrated from Switzerland to make something of himself in America. There wasn't enough work in his native land for all seven kids. The hard-working dairy farmer, who married a handsome woman from New Zealand and built a life in Ferndale, died suddenly at 53. Joe isn't sure how the family survived under the weight of all that grief. But the Mosers pulled

Joseph Moser Sr. emigrated from Switzerland to build a life in America. His strong work ethic inspired his son long after his death. *Joe Moser collection*

together in hard times the way families do. Joe shouldered immense responsibility in the absence of his mentor and namesake. Mary Moser, a widow at 31, stood faithfully by her children and their dreams.

In 1939, Joe Moser dreamed of flying one of the fastest fighters on the planet. He was a senior in high school when he thumbed through an airplane magazine and saw a picture of the Lockheed P-38 Lightning. The coveted fighter with a menacing nose could reach speeds in excess of 400 miles per hour. The German Luftwaffe dubbed the P-38 "der gabel-schwanz-teufel" or the fork-tailed devil because of the aircraft's horizontal stabilizer and twin booms with vertical rudders. "Oh, gee, I just fell in love with it," Moser said. "I wanted to fly it. But you had to have two years college education. We couldn't afford me going to school because I was running the farm for mother, so I kind of put it off."

"It was just something I dreamed I wanted to do," Moser said of his dream to fly the Lockheed P-38 Lightning. Dubbed the "Fork-Tailed Devil" by the Germans, the twin-eingine fighter flew over Europe, North Africa and the Pacific. *United States Air Force*

Joe's dream was left unanswered until a few weeks before Christmas in 1941. He was out cleaning the barn after breakfast when news broke over the radio that the Japanese bombed Pearl Harbor. Everything changed for the country and for Joe on "a date which will live in infamy." President Roosevelt declared a state of war between the United States and the Japanese Empire, and college requirements for the U.S. Army Air Corps relaxed. Moser could be inducted if he passed a special exam. He was initially told he failed, but his test had been mismarked. Joe Moser was officially welcomed into the AAC on May 18, 1941. "Oh man, my dreams were coming true," he remembered.

Moser's big plans unraveled quickly, however, during his 44th mission, about two miles north of Dreux, France. Moser was on a strafing run with orders to attack anything that moved when he spied a truck convoy. He flew at just 200 feet with his heart pounding, when a 37-millimeter shell pierced his left engine. Flames erupted. He shut the left engine off hoping the airstream would kill the fire, but the blaze persisted. A window broke. Shards of glass flew underneath his flight suit. Flames began licking at his elbows.

Joe Moser as a young U.S. Army Air Corps officer. *Joe Moser collection*

Moser had one option—to bail out and let it go, a particularly dangerous maneuver at lower speeds in a P-38. He inverted the plane and desperately tried to shake himself free. But the toe of Moser's left boot caught on the canopy. Moser's dream to fly was turned upside down, hanging precipitously, like him, from his coveted aircraft. He descended toward the earth attached to the plane he loved.

The toe of Moser's boot finally broke free and the tail dropped away from view. Free falling, Moser raced for the surface of the earth at 400 miles per hour before he pulled the ripcord. The chute opened and stopped him with a lurch. The P-38 exploded beneath him, near a stone farmhouse in the French countryside. Moser landed a second later and watched the smoke rise from a mass of wreckage dangerously close to the home. He quickly stripped himself of anything that might give him away to the enemy, like his parachute or his helmet. French farmers greeted him and thanked him for fighting in the war. Two young boys took him off to the woods to shield him. All too soon, however, they found themselves exposed and staring into rifles.

Escorted to Marchefroy in northern France, Moser was interrogated by the Gestapo. His training took over. Regardless of the question presented by the interrogating officer, Moser repeated: "Joseph Frank Moser, First Lieutenant, United States Air Corps, 0755999. Joseph Frank Moser, First Lieutenant, United States Air Corps, 0755999." He was led to a dark wine cellar and tossed inside. A truck backed against the wooden door to block his getaway. Joe started digging for his life with a garden hoe. But he was forced to cover his tracks when the truck moved and two more prisoners, French farmers who'd emerged in the aftermath of the crash, were thrown into the cellar.

Moser was transported to a cell at Fresnes Prison that had held political prisoners since the beginning of the German occupation of France. There, just outside Paris, Moser sat alone in his cell pondering his fate. Within two days, Moser and 167 other airmen were branded "terrorfliegers" (terror fliers) and loaded into cattle cars like animals with the other prisoners. It was pandemonium. Ironically, Paris was liberated just days later.

The German SS (Schutzstaffel), the officers who controlled the camp system, jammed nearly 100 prisoners into a single car. Each was equipped with only two 4x18 slats for ventilation. They made an unbearable journey, witnessing a 17-year-old boy dare to stick his arm outside the railcar and pay first with his hand and then with his life.

ON SLOPES OF THE ETTERSBERG in north-central Germany, guards and dogs appeared on a wooded hill when the prisoners arrived by train. Moser assumed he would be held captive at a POW camp. What he discovered was a kind of surreal inhumanity.

It was August 20, 1944, and the scene of prominent and mass killings. Buchenwald concentration camp, one of the largest on German soil, was surrounded by a barbed wire fence and sentries equipped with machine guns. There were prisoner barracks to the north, SS quarters to the south, working factories and a stone quarry. Buchenwald was a haunting place where people were mistreated, starved and executed. On Hitler's orders, the SS here murdered Ernst Thalmann just two

The view for Joe Moser, a devout Catholic, who prayed daily while in confinement: "I questioned why—how could this happen. But I was never angry."
Doug Richter-Bisson photo

days before the airmen's arrival. Thalmann was leader of the Communist Party during the Weimar Republic, the government of Germany between the wars. He was captured during a mass arrest of communists in 1933 and spent the next 11 years in solitary confinement.

It was the other killings that would silence Moser for years after the war. And there was evidence of them everywhere. There was a crematorium, just to the right of the gatehouse as you entered, and a death room below with hooks on the wall. A chimney spewed smoke and a searing odor wafted through the air.

The eerie images of the camp and the pungent smell didn't stay with Moser like the poignant faces he saw. Political captives and slave laborers—people from 30 nations—appeared dazed and vacant, as if no one lived inside. There were thousands of them—11,000 in 1939 and 86,000 by 1945. (The population at Buchenwald concentration camp has grown since *Kristallnacht*. During the "night of broken glass," Nazis burned hundreds of synagogues and destroyed thousands of businesses before rounding up the Jews.) The interred may have been Jewish, or Jehovah's Witnesses or unemployed or prisoners of war or Roma and Sinti (Gypsies). Their bodies

Stripped of their clothes and belongings, the interred are given uniforms. The lucky wear shoes. "You're a prisoner," Moser said. "Your life is not your own."
Margaret Bourke-White/Time & Life Pictures

were reduced to skin and bones. Their shapeless figures were covered in gray, tattered clothing bearing identification numbers and badges. The lucky prisoners wore shoes.

Moser, an airman who by rights under the Geneva Convention should have been held at a prisoner of war camp, was ordered inside. A guard informed a prisoner in their group that no one leaves Buchenwald, except through the chimney. Moser learned that so many died behind the barbed-wire fence that the brick ovens couldn't keep up. They shot people in the stables or hanged them in the crematorium. "I was so close to being killed," Moser said. "It's just so unbelievable."

Almost 100,000 people were admitted to Buchenwald

in 1944, the year Moser arrived, and more than 8,600 died, without a goodbye to family or proper burial. The act of mass killings was routine, an ordinary step at the end of an assembly line. The months Joe was held captive, 742 people disappeared in August, another 497 in September, another 732 in October. By the time operations at Buchenwald ceased, some 240,000 prisoners had been incarcerated here and 43,000 had died.

Inside the camp, Moser experienced the cruel existence of the living and near dead. He suddenly had no name, no family and no home. His dreams—burned away someplace over north-central France—were never born. It was as if Joe Moser, the farm boy who dreamed of sitting in the cockpit of the P-38, never existed. Moser lost his identity when they stole his clothing, and his dignity when they brusquely shaved him from head to toe with a dull razor and clippers. He was treated like an animal. He showered without warm water or soap, and his raw skin stung after guards applied disinfectant with a rough brush.

The wooden barracks at Buchenwald were full, forcing Moser to spend his first two weeks in the camp sleeping on rocky ground and sharing a blanket with three other men. He was thankful for the warmth of August. He dreamed of fried cornmeal cakes, a Swiss dish, but he stomached cabbage soup with worms and foul bread. The food began to taste good, eventually. The toilet—a makeshift community basin of filth—never improved.

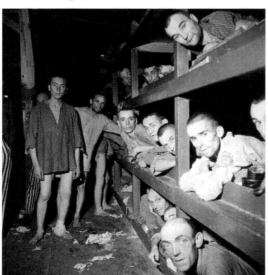

Buchenwald prisoners live on a diet of cabbage soup with worms and foul bread. "Lots of people were just skin and bones," Moser remembered. *Margaret Bourke-White/Time & Life Pictures*

Moser feared for his life on day four.

The Eighth Air Force bombed a German facility adjacent to the camp that made parts for V-2 rockets used to target civilians in Europe. The airmen spotted a squadron of B-17s overhead. One of them yelled, "They're going to bomb this place!" But there was no place to go. The airmen crouched down. The bombs destroyed the munitions factory and some of the SS living quarters. Hundreds perished in the assault when SS guards refused to allow prisoners working in the factory to take cover.

"After the raid, the 168 of us Allied fliers that were there ... were told to go to a certain spot, a prison camp there. We got there and there was a machine gun set up. We all thought that they were going to kill us ... for what the Air Force did. But then we were told to fight fires. Maybe half of us had shoes; I wasn't one of them. We were told to go into these buildings that were burning and haul out something, whatever was available." Moser pretended to cooperate but hauled the same equipment in and out of a burning building.

Joe Moser was finally placed in barracks. Approximately 900 young kids were housed in nearby quarters. He and the other airmen later learned that the children—labeled Gypsies and more—were "disposed of." "That's one of the things that hurts me," Moser said, "to see so many children that didn't make it. That you wanted to help, but you couldn't."

The calendar changed from August to September, and September to October. Moser made a conscious decision to live. He longed to see his mother again and he thought often of his late father. He ate the dehydrated cabbage, used scraps of his extra-large shirt at the toilet and he prayed. Every day Moser, a devout Catholic, talked to God: "Why? Help me get through this!" Never once did Moser ask, "Why me?"

For all his spirit and determination to live, Moser grew weaker. He dropped 35 pounds in two months. "Myself, I'd figured that another month or two and I would be one of those corpses. Every day the wagon would go and pick up dead people, where they just fell and died. So you had that feeling. It was going to happen to you. You were hungry, oh, so hungry. Even the worm-filled cabbage soup, it just didn't bother you anymore. You ate it because it was—it kept you alive, for a while anyway."

But the airmen at Buchenwald didn't have much time.

They began to hear rumors and their ranking officer, a much-respected New Zealander named Phil Lamason, had learned their fate. "We were scheduled to be executed on October 24," remembered Moser.

THERE'S A CODE BETWEEN AIRMEN, a comradery and a shared respect that transcends battle lines, even in worldwide conflict. Stories of the airmen had crossed the desk of Hannes Trautloft, a German ace fighter who fought in the Spanish Civil War and commanded a German fighter squadron in World War II. Trautloft was inspector of day fighters when he heard that Allied airmen were imprisoned and under brutal treatment at Buchenwald. Trautloft requested a camp tour under the pretense of checking out nearby bomb damage. The German SS told him that the camp housed political prisoners who worked in the factories. Trautloft was winding up his tour when a German-speaking airman called out to him and explained that he was one of more than 160 airmen unlawfully imprisoned at the concentration camp.

Hannes Trautloft, the respected German airman who liberated Moser and more than 160 pilots from the Buchenwald concentration camp.

Within days of Trautloft's initial visit, the airmen were ushered into a building and given their original clothing. Moser was then handed his ankle-length flight boots—even the left shoe with the missing toe. Heinrich Himmler, Reich leader of the German SS, was reportedly so angry about the airmen's release from Buchenwald that he threw a wine glass against the wall. Later, when the airmen arrived at a POW camp, the interrogating officer believed the information they revealed about their time at Buchenwald was critical for future trials of war crimes. He reputedly hid four pages of notes in the lining of his coat.

WITHIN DAYS OF THEIR SCHEDULED EXECUTION, the airmen were freed. They were sent back to boxcars and on to Stalag Luft III, a POW camp in Poland approximately 100 miles southeast of Berlin. Moser weighed 113 pounds. Stalag Luft III housed Allied airmen captured during the war and later spawned *The Great Escape* starring Steve McQueen. The film chronicled the breakout of Allied POWs who tunneled their way to freedom. "I was put in that same barracks where that tunnel had started," Moser recalled.

For Moser, if Buchenwald was the dark of night, then Stalag Luft III was the light of day. Some modicum of life had returned at the POW camp. They bathed regularly, slept in straw beds and ate from large Red Cross parcels. "We got into a room with two American fliers and four Polish fliers. Each room cooked their own meals. ... We got our meat from our Red Cross parcels. We got corned beef and cabbage, sauerkraut and wieners, Spam."

"RAUS! RAUS!" The order to get out came on January 27, 1945, as the snow fell. Russian forces were advancing across Poland, triggering the Germans to move the prisoners out of POW camps and across rough terrain despite a bruising cold. Many would march until their deaths in one of Europe's coldest winters of the 20th century.

Some of the walkers slathered their faces with margarine to protect the skin from the chill. Joe Moser, thinner and weaker, wore everything he had—pants, a shirt, a coat and shoddy gloves. His footprints froze as he pulled a sled two feet long. "We had a little wagon the first couple of days," Moser remembered. "Then, that got too heavy to pull anymore. So we abandoned the wagon. So then we just bundled what food we had in extra clothes."

The prisoners figured they walked 21 miles the first day, and 15 or 16 the next. With every excruciating step, they could hear the German warning: anyone who fails to keep pace will be shot. For the first time since his capture, Moser was about to give up.

Moser's identification card as a prisoner of war. *Joe Moser collection*

As they walked, some prisoners dropped off and huddled in the snow banks. The walkers still pressing on behind them stopped. They slapped their faces and steadied them on their feet. "There were times when the people following long behind would pick up those people and help them," Moser recalled. "And then there were other times when nobody would help. They couldn't anymore. To see fellow walkers just collapse, and most of them that collapsed died right there. I don't know what it was but I just didn't want to die yet."

Other marchers lost all hope and summoned the chaplain. Recalled one Brit of discovering a man: "I found [him] on his back in the snow. He insisted on giving me what remained of his scanty rations. I stayed with him till he died, closed his eyes and ran to catch up with the main column, three miles away. The summons came again and again."

The unbearable walk eventually became too much for Moser, who passed out. Two American pilots pulling a sled hoisted him up and carried him, unconscious, for a quarter-mile. "I remember waking up in bed. I was halfway warm. We had been walking, I don't know, 40 or 50 miles." Moser found himself in a makeshift hospital in a village called Bad Muskau, on the current border between Germany and Poland. He realized he could have been left for dead along a country road in Poland.

"I started walking again and we walked 65 miles in five days to a town called Spremberg. [They] put us in boxcars again and then I went to a prisoner of war camp in Nuremberg, Germany. ... I was in Nuremberg for just about two months. ... Then, the American army got close so they marched us out of Nuremberg and we went south to Moosburg."

IT WAS APRIL 1945. Joe Moser was living in filth at Stalag VII/A near Moosburg, an ancient city in southern Germany where he'd been confined for a couple of weeks. He slept in overcrowded tents, in a camp built for 10,000 POWs that held some 80,000 people. Moser and 15,000 POWs had just completed a 70-mile march from Nuremberg, the site of their last POW camp. During their long journey, a farmer told the passing men of President Roosevelt's death from a massive cerebral hemorrhage.

The sloppy weather at Moosburg began to warm. The war was ending. Allied forces were coming. After a fierce battle, the Allies captured the town of Moosburg. "I was right close

"I think we all just cried. ... No feeling like it, really." Joe Moser on the day of liberation, April 29, 1945.

to the gate when a big American tank came and run right over the gate. Come in and they took down the German flag and raised the American flag. You're a prisoner. Your life isn't your own. And all of a
sudden, you're free. The joy is tremendous. It's something that is hard to describe because we're a free nation; we can do just about whatever we want. And to have all of that taken away. And to have all of that given back to you. I think we all just cried. ... No feeling like it, really."

After the war, Joe Moser was reunited with his mother, Mary. "We had walked down by Tacoma when I first saw her. She had drove up in her car and I was walking. She got out of the car and I saw her for the first time. I think I bawled like a baby."

Moser gave up his career as a fighter pilot. He married, raised five kids and kept up his faith in the Catholic Church. He became an avid Seattle Seahawks fan. Moser earned his living repairing furnaces, quietly exchanging pleasantries with neighbors. They knew nothing of his past as a fighter pilot. Moser tried to open up about the war. But like the American officers who'd balked at his claims when he applied for his discharge papers —"No Americans were there!" they'd accused— people in his own community also doubted his assertions. "I don't believe a word he said," a gentleman said after Moser spoke at a community Lions Club. The hurtful response silenced Moser for decades. "So many didn't believe it, and that's in the back of my mind. So many people didn't believe a person could be treated that way."

Then, in the 1980s, a reporter at a POW support group meeting wrote a story about Joe, breaking through the wall of silence. It was the first time his family learned the truth. His children understood why their father's story had to live on. They collected all they could—pictures, war documents, newspaper articles and stories. They urged their father to speak up, especially around young people. "Kids don't know," said daughter Jaleen Bacon. "They don't know how cruel people can be. It's not in the history books."

The nightmares stopped and Moser found peace. He harbored no ill will, not even toward his captors. He was especially grateful to three men, Hannes Trautloft, the German fighter ace who helped liberate the Buchenwald airmen, and his fellow marchers who trudged through the snowy cold and carried him to safety. His deepest regret was that he never knew their names. "If they hadn't carried me," he said, shaking his head, as his voice trailed off. "Over the years, I've thought of those guys so many times. I've blessed them many times. What I wished all my life, really, is that I could remember their names."

Often, Joe Moser returned to August 13, 1944, the day he dangled from the prized aircraft, a young man with big dreams gone astray. But a moment later he was back in Ferndale and grateful for the life he'd lived. "I've had a wonderful life. ... I would go through it again to keep our freedom, really. ... I know I could be angry for what I had to go through, but it made life worth living."

Capt. Joseph F. Moser died on December 2, 2015.

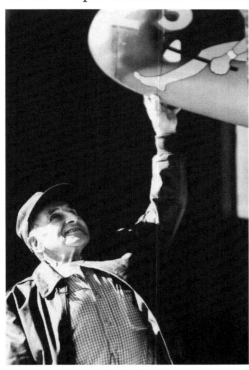

Joe Moser reaches for his beloved P-38.
Joe Moser collection

Trova Heffernan

ARNOLD SAMUELS

Eyewitness to the Holocaust

"The Weimar Republic, with all its liberal trappings and blessings, was regarded as an imposition of the enemy. ...and into that void after a pause there strode a maniac of ferocious genius, the repository and expression of the most virulent hatreds that have ever corroded the human breast—Corporal Hitler."

– Winston S. Churchill

Anyone who lost aunts, uncles and cousins in the Holocaust never forgets. So it seemed fitting that the shades were drawn on an otherwise sparkling winter's day at Ocean Shores, Wash. It was February 6, 2015. Arnold Samuels, 91, pointed toward a binder of photos he took 70 years ago when he arrived at Dachau, the Nazis' first concentration camp. Ordinarily, he's so playful that what happened next was startling. He closed his eyes, held his head and made a low keening sound—an anguished "Awwwwwwww"—as the memories flooded his brain. "People need to see them," he finally said. "But they give me nightmares. I just couldn't visualize how a cultured nation could do that to other human beings."

A cuckoo clock chirped. Its cheerfulness seemed hollow.

"Take a look at the pictures!" Samuels implored. "You say to yourself, 'Why?' It's just un-understandable."

U.S. ARMY PRIVATE FIRST CLASS SAMUELS, a German Jew whose family had escaped to America, was back in Bavaria in the spring of 1945. Since entering combat with the 70th Infantry Division's Artillery around Christmas, he had gone on many reconnaissance missions behind enemy lines. His flawless, idiomatic German yielded crucial information about Nazi defenses. Sometimes he wore civilian clothes and carried phony German identification papers. Now, however, the Americans were meeting little resistance as they mopped up what was left of the Third Reich.

Arnold's fake German ID papers when he was working behind enemy lines.
Arnold Samuels collection

On April 29, two infantry divisions converged on Dachau, 15 miles northwest of Munich. They discovered a hell on earth. To call it bestial, someone said, was to give beasts a bad name. When Samuels arrived two days later to help with the interrogations, "there were still bodies all over—all over. Unbelievable. Oh God, unbelievable! You've never seen anything like it and you can't describe it. Never leaves your mind. Never, never, never! The inhumanity of man to man is unbelievable!"

Samuels was one of the liberators because he had been liberated. He had arrived in America a few days after the Fourth of July, 1937. Two years later, his Aunt Johanna and Uncle Leon weren't so fortunate. Refused sanctuary by Cuba and the U.S., both perished in the Holocaust. Leon Joel was also Billy Joel's uncle. Six degrees of separation don't get more tragic than that. The famous singer-songwriter and the gregarious former

Ocean Shores City Council member are united by the broken branches of their family trees—and the un-understandable.

ARNOLD SAMUELS—originally Kurt Daniel Samuel—was born on December 15, 1923. A month earlier, Adolf Hitler and his Brownshirts, the paramilitary wing of the fledgling Nazi party, had failed in their attempt to overthrow the Bavarian government and spark a national revolt. Bavaria was a hotbed of resentment over the steep reparations the victorious allies imposed after Germany's defeat in World War I. Hitler preached that the Weimar Republic, with its ruinous hyperinflation, was rife with Jews, Bolsheviks, Socialists and other traitorous "parasitic vermin" who spread liberal "defeatism and degeneracy." They had "stabbed Germany in the back."

Hitler's abortive coup landed him in prison, supposedly for five years. He was coddled by sympathetic guards, entertained a stream of visitors and dictated his autobiography, *Mein Kampf,* to Rudolf Hess, his slavish follower. Prison burnished his celebrity. Freed after only nine months, he was now a nationally known right-wing leader with a growing band of fanatical followers, many little more than street thugs in spit-shined new jackboots.

Wilhelm "Willi" Samuel, Arnold's handsome bald father, was the son of a kosher butcher in Bad Königshofen im Grab-

Arnold's father, Willi Samuel, in his beloved Mercedes in front of the "Chocolate House" café in Hammelburg in the early 1930s. *Arnold Samuels collection*

Arnold, his brother and parents lived downstairs, his grandfather and aunt upstairs.
Arnold Samuels collection

feld, a spa town in Bavaria. Willi was studying at a trade school in England in 1914 when Europe erupted in war. He was interned by the British as an enemy alien for the next four years—one of some 24,000 German citizens held captive in camps. Willi emerged from the ordeal near-fluent in English but told his family he was treated poorly.

In 1920, Willi Samuel married Blanka Sichel, the sturdy daughter of a grain merchant in the pretty little town of Hammelburg about an hour away. Willi joined his father-in-law's business, roaming the countryside to meet with farmers and supplying wheat—"Weizen"—to breweries. Samuel Sichel and Willi Samuel had their office in the quaint building where both families lived. Sichel by then was an elderly widower who shared an upstairs apartment with Arnold's Aunt Fanny. A pious man, Sichel was the doyen of Hammelburg's small Jewish community, some 50 families in a largely Catholic farm town of 3,000.

Willi and Blanka Samuel's firstborn was Gerhard. Two years later came Kurt, an inquisitive boy with a mischievous grin. The Samuels were generous people who loved music, books and bowling. Willi owned a Mercedes-Benz cabriolet and an elaborate new radio that struck his youngest son as magical. When Arnold remembers what it was like to be Kurt, he sees himself roller-skating through town, playing cops and robbers and roaming the hills with his brother and their school pals. When the grapes were ripe in the vineyards, school closed for a week so the kids could help with the harvest. On Sundays, Kurt's job was to take his white-bearded Grandpa Sichel to the beer hall to spend the morning with the other town elders.

Sometimes he would accompany his grandpa to the warehouse. "He was nearly blind, but he loved to smell the grain. As it flowed through his fingers he could tell whether it would make good beer."

Arnold and his father. *Arnold Samuels collection*

There had been little distinction as to race or religion in Hammelburg, especially among the kids. Gerhard and Kurt attended Catholic kindergarten, where the nuns were uniformly strict. Kurt's best friend was Markus Hofstetter, a Christian whose genial father was the town barber. In the winter of 1931, when the boys were 8, they went sledding two miles outside town. Markus lost control of his sled and careened down a steep hill. "I was almost right behind him," Arnold remembers. "He flew onto the road, right into the path of a truck. I threw my sled down, got him out from under the vehicle and ran back to Hammelburg to tell his father, who was a medic in World War I." Soon the town ambulance scooped up poor Markus and rushed him to the nearest hospital. A shattered leg had to be amputated. That likely saved his life when the other boys went off to war. Few came back.

EVERYTHING CHANGED IN 1933, the year Kurt turned 10. When Hitler became chancellor on January 30, he moved quickly to crush all democratic impulses. The Communist Party was banned; trade unions forbidden. With a metastasizing vengeance, *der Führer* set about rearming Germany in defiance of the Treaty of Versailles. Anti-Semitism became the official state ideology. The concentration camp outside Dachau, a charming

Grandpa Sichel with Arnold's mother and aunts: From left, Blanka Samuel, Meta, Rosa and Fanny. Rosa and Fanny perished in the Holocaust together with Fanny's daughter and Rosa's two grandchildren. *Arnold Samuels collection*

village, opened on March 22; the Gestapo, a fearsome police force, was formed a month later. And on May 10 in Berlin 40,000 spectators gathered in a plaza as "thousands of students proudly wearing their university colors walked through the foggy streets by glittering torchlight" and consigned to a mammoth bonfire armloads of books written by Jews. Joseph Goebbels, Hitler's reptilian Minister of Propaganda and National Enlightenment, soon arrived to celebrate the moment when the birthplace of the printing press became the epicenter of thought-control. "Jewish intellectualism is dead!" Goebbels declared. "The German folk-soul can again express itself. These flames do not only illuminate the final end of the old era, they also light up the new." Then the crowd sang "The Nation to Arms." What some called a "literary holocaust," or as *Time* magazine put it, a "bibliocaust," was a prelude to human smoke.

"A gloominess came over my parents," Samuels remembers. "My father told me years later that he had remarked to Christian friends at the bowling alley that anyone voting for Hitler should have his hands cut off. It appears no one ratted him out at the time, but all of a sudden the gentile kids didn't play with us anymore. They had joined the Hitler Youth—the Hitlerjugend—and the Hitler Youth taught them 'You can't play with Jews!' The girls had to join the BDM—the Bund Deutscher Mädel, the league of German girls. Our Christian friends and classmates fell away from us and we were isolated. Some of them started fights with Jewish kids and called us 'Judenstinkers.' I really didn't understand it—the politics of hate. Then in school we were separated from the other kids. I had to sit at the back of the class. I couldn't sit with my friends on the same benches. Hitler had a helluva machine going when he got into power. People were struggling. They wanted Germany to be great again. He mesmerized the masses. Especially German youth. Everyone got in line. It was 'Heil Hitler! Mein Führer! Our great leader!' "

Everything changed in 1933, the year Arnold turned 10. Hitler came to power and anti-Semitism soon became the official state ideology. *Arnold Samuels collection*

Heinz Kissinger, seven months older than Kurt Samuel, was growing up two hours south in Furth. The future U.S. secretary of state recalls that he and his friends were barred from the swimming pool, the dances and the tearoom. "We couldn't go anywhere without seeing the signs Juden Verboten! (No Jews!)" Fate would have it that Henry Kissinger and Arnold Samuels, their names Americanized, would become colleagues in postwar Germany.

THINGS GOT SO BAD, even in Hammelburg, that in 1934 Willi and Blanka Samuel sent their sons 50 miles away to live with a sympathetic family in a town where there was a Hebrew school. But the pox was relentlessly spreading. "The main object in those days was to get rid of the Jews," Samuels remembers. "In every little town, the mayor and rulers of the town would hang a banner across the main street that declared *Diese Stadt ist judenfrei*!

'This city is free of Jews!' And the faster they could put those banners up, the higher rating they got in the Hitler regime."

In 1935, when Samuels was 12, the triumphant Nazis assembled en masse at Nuremberg and promulgated their new laws on "Aryan" racial purity. Jews, Gypsies and ethnic Poles were deprived of German citizenship and prohibited from sexual relations or marriage with "true Germans."

That was just the beginning. Soon Jews were barred from the professions, made to carry special ID cards and publicly humiliated. Crackpot Nazi eugenicists measured their noses and skulls. An "Aryan" woman under the age of 45 could not work as a servant for a Jewish family, underscoring the Nazi characterization of Jewish males as loathsome lechers.

One of the most compelling studies of German anti-Semitism is Götz Aly's 2011 book, *Why the Germans? Why the Jews?* Aly notes that Siegfried Lichtenstaedter, a retired Bavarian civil servant and author "who spent much of his life pondering his dual identity as German and Jew," believed "Nazism was propelled by the least pleasurable of the seven deadly sins: envy." It "dissolves social cohesion. It destroys trust, creates aggression, promotes suspicion over proof, and leads people to bolster their sense of self-worth by denigrating others. ...Upset by others' success, they dismiss those they envy as immoral, egotistical and despicable, while they themselves pose as respectable moral authorities." Working underground during the war, Samuels met a German university professor who at great risk was doing what he could to undermine the Nazi regime. Samuels said he couldn't fathom anti-Semitism. And the professor said, "You know, Kurt, we love you for your talents and we hate you for your success."

One night in 1936, Willi Samuel had a surreptitious visitor. It was Herr Stumpf, who owned the garage where Willi took his Mercedes. "Herr Stumpf was a gentile," Arnold remembers, "but they were good friends and secretly had remained so even though Stumpf had to join Hitler's SA Brownshirts and parade through town with a swastika banner. 'Willi, get out of Hammelburg,' he said. 'I can't protect you anymore.' In gratitude, my father gave his car to Stumpf and transferred title of his property to the Nazi party in exchange for papers allowing him to pursue leaving Germany."

Cantor Heinz Heller, Arnold's uncle, became a fixture at Tremont Temple in the Bronx. *Arnold Samuels collection*

Willi Samuel began corresponding with relatives in America. His sister Paula and brother-in-law, Heinz Heller, a cantor and teacher in Königshofen, had made it to New York in the summer of 1936. (Heinz became "Henry" and was a beloved cantor at Tremont Temple in the Bronx until his death in 1964). Then practically overnight, Arnold remembers, his father closed his office. "They packed up as much as they could as fast as they could and we took the train to Hamburg. To my brother and I it was an excitement— an adventure! We didn't realize we were in such danger. Hey, we were getting out of Hammelburg! And Hamburg seemed safer. The Nazis had a lower profile in the big cities—at least for a while, especially during the 1936 Olympic Games when they made nice and wanted the world to think the new Germany was peaceful. But the Gestapo was working in Hamburg underground. Now it was everywhere. After *Kristallnacht* in 1938, when the SA smashed the windows of Jewish stores, burned synagogues, murdered hundreds of Jews and rounded up thousands of others, the Nazis took all my grandfather's property in Hammelburg. They smashed his windows and his big grandfather clock that I always had my eye on as a child. They put him in jail for two weeks. Then for some reason they let him go to a nursing home in Würzburg, where he died as a lonely man within a year. Aunt Fanny, whose husband had died for the fatherland in World War I, moved to Holland where her daughter was a doctor. When Hitler invaded Holland, they just disappeared. We never heard from them again. Now I know what happened to them because I have done a lot of research. They all went to the concentration camps. My family was one of the lucky ones. We made it out alive. There's an old German saying, 'The fatherland thanks you for your sacrifices.' To a Jew it became 'The thanks of the fatherland is to shoot you.' "

Arnold turned 13 in December of 1936. He was studying for his Bar Mitzvah when Mussolini declared that Italy, Germany and Japan had formed an "Axis" to oppose the Jews' alleged handiwork, International Communism. Hitler's armament factories were working overtime. In New York, the best kind of friend an endangered family could hope for was too.

Morris L. Ernst, at 47 was one of the most influential attorneys in the United States and a cosmopolitan civil libertarian, serving on the board of the American Civil Liberties Union. Ernst in 1933 had famously defended James Joyce's groundbreaking novel *Ulysses* against obscenity charges. He aided advocates of birth control and sex education and championed consumer rights. The natty, pipe-smoking lawyer was also a contributor to the *New Yorker* magazine. Ernst counted as a friend U.S. Supreme Court Justice Louis Brandeis and had a wide network of acquaintances and admirers in politics, publishing, entertainment and the literary world. These included Franklin D. Roosevelt, J. Edgar Hoover, Walter Winchell, H.L. Mencken, Henry Luce, E.B. White and Groucho Marx. A widower, Ernst in 1923 had married Margaret Samuels, a Phi Beta Kappa Wellesley graduate who was a writer, teacher and librarian. Margaret's father, Emanuel Samuel, had come to America as a teenager in 1883. He became a successful businessman in Mississippi, adding an "s" to his surname, as Arnold would later.

Morris L. Ernst, who saved the Samuels. *Arnold Samuels collection*

Here's the family connection that rescued four people from almost certain death: Emanuel Samuels was Willi Samuel's uncle. Put another way, Arnold Samuels' grandfather Max was Emanuel Samuels' brother. Moreover, Margaret Ernst's brother, Frank L. Samuels, was a Yale graduate with a successful real estate practice in Manhattan.

Strict immigration quotas had been established by Congress in the 1920s "in the name of preserving 'the ideal of American homogeneity,' in part to stem the flow of Jews who had fled Poland and Russia." Germany was allotted 25,957 slots per year. But high-ranking officials in the State Department were anti-Semites who encouraged strict enforcement of the "likely to become a public charge" clause. "LPC" was designed to discourage immigration of the penniless and downtrodden, especially during the Depression. *In the Garden of Beasts*, a chilling book about the American ambassador to Berlin navigating State Department intrigue during the early years of the Third Reich, Erik Larson writes, "Jewish activists charged that America's consulates abroad had been instructed quietly to grant only a fraction of the visas allowed for each country, a charge that proved to have merit."

The Ernsts and Samuels cut through the red tape and loaned Willi Samuel money to help with travel expenses and Nazi palm-greasing. Not counting forfeited property, it cost Willi Samuel upwards of $5,000—$82,000 in today's dollars—to get his family out of Germany, he told his sons after the war. Crucially, Morris Ernst also vouched with Immigration that Willi would have a job. And once settled in, Willi was assured his family could soon follow.

Arnold, his brother, mother and family friends hugged Willi and posed for photos dockside before he boarded the *S.S. Manhattan* at Hamburg, immigration documents secure in a breast pocket. He waved from the ocean liner's railing as they shouted "Auf Wiedersehen." On January 25, 1937, when Willi disembarked in New York City, the Ernsts and Hellers greeted him with outstretched arms.

In March, as Willi Samuel was getting a start selling cleaning supplies in Brooklyn, Stanley Baldwin, the British prime minister, was meeting with a delegation of peace advocates. "I know some of you think I should speak more roughly to Hitler than I do," he said, "but have you reflected that the reply to a stiff letter might be a bomb on your breakfast tables? ...The peace of the world lies in the hands of these dictators. For all I know, they may be insane, and unlimited power drives men mad."

In April, the Luftwaffe tested its new warplanes by pounding the Basque town of Guernica for its ally, the Spanish nationalist government. The charred bodies of women and children were but collateral damage to the Nazis—"guinea pigs in an experiment designed to determine just what it would take to bomb a city into oblivion."

On July 8, as a new concentration camp opened at Buchenwald, Blanka Samuel and her sons sailed past the Statue of Liberty. Fate and the long arm of the Gestapo conspired against other family members.

IN MAY OF 1939 with war looming and trains leaving for the death camps, Arnold Samuels' Aunt Johanna and Uncle Leon were desperate to escape the Third Reich. Four months earlier, Leon Joel's brother Karl, sister-in-law Meta and nephew Helmut had made it to Cuba. "Hurry," they wrote.

Leon and Johanna Joel and their 10-year-old son, Gunter, departed Hamburg for Havana on the German liner *St. Louis*. All but a handful of its 938 passengers were "Hebrews," as the newspapers put it. What came to be called "The Voyage of the Damned" made headlines around the world. When the ship arrived in Havana, only 28 passengers were allowed to disembark. Cuba, like the United States, was slow to recover from the Great Depression. The Cuban branch of the Nazi Party stirred up anti-Semitism. "Corruption and internal power struggles" were also rife, and "many Cubans resented the relatively large number of refugees (including 2,500 Jews) whom the government had already admitted into the country, because they appeared to be competitors for scarce jobs." The same sentiments prevailed in the U.S., where anti-Semitism ran wide and deep. Forty-one percent of respondents to an opinion poll believed Jews had "too much power in the United States." Father Charles Coughlin, the Michigan priest who railed against Jewish bankers, had a radio audience of millions and gave the Nazi salute

It's June 17, 1939. The *M.S. St. Louis* has just docked at Antwerp. The man in the middle, surrounded by happy passengers, is Morris Troper, European director of a Jewish refugee assistance organization. His wife Ethel is wearing a hat. The smiling, round-faced woman at left is Arnold Samuels' aunt, Johanna Joel. Safety was short-lived. Johanna and her husband Leon died in the gas chambers at Auschwitz in the fall of 1942. *Arnold Samuels collection*

at one speech. After an anti-war America First rally in Boston, someone defaced a poster on a lamp-post, changing the "United States of America" to the "Jew-nited States of America." While American media "generally portrayed the plight of the passengers with great sympathy, only a few journalists and editors suggested that the refugees be admitted into the United States," the U.S. Holocaust Memorial Museum notes, adding:

> Sailing so close to Florida that they could see the lights of Miami, some passengers on the *St. Louis* cabled President Roosevelt asking for refuge. Roosevelt never responded. The State Department and the White House had decided not to take extraordinary measures to permit the refugees to enter the United States. ...A *Fortune* magazine poll at the time indicated that 83 percent of Americans opposed relaxing restrictions on immigration. Roosevelt could have issued an executive order to admit the *St. Louis* refugees, but this general hostility to immigrants, the gains of iso-

lationist Republicans in the Congressional elections of 1938, and Roosevelt's consideration of running for an unprecedented third term were among the political considerations that militated against taking this extraordinary step in an unpopular cause.

After his re-election in 1936, Roosevelt had moved to loosen restrictions on Jewish immigration and promote Palestine as a Jewish homeland. That he was ill for several days as the *St. Louis* drama unfolded clouds his role in the affair. The political calculus was indisputably tricky. As the *St. Louis* sailed back to Europe, its passengers "hanging between hope and despair," the State Department was attempting to make sure they weren't returned to Germany. Jewish welfare organizations managed to secure entry visas with England, the Netherlands, Belgium and France. In a photo on the Holocaust Museum's website, Johanna Joel can be seen smiling in a crowd of passengers as the *St. Louis* arrives at Antwerp on June 17, 1939. "That's my Aunt Johanna," Samuels says, pointing to her happy face. "They were mishpuchah—family. I've always wondered what the Statue of Liberty thought when those people were turned away."

A cartoon in the *New York Daily Mirror* dramatizes the plight of the *St. Louis*. Arnold Samuels collection

Leon, Johanna and Gunter Joel found temporary refuge in France. But together with some 500 other Jews who had staked their hopes on the *St. Louis*, they fell back into the Nazis' clutches as Hitler conquered Europe. Johanna and Leon died in the gas chambers at Auschwitz in the fall of 1942. Their son escaped to Switzerland, aided by the underground, and eventually made it to America. Gunter's musical 16-year-old cousin, Helmut Joel—his name anglicized to Howard— was already here, his family having gained entry to the U.S. after a stay in Cuba. "I was lucky because my parents had some money left. That's why I'm still alive," Howard Joel said in 2001 as his famous son, Billy, explored the fate of family members sent to the concentration camps.

Arnold and his brother with their parents in America in 1940. *Arnold Samuels collection*

We now know that Arnold Samuels and Howard Joel, whose battalion was also part of Patton's Third Army, were at the liberated Dachau the same week. But the two young Jewish GIs, related by marriage and their revulsion at what they saw, had no way of knowing they were simultaneously staring into the abyss of the un-understandable.

IN THE SUMMER OF 1937, when the Samuels were reunited in Brooklyn—a borough of 2.7 million in a city of 7½ million— they moved into a small but decent second-floor apartment in a largely Jewish neighborhood. Willi's new job as a salesman supplying hotels with toilet paper, towels and soap was a far cry from his days as successful grain merchant with a Mercedes-

Benz. They took in a boarder, and Mrs. Samuel did piece work in the apartment, sewing leather gloves. Though happy to be alive, the adjustment was still difficult—but less so for their boys. Kurt and Gerhard, at 14 and 16, had been practicing their English. They made new friends quickly and were enrolled at Erasmus Hall High School. The German teacher there was eager to become more fluent. "He made a deal with us," Samuels says. "After school, he spent an hour teaching us more English and we taught him more German. We developed our vocabulary by making lists of words—10 each. When we got home, we'd get the English-German dictionary and look up the translation into German. Then I interrogated my brother with my 10 words and he interrogated me with his 10 words." The English phrases they learned on the streets of Brooklyn turned out to be ones they couldn't share at home. "They were always bad ones!" Samuels says with a chortle. The boys soon found odd jobs. Arnold delivered meat for a kosher butcher—at 50 cents for a morning's work, plus leftovers to take home.

When both boys posted stellar test scores, they were accepted at Hebrew Tech, an ambitious private school, only to see its funding run dry. They landed next at one of the nation's top

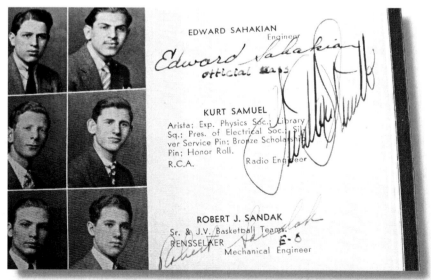

Arnold—still Kurt—graduated from New York's famed Stuyvesant High School with honors in 1941. *Arnold Samuels collection*

public high schools—Stuyvesant, which offered rigorous, college-prep courses in math, engineering and the sciences. It was an all-boys school, which suited Arnold fine. He liked girls, one especially, but found them "too distracting" when he was trying to listen to the teacher. Arnold was excited to study electronics. When he was around 6 his father had brought home a wondrous new radio. "One night when my folks came home from bowling, they found all the tubes and coils out of the radio. Dad woke me up and demanded, 'What did you do to my radio?' I said, 'I was looking for the man that always talks in that thing!' My Dad always said, 'That's when I found out you were going to become a radio man.' " It was the beginning of a lifelong fascination and vocation that took him around the world. At Stuyvesant Samuels was a straight-A student. He joined the amateur radio club, qualified for extracurricular courses at the RCA Institute's School of Radio Technology and attended workshops underwritten by Westinghouse at Columbia University. He experimented with UHF and VHF broadcast signals and RCA's latest tubes. During the futuristic 1939 New York World's Fair, Arnold represented Stuyvesant High at Westinghouse's exhibit. He had the run of the fair for free, and Westinghouse paid the carfare.

Arnold represented Stuyvesant High at Westinghouse's exhibit during the 1939 New York World's Fair. *Arnold Samuels collection*

At the Flatbush Jewish Center a year earlier, he had met a girl who was very distracting. Her name was Phyllis Krasner. She was only 15—nearly two years younger than him—but she was smart and vivacious, with an infectious laugh. When she stopped by the Westinghouse exhibit to say "Hi," Arnold was hooked. She was now a knockout. Moreover, her family loved classical music, one of his passions; her mother's gefilte fish and fried chicken were heavenly. His parents thought they were too young to be so serious. Sometimes they met in secret.

Arnold—still Kurt—graduated from Stuyvesant with honors in 1941.

He was a slender young man, six feet tall, with dark, tousled hair and a contagious smile. While attending night school classes at the RCA Institute he landed a series of jobs repairing radios at small shops before being hired at Goldsmith Bros. department store, which sold a lot of radios, phonographs and records.

AFTER PEARL HARBOR, the Samuel brothers volunteered for the military. "They told us, 'Oh, you can't volunteer. You're not citizens. You're enemy aliens. But we can draft you when we want you.'" Arnold returned to his studies. His brother was called up first. Gerhard, now called "Jerry," was sent to the South Pacific as an aerial photographer. When Kurt was drafted by the Army at the beginning of 1943, he became "Arnold" and added an "s" to his surname. The Americanization of two German boys was now complete. Both became naturalized citizens. There were 550,000 Jewish soldiers in the Army. Minorities served in the U.S. military in higher percentages proportionally than Caucasians. "We knew what we were fighting for," Samuels says, "and some of us had actually lived under the Nazis." Despite

Arnold in basic training at Camp Croft near Spartanburg, S.C., in 1943. He entered combat with the artillery of the 70th Infantry Division in 1944 in France. *Arnold Samuels collection*

that, slanderous "stereotypes portrayed typical Brooklyn Jews as quintessential draft-dodgers," Deborah Dash Moore writes in her 2006 book, *GI Jews*. "As one professor at City College joked, 'The Battle Hymn of the Jews is *Onward Christian Soldiers*, we'll make the uniforms.' "

During basic training at Camp Croft near Spartanburg, South Carolina, Samuels met Henry Kissinger. "But so what?" Arnold says with a chuckle. "He was then just another schmuck like the rest of us."

Based on his test scores and schooling, Arnold was selected for the Army Specialized Training Program—ASTP— in electrical engineering at Georgia Tech in Atlanta. After a year there, he applied for flight school but was rejected on the grounds he had not been a U.S. citizen long enough. Frustrated, he nevertheless ended up in a job for which he was well suited—that of a field artillery "surveyor." At Fort Leonard Wood in Missouri, he was trained to assess target data— angles, elevations and distances. "It was a good thing I was handy with a slide rule and liked trigonometry. Once trained and assigned, we were considered the artillery commander's pets, since the effectiveness of artillery is totally dependent on the accuracy of the survey team's computations." Attached to the 70th Infantry Division—the "Trailblazers"— Samuels arrived at Marseille, France, on December 10, 1944.

A GI in Arnold's 70th Infantry Division guards a group of captured German soldiers carrying their wounded from Wingen, France, on January 6, 1945. *National Archives*

It was rainy, muddy and cold. And for two weeks at least, uneventful save for the night a Nazi reconnaissance plane dropped a flare to monitor their advance. "Everyone ran out of their tents and urinated on the flare to extinguish it," which struck Samuels as hilariously symbolic of something. Maybe that war was insane. Things soon became deadly serious.

THEIR GOAL WAS TO SECURE ALSACE-LORRAINE along the border between France and Germany, then punch through the heavily fortified, 400-mile-long Siegfried Line. The Germans were fighting ferociously—often willing to die before surrendering. "The battle through France was swift, at least for a while," Samuels remembers, "with the Germans retreating and regrouping along the whole front." Then crack SS mountain troops, supported by artillery and tanks, dug in and began to infiltrate the advancing 70th Infantry. Its casualties mounted. Samuels was temporarily assigned to the legendary 3rd Infantry Division, which had seen heavy combat since 1942.

Arnold holding a stray Dachshund the GIs dubbed "Schnapps." The patch on his shoulder is that of the legendary 3rd Infantry Division, to which he was attached as the U.S. Army advanced into Germany. *Arnold Samuels collection*

"I went on reconnaissance missions practically every day with my buddy Jimmy Mitchell. One day, snipers spotted us. Then came an 88-millimeter German artillery round. And mortar rounds— "Screaming Meemies" we called them. They exploded into a million little shrapnel. We lost our Jeep and barely escaped, really shook up. Another time when they started shelling us,

I jumped into a pile of horse manure! I'll never forget that! I crawled in and ducked myself under the goddamn horse manure and, boy, I came out smelling like a rose! It was the first time in my life," he cackled, "that I ever thanked a pile of shit!"

"Because of my background, they often sent me behind enemy lines in civilian clothes. Sometimes we met with informants. One night, the Gestapo got wind of us. One of the farmers who was anti-German hid me in the attic under the straw that they used for the cows. The Gestapo came in, looking all over with their flashlights. But they couldn't see me and I got away! Sometimes I stayed behind enemy lines for days. And I wrote Phyllis not to worry if she didn't hear from me. I carried a pistol in a shoulder holster and my phony German papers identifying me as Joseph Wagner, a writer from Hammelburg born in 1919. Of course it said nothing of my race. If they had caught me and decided I looked Jewish and in any case wasn't in the military like every other young true Aryan, that would have been a death warrant.

"By February [of 1945] we were in Forbach, a coal-mining area, and advancing on Saarbrücken, along the Saar River in southwest Germany, when we got in a fierce standoff with a fanatical German general who didn't realize the war was lost. I slipped into Saarbrücken and found out where the military installations were. The next day, all hell broke loose: Our planes bombed their strongholds for what seemed like hours." Still, the Nazis held on until the middle of March.

When the Americans finally occupied the city, Mitchell and Samuels poked around the basement of a camera shop. An unopened crate yielded dozens of fine German cameras. They each kept one and gave the rest to the supply officer.

After the fall of the Saar area and the capture of the famous bridge across the Rhine at Remagen, the Allies advanced rapidly. Thousands of German troops were surrendering to the Americans, a fate far preferable to falling into the hands of the vengeful Russians closing in on Berlin from the east.

Samuels found himself near Hammelburg, his home town, which was now in American hands. Weeks earlier, General Patton had ordered a disastrous raid on a POW camp just outside Hammelburg. His son-in-law was a prisoner there.

The rescue mission met with heavy German resistance, fell into an ambush and ended up as a debacle. Samuels views Patton as a bold and talented commander, "except if you were a GI he didn't particularly worry about your life. His rescue mission got its butt kicked." (Patton's nickname was "Old Blood and Guts," which some GI's derided as "Our blood, his guts!" Some of them even "had parties" after he was fatally injured in an auto accident a few months after the war was over, according to Samuels.)

Samuels requisitioned a Jeep and headed for Hammelburg. He encountered the mayor, who expressed thanks that the Allies hadn't reduced his town to rubble. "Then I walked up the road and saw a guy, still in Nazi uniform, coming down on a motorcycle. He was a messenger. As he got closer, I saw that he resembled my boyhood friend Markus Hofstetter, who had lost his leg after the sledding accident. I said, *"Markus, bist du es?"* [Markus, is that you?] He came to a stop, looked at me and said, *"Kurt! Du bist hier!"* [Kurt! You are here!] He threw his motorcycle down and we hugged and kissed and cried. You weren't supposed to fraternize but how could we stop such emotions? The word got around Hammelburg like lightning—'Willi Samuel's son is here!' The next person in my arms was Herr Fuchs, my dad's old friend. Then I saw my favorite teacher, Herr Seufert, who was never a Nazi."

Samuels soon returned with several other GI's. He took them sightseeing and to the beer hall. To call what happened next sobering would be the understatement of the 20th century.

PFC. SAMUELS had heard what the 45th and 42nd Infantry Divisions saw when they first arrived at Dachau. Yet when he pulled into the courtyard on May Day, 1945, he was still unprepared. Chalk-white, skin-and-bones former human beings were stacked like cordwood and protruding from the ovens. Samuels turned a corner and saw a silo filled with ashes. The stench of death was inescapable. Some American soldiers had been so incensed by what they saw that they mowed down a row of SS guards before their colonel rushed over, fired his pistol in the air and told them there'd be none of that. Elsewhere in the camp, two emaciated inmates had summoned the strength to arm themselves with shovels. No one tried to stop them as they beat to death one of their cowering former guards— a member of the pitiless SS Totenkopfverband who administered the concentration camps, strutting about with the death's-head em-

What struck Samuels as singularly chilling was the sign above the wrought-iron gate to the inner camp at Dachau: *Arbeit Macht Frei*. "Work Makes [You] Free."

blem on their caps. This guard was one of the most hated. He had castrated a prisoner.

What struck Samuels as singularly chilling was the sign above the wrought-iron gate to the inner camp: *Arbeit Macht Frei*. "Work Makes [You] Free" was the biggest Big Lie in the checkered history of humankind—a cruel, perverted mockery of civilized speech. Most sent by the boxcar load to Dachau and its subcamps were worked to death; some became guinea pigs for unspeakable medical experiments; others, including women, children, the elderly and the already sick or infirm,

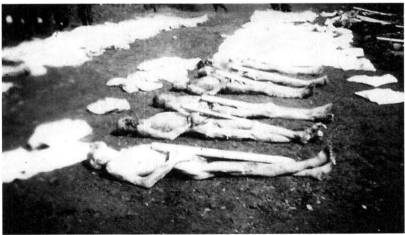

One of the horrifying photos Arnold took when he arrived at Dachau to help with the interrogations. *Arnold Samuels collection*

were shipped off to be exterminated at camps that specialized in wholesale murder. At least 32,000 died at Dachau.

"I was sick to my stomach," Samuels remembers. "I wept. I had not said the 'Shema Yisrael' prayer for a long time—the prayer I learned as a child. But I found myself praying: 'Hear, O Israel: The Lord is our God, the Lord is one. And you shall love the Lord, your God, with all your heart, with all your soul, and with all your might.' The survivors I spoke with were living skeletons—sick, diseased, too starved to really eat. Some were stunned that an American GI was speaking German. Most could hardly talk or fully comprehend they had been liberated. But some were able to help us separate the SS from the ordinary soldiers. We found some of the killers who were trying to pass as innocent civilians. They all had the same slogan: 'I followed orders. And if I didn't follow orders I would be in here (Dachau), too.' I took pictures. But I never showed my parents the pictures of what they might have looked like had they been in the camps like so many of our relatives. Never dared! Never dared to show them those pictures! They're too horrible. ... But no matter how many pictures you see, you can't imagine what war is really like until a friend shot dead right beside you crumples to the ground."

Henry Kissinger, meanwhile, was writing his parents that he had visited places they all once knew so well, including the apartment where they had lived when he was a boy—happy memories clouded now by the rubble of war and the years of "cruelty ... and nihilism" that had poisoned Germany since their escape to America. "Those who live by the sword shall perish by the sword," he wrote, adding that on a hill overlooking the ruins of Nuremberg "I said farewell to my youth."

Hitler killed himself in his Berlin bunker on April 30 as the Russians savaged the capital of his "Thousand-Year Reich." His goal had been to "murder every single person of Jewish ancestry on the European continent."

The Nazis estimated they needed to exterminate 11 million human beings to make the world safe from "the universal poisoner of all peoples, international Jewry." Six million Jews perished, together with almost two million Poles, three million Russian POWs and hundreds of thousands of others—Gypsies, Jehovah's

Arnold's ID card with the Counter Intelligence Corps. *Arnold Samuels collection*

Witnesses, homosexuals, infants with birth defects, the mentally ill and otherwise infirm. These were the *Untermenschen*—"subhumans," inferior people deemed unworthy of life.

Ironically, Hitler's delusional, hate-filled last will and testament was discovered by another German-born U.S. soldier, a Jewish GI named Arnold Weiss. Like Kissinger and Samuels, Weiss had been selected for the Army's Counter Intelligence Corps, the CIC, as the war wound down. The job now was to identify war criminals and create a de-Nazified postwar government to restore infrastructure. At Nuremberg, where top Nazi leaders would face trial before an international tribunal, most of the 900-year-old city had been bombed beyond recognition. The U.S. Office of Military Government—OMGUS—fired more than 2,000 complicit municipal officials and workers. It installed new managers and hired and trained a new civilian police force. By the fall of 1945, 25,000 children were back in school with new teachers.

PROMOTED TO SERGEANT, Samuels was sent first to the Military Police school in Heidelberg, the storied university town that had been a regional stronghold of the Nazi party. The city had escaped allied bombing because it was not an industrial center.

It became a postwar hub of U.S. Army operations.

After several intense weeks of law enforcement training and undercover work ferreting out important Nazis and collaborators, Samuels was sworn in as a special agent of the Counter Intelligence Corps. He became an operative with the Army of Occupation, assigned to Bensheim, a picturesque, tree-lined town of some 17,000 between Darmstadt and Heidelberg. Though some of its oldest structures had been destroyed by incendiary bombs, much of its medieval architecture had survived. The Allies established a displaced persons camp there. Hardcore Nazis desperate to escape detection tried to blend in with the floodtide of refugees. Some tried to bluff their way into new jobs by denying any involvement with slave-labor factories or the death camps.

The CIC's detachment in the region, which included 20 towns, was headed by Kissinger, who had just turned 22. Three months earlier, when the 84th Infantry Division captured Krefeld, a major port along the Rhine, no one in its Counter Intelligence detachment spoke German. Private Kissinger did. Kissinger helped restore essential public services for a city of 110,000 reduced to rubble by air raids. The CIC soon snapped him up. "Suddenly the Army needed men who could quickly and accurately carry out background checks on potential German collaborators to weed out the committed Nazis," Kissinger biographer Niall Ferguson notes. Kissinger and Arnold Samuels were ideally suited to the task.

"Mr. Henry" proved to be a particularly crafty interrogator. "He would tell each suspected Nazi, 'We know you're not important, you're just a small fry,' until the suspect's pride would cause him to erupt that he was in fact a high-ranking local Nazi."

"Kissinger commanded respect," Samuels remembers. "You could tell he was going to be someone important—a teacher like his father, or a diplomat. In the CIC we had a lot of power, and the frightened local Nazis did everything they could to downplay their importance. Henry's interrogation techniques impressed me. I never heard him use a foul word or threaten any of the people we interrogated. He got more information from suspected Gestapo men and other significant Nazis and collaborators than the CIC agents who used shouting and pro-

Arnold snapped this photo of Sgt. Henry Kissinger at his desk in their office at Bensheim. The Counter Intelligence Corps detachment in the region, which included 20 towns, was headed by Kissinger, who had just turned 22.
Arnold Samuels collection

fanity. I emulated him. When I interrogated suspects—and some of them were vicious bastards—I did my best to be nice. What do they say? 'You catch more flies with honey than with vinegar'? Same way in the Counter Intelligence Corps. Though we were both Jews, we were careful not to make it seem as if we were extracting revenge. We were both sergeants by then, but Henry was in charge of the whole detachment. To all appearances, we really had no ranks. I never wore a uniform because the Germans are very rank-conscious. If you would show that you're only a sergeant, they'd never talk with you.

"We belonged to the Officers' Club and had ready access to military vehicles. Kissinger had a nice villa and gave parties. We had ration cards for whiskey and champagne. He had confiscated a white Mercedes from a local industrialist who was in bed with the Nazis. Henry had all that power, but he wasn't arrogant about it. After all the horrible things we'd seen, the luxuries and power were nice, but we never forgot our job: We were there to identify the war criminals and screen applicants for jobs in the postwar government. We got our region back on its feet and identified several Nazis who were prosecuted at Nuremberg and Dachau. When Henry left to become a teacher at the military's European Theater Intelligence School at Oberammergau in 1946, I was placed in charge of the Bensheim area. And he gave me his Mercedes."

Arnold resisted a wink. His smile said it all. He might have been thinking about the jaunty cabriolet his father gave up when they fled Hammelburg.

Samuels "lost no time" in impressing on the local burgermeister "that he was not weaker" than Kissinger, Ferguson notes. "The mayor should not make the mistake of thinking that 'another policy would be pursued because Mr. Henry was no longer in charge.' "

ON HIS FURLOUGH IN BROOKLYN, Arnold and Phyllis were married on June 30, 1946, by Arnold's uncle, Cantor Henry Heller. Arnold had been told his bride could join him in Germany. When he returned to Bensheim, however, he learned there would be at least a six-month wait for housing. It was clear, too, that he lacked the leverage Kissinger had enjoyed. With the war won, by-the-book bureaucracy was coming down from higher-ups who had never seen combat. In his absence, another agent had taken the Mercedes for a high-speed spin on the Autobahn, crashed it and died. It seemed like an omen.

Samuels transferred to another region and went undercover to foil an escape scheme at a camp where Nazis awaiting trial were being held. "That November I was told that due to the postwar housing shortage, policies had been changed. It was unlikely my bride would be able to join me anytime soon. I told my captain—a helluva nice fellow—that it was time for me to go home." Samuels was discharged from the Counter Intelligence Corps on March 1, 1947. "I was offered a job with what became the CIA, but I just wanted out. I'd had enough cloak-and-dagger stuff to last a lifetime."

Phyllis and Arnold on their wedding day in 1946. *Arnold Samuels collection*

The young couple moved in with Phyllis's family. Arnold decided to go into partnership with a boyhood friend and start a radio repair business in the basement of an apartment house. After a year, however, his friend decided to take advantage of the GI Bill and go back to college. "I should have, too," Arnold says. "That was the biggest mistake I ever made."

Arnold found a new business partner. They borrowed money for inventory to start selling radios and TVs and moved into a small storefront. The rent was $50 a month. "Television sets were just coming on the market—tiny things with seven-inch tubes. We used to leave one on in the front window, turning it around so the screen faced the street. When Milton Berle's variety show came on the air in 1948 the whole neighborhood brought their chairs and sat on the sidewalk watching 'Uncle Miltie.' But as TVs grew more affordable, I was barely making a living. The big outfits like Sears and Roebuck and Macy's opened outlets in Brooklyn and I couldn't compete with them."

When Arnold and Phyllis's first son arrived in 1950, Arnold was working two jobs and attending weekend classes at New York University for a teaching certificate in electronics. "It was a rat race. One day in 1952 I saw an ad from the Voice of America seeking technicians. Since I had a first-class commercial radio operator's license, they gave me a top rating and offered me a job overseas. Phyllis was all for it. We didn't have much to lose. And it sounded like an adventure." It was. Nearly 30 years' worth.

Arnold, Phyllis and their growing family—there would be three sons in all—spent the next five years in the Philippines. Samuels helped maintain the huge transmitters that beamed Voice of America programs to Southeast Asia and behind the Iron Curtain. The U.S. was intent on counteracting communist propaganda as the Cold War heated up. Voice of America's programming featured news shows, dramas and American jazz, which was hugely popular in the Soviet bloc. "We were America's propaganda machine. The communists tried everything to jam our signals." Arnold soon was named security officer for the region. Life was good. The fishing was great, the beaches lovely. Arnold joined the Lions Club, became a Mason and, in

Arnold with two boyhood friends, Alfred Stuhler, center, and Markus Hofstetter, right, at a reunion in Germany during the 1980s. *Arnold Samuels collection*

his spare time, one of the most active amateur radio operators in the Pacific as "KH6COY." In 1957, he accepted a transfer to the relay station at Honolulu. Five years later he was hired by a defense contractor to manage the U.S. Army Strategic Communications Command's strategic station on Wake Island, a beautiful coral atoll in the mid-Pacific. "Free housing, free car, no crime and a lagoon where the kids loved to swim." Mother Nature was the wild card. When a typhoon devastated Wake a year later, the Samuels were back in Hawaii. Arnold had landed a job as quality control officer with the U.S. Air Force. He did another stint in the Philippines before retiring in 1980 with a government pay-grade equivalent to lieutenant colonel.

Before they left Wake, the Samuels met an airline pilot working part-time for the real estate company that was developing a resort community along the north beach of Grays Harbor in Washington State. "We looked at his brochures, and the wife said to me, 'You know, honey, we've been around the moon now for the last 30 years and it's about time we bought a little bit of terra firma.' " Sight unseen, they invested $1,800 in an undeveloped lot. On a trip back to the states a decade later, they visited Ocean Shores for the first time and liked what they saw. Before the day was out, they had consummated a deal to sell their lot and buy two more so they'd have more room for their retirement home along a canal a mile and a half from the ocean. On Wake Island, they'd been flooded twice in the middle of the night. "I don't want to be that close to the ocean ever again," Phyllis decreed. They built a comfortable rambler, joined everything and made hundreds of friends over the next 20 happy years.

In 2000, Arnold lost his best friend of 54 years. Cancer claimed the vivacious Phyllis. He sublimated his grief by becoming even more active. He was elected to the Ocean Shores City Council as a write-in candidate and served four years. Almost 93 at this writing, he still seems to be everywhere at once. He's the honorary photographer for the weekly *North Coast News* and helped establish an all-volunteer FM radio station. He buys cookies from the Relay for Life ladies at the bank—they're some of his favorite "mermaids"—and makes the rounds of the Eagles, Elks and VFW. He's a stalwart among the aging congregation at Temple Beth Israel, 25 miles inland at Aberdeen. During the holidays, he's a Salvation Army bell-ringer. "Being active is what keeps you alive," Arnold says. "And I drink two glasses of wine a day." He wrote 235 personalized Christmas and Hanukkah letters in 2014, faithfully maintains a diary and is constantly tidying his scrapbooks and photo albums. His kids and grandkids live a long way away. "Maybe someday when I'm gone, they'll go through all of this stuff and just throw it away. I hope not, because there's history here and important lessons."

In 1995, when Arnold visited his old hometown, Hammelburg honored his grandfather by erecting a handsome sign in front of a park where the family's grain warehouse once stood. It is now *Samuel Sichel Platz. Arnold Samuels collection*

In 1995, when Arnold visited his old hometown, Hammelburg honored his grandfather by erecting a handsome stonework sign in front of a park where the family's grain warehouse once stood. It is now Samuel Sichel Platz. He sends the Jewish congregation in Würzburg $50 a year to take care of his grandfather's grave, which was once desecrated by the Nazis.

Samuels is proud of America's role in rebuilding post-war Germany. "We didn't repeat the mistakes we made at the end of World War I." But he believes the war-crimes trials were a waste of time and money. Thirty-six Dachau officials, including the camp's commandant and a sadistic doctor, went to the gallows, together with some of Hitler's top generals, the Reich's slave labor czar and the nauseatingly anti-Semitic editor of the Nazi house organ. Samuels, like Winston Churchill, had favored summary executions. "We knew these bastards were guilty but we made a political deal out of it, a big spiel, to show the world that we are a democracy ruled by law. They should have been shot the next day!"

Arnold and a fellow member of the VFW sell Buddy Poppies at Ocean Shores. *Arnold Samuels collection*

Told that a Pew Research Center study in 2014 found a sharp increase in anti-Semitism, particularly in Europe, Samuels was unsurprised. "I wonder whether the world learned anything from Hitler and the Holocaust? Look at all the wars still going on—people killing one another over religion, which is supposed to bring people together and foster good will, not hate. My dad used to say, 'Religion is the root of all evil.' If the whole world would live by the 10 Commandments and The Golden Rule we'd have peace. Everything else is hocus pocus. The only way I can fight hate and pessimism is to be optimistic and try to do my part. But I worry, especially about the politicians."

When Arnold Samuels opens his front door on springtime mornings, five of his doe-eyed deer friends are usually waiting on the lawn for the apple slices he serves up. His other faithful companion was a petulant Siamese cat named "Shadow," who was 18 and looked it. He lost his pal last year and is searching for a replacement.

There's a sign just inside the front porch. It says "Shalom."

Sciatica is slowing him down. He knows he's heading down the stretch. "No regrets. I've had a good life. I don't feel that I've done anybody any harm. I helped a lot of people. I donated a lot of money to a lot of causes. I feel I've done my thing for God, country and Ocean Shores!"

He laughs and says we need a nice glass of wine at the Elks Club.

John C. Hughes

Arnold sleeps with this mermaid.
John Hughes

I AM WAR

Arnold Samuels believes this editorial is one of the most poignant—and prescient—he has ever read. It was written in 1939 by Edwin Van Syckle, a young editorial writer for The Aberdeen Daily World in Washington State. "I Am War" was reprinted nationwide and nominated for a Pulitzer Prize. The newspaper reprints it annually on Memorial Day.

Yes, you know me; but there are grass and flowers covering the scarred fields where we met before. You daintily balance your tea cups, and relish your wine, and you talk small talk with your neighbors over back yard fences. You have replanted your groves, and the grain waves in the gentle winds. You work and play and dance, and trifling things amuse you. So you are prone to forget me. But you should not.

For I am War. Remember? I have called on you before. I have taken from your huts and your castles, your great buildings that gleam so magnificently in the sun. You came to me from your hills and your plains, and the secluded valleys where you felt so safe and secure. I demanded it. I took you from your firesides, the peace of your quiet lanes, the mills and factories, from the oceans and all the lands that you call home. And some I did not let return. Thousands, millions, did not return.

For I am War. I kill. I ravage and despoil. I am the waster of flesh and brains ... and youth. For if I do not take you I will take your son. And I will leave only a stench on the battlefield. I do not care if he is brave or cowardly. I will sprawl his body by some tiny pool made by the rains. And the curly head you fondled and the smile that lifted your heart will be smeared with blood.

Yes, it will be ghastly.

I will torture you with anguish and fear. I will rend your body until you wish death to ease the pain. I will tear the white throats of your children. On the pavements they will lie and gaze into the heavens with staring but not understanding eyes. I will leave your cities in shambles, and your peoples will strew the streets in death.

Your homes will be ruins, or gaping craters where they once stood. You will search in vain for those who lived there, for one small trace; and you will hope to God it cannot be found. A whole generation of you will die. Or it will come back in torment, and scarred and broken, with faces hardened by agony and bitterness. And the memories torturous, the hatreds, the broken faiths, the spending of your substance, the losses that even God cannot replace ... they will scourge you for generations and generations to come.

Yes, you will remember me. For I am War.

A DAY IN THE LIFE OF AN INFANTRYMAN

Bill Mauldin, the legendary cartoonist for Stars and Stripes newspaper during World War II, won a Pulitzer Prize for his work depicting the life of two fictional GI's—"Willie and Joe." Mauldin was an accomplished writer as well. This piece gives us an idea of what an infantryman in Europe faced daily in 1944:

Dig a hole in your backyard while it is raining. Sit in the hole while the water climbs up around your ankles. Pour cold mud down your shirt collar. Sit there for 48 hours, and, so there is no danger of your dozing off, imagine that a guy is sneaking around waiting for a chance to club you on the head or set your house on fire. Get out of the hole, fill a suitcase full of rocks, pick it up, put a shotgun in your other hand and walk on the muddiest road you can find. Fall flat on your face every few minutes as you imagine big meteors streaking down to sock you. ...If you repeat this performance every three days for several months, you may begin to understand why an infantryman sometimes gets out of breath. But you still won't understand how he feels when things get tough.

HENRY FRIEDMAN

IN FOCUS
JEWISH BOY IN HIDING

> " All I did was pray and sleep ... pray to a God who at that time I was afraid had abandoned the Jewish people and closed His eyes and ears to their suffering. But I had no choice but to pray, because that was the only way to communicate, and it gave me some hope. "
>
> – Henry Friedman, Holocaust Survivor

Henry Friedman and Julia Symchuck reunite in America in 1989. The Ukrainian woman warned Henry's father in 1942 that he was wanted by the Gestapo. That October, Julia's parents took Henry's family into hiding. *Henry Friedman collection*

Henry's father hid near his family, in the barn of Maria Bazalchik, for nearly two years. Henry stayed with him temporarily in what he described as the worst months of his life. *Henry Friedman collection*

Wracked by hunger, 14-year-old Henry Friedman evaded the Nazis in a barn loft as small as a queensize bed. His diet of scraps—soup, bread, an occasional piece of meat—was eventually reduced to a single slice of bread. For 18 months, the Jewish boy found solace in prayer.

Christian farmers gambled with their lives to hide Henry, his mother, his brother and a teacher. By liberation in 1944, only 88 of 10,000 Jews from his hometown of Brody, Poland, had survived.

Friedman became a well-known Washingtonian for his role in establishing the Holocaust Center for Humanity in Seattle, and for bravely sharing his unthinkable experience with students. "I want them to know life is precious," he said.

ROBERT GRAHAM

Country Boy in the South Pacific

*" 'Greatest Generation' is kind of flattery in a way.
But I feel we really did something.
Individually and collectively. We stepped up."*

–Tech. Sgt. Robert graham, U.S. Army Air Forces

In the summer of 1937, Bob Graham and his pals were heading home from a swim in the Humptulips River near Copalis Crossing, a wide spot in a two-lane road meandering through the forested hills of Grays Harbor County. When someone offered them a ride, it changed the direction of Graham's life.

He was 16 then. He was 93 when we sat down to talk in 2014. At his home in Olympia, Washington's former seven-term state auditor flipped through school annuals, tattered clippings and the sepia-toned pages of a booklet about his Air Transport Command squadron during World War II. Lloydine Ryan Graham, the Hoquiam girl whose letters were his lifeline to home, sat nearby.

Robert Graham collection

They'd been married for 69 years. Bob's legs were tentative but his memory was remarkable. He still had a head for numbers. One in particular. "If you were in the war, you'll never forget your serial number. Mine is 39185223." Just for drill, he said it again, ending with a satisfied smile.

Technical Sergeant Robert Vincent Graham was a flight engineer on cargo planes that shuttled everything from C-rations to atomic bomb parts ever deeper into the Pacific Theater. Every island and atoll extracted an awful price. On flights back to home base in California, their C-54's were jammed with sick, maimed and otherwise wounded men. Some cried out for loved ones and more morphine. "There were always a number of nurses on board," Graham recalled. "They were great, but they had their hands full. There'd be two rows of litter cases in the middle; then there was an aisle on each side, and another row of litter cases, five high, the length of the airplane. Our motto was 'We always deliver the goods.' To me, that particularly precious cargo came with a real feeling of accomplishment and an appreciation for the overall struggle we were in. I felt lucky to be alive."

Luckier yet was his big brother, Ralph Graham—"Moonie" to family and friends. For a while they feared he'd been killed in the Battle of the Bulge in Belgium, the Nazis' last-ditch attempt to halt the advancing Allies. The week before Christmas, 1944, found Moonie and a buddy holed up in

Graham points out an island on a World War II map of the South Pacific. The interviewer is John C. Hughes, a Legacy Washington historian. *Laura Mott*

a cellar after their squad was surrounded by German tanks. Twenty-five other GI's were rousted out in a house-by-house search and summarily executed. Moonie and his pal were spared for reasons unknown. They spent the rest of the war in POW camps, each progressively worse as the Third Reich was reduced to rubble. Malnutrition was rife. Some of the captive Americans died in allied bombing raids. The survivors were detailed to bury the dead—foe and friend alike, soldier and civilian. "We didn't learn any of that until after the war ended in Europe," Bob remembered. "We just prayed. My mother was a prayer warrior. Her primary prayer was for our family, that the chain would not be broken—our family chain. That was always the way she put it, that 'the chain would not be broken.' Her sons made it home. The chain was not broken."

Throughout the war, Graham's thoughts often turned to the fate of his best friend at Grays Harbor Junior College, "a wonderful guy named Perry Saito" who happened to be Japanese, a pacifist and as American as a sock hop.

A man of deep faith, Graham saw God's hand, and startling coincidences, everywhere in his eventful life. For instance, when he decided to transfer from Hoquiam to tiny Moclips High School he never imagined he would be elected student body president. He also caught the eye of the school superintendent, who saw bigger things for the strapping kid with wavy hair and the radiant smile of a natural born politician.

Some of Bob's classmates had dropped out of school to work alongside their dads, brothers and uncles in the logging camps and mills that dotted the area. They came home every night with banged up hands and sawdust in their ears. You could tell a "shake rat" by his missing fingers. Bob respected them for their plain talk and resilience.

There were loggers in Graham's family tree. Its roots run deep in Scotland. The Grahams and Bob's maternal grandfather's people, the Smiths, were dairymen, farmers— "crofters"—and tree cutters in the Highlands and islands county called Ross and Cromarty. Like his fellow proud Scot, former longtime secretary of state Ralph Munro, Graham had made a sentimental journey to the land of his ancestors.

Growing up, the forest was Graham's neighborhood.

The teacher and students at the tiny Newton School in rural Grays Harbor in the 1920s. This group appears to be slightly ahead of Bob Graham's days there. His passing prevented us from getting identifications. His brother Ralph may be in this group. *Polson Museum collection*

When he was a young state worker, he spent his days off at the headwaters of the Copalis River, cutting the clear-grain cedar that was milled into siding for their new rambler. It's a very good house, with a flag out in front. He and Lloydine raised four sons and a daughter there. The grandchildren and great-grandchildren visit often.

GRAHAM'S PATERNAL GRANDPARENTS came from Scotland to Ontario in 1877 and moved across the river to Sault Sainte Marie, Michigan, two years later. They took up farming at a hamlet called Dafter. Bob's father, Ralph V. Graham, got itchy feet when he turned 17. He hopped a train and landed at Sumner near Puyallup in Pierce County. Before long he was in love with a pretty schoolgirl named Hazel Smith, whose father divided his energies between building lumber mills and running dairies. In the 1920s at Moclips, overlooking the gray Pacific north of Grays Harbor, L.T. Smith built what was reputedly the largest shingle mill in the world. A few miles southwest, in the green fields along the Humptulips, Smith also launched the Riverside Dairy. His son-in-law became his partner. The Northern Pacific Railway, collecting lumber and shakes along its route from Hoquiam to the beach, ran right through the Grahams' back yard.

Two of Graham's classmates at the Newton School enjoy a homemade car. *Polson Museum collection*

Bob, his siblings and a dozen other kids attended the tiny Newton School just below Copalis Crossing. Every weekend the schoolhouse doubled as Sunday School. In first grade, despite being its youngest member, Bob got himself elected president of the choir. When seventh grade rolled around, he rode the school bus in to Hoquiam. It was during the summer after his sophomore year at Hoquiam High that he and four other "big lugs" were heading home after a swim.

A car pulled alongside.

"Like a ride?" said the driver. He was a big man with a friendly face.

"We just live up the road a little ways."

"Well, that doesn't matter. Hop in."

A mile later, when it was time to hop out, the driver said, "Just a minute. Do you boys play football in Hoquiam?"

Nope, said Graham. "If we're not on that bus at 2:30, it's 18 miles back out here and we're out of luck."

"I'll tell you what: My name is Doug Dreeszen. I'm the football coach at Moclips. I'm also the bus driver and we never leave until after practice."

Graham and his buddy, Bill Campbell, transferred from Hoquiam High School to Moclips High School and became starters for Dreezen's Moclips Hyaks. In their senior year, they drubbed the Aberdeen and Hoquiam B-squads. At 6-feet and

190 pounds, Graham was still burning through his baby fat. Dreeszen dubbed him "Chub." Graham's good friend, Gene "Cubby" Jackson, son of the chief of the Quinault Nation, was their team captain and quarterback.

There had been 156 kids in Graham's sophomore class at Hoquiam. At Moclips, he was one of only 23 in the Class of 1939. "Suddenly being a big fish in a small pond" gave him enormous confidence. He was elected student body president his senior year, lettered in football, joined the band and glee club and appeared in three plays. Jackson took him up the Quinault River and showed him how the Indians reeled in nets squirming with salmon. In his spare time, Bob had become the Grays Harbor County 4-H Club swine-raising champion, winning a week's stay at Washington State College in Pullman. "And that was really something!" Still, his horizon hadn't stretched much farther than Hoquiam where a cute girl named Lloydine Ryan was a junior.

On graduation night, the school superintendent, Eli T. Moawad, cornered him:

"What are you going to do now that you've graduated, Chub?"

Graham, right, and the other student body officers at Moclips High School in 1938-39 proudly wore their letter sweaters for the yearbook photo. *Moclips High School Neptune, 1939*

"Well, I'll probably go to work in the shake mill with the family."

"*I don't think so,*" Moawad said, italicizing every word. "Tomorrow morning at 9 o'clock I'd like to have you put on your best bib and tucker, wash behind your ears, and we're going to Aberdeen."

"What are we going to do there?"

"I'll show you when we get there."

High on a hillside stood the four-story Terrace Heights School. Built in 1892 to house the first Aberdeen High School, it was an unpainted, abandoned grade school when in 1930 it became the first home of Grays Harbor Junior College. With unemployment rapidly rising in the wake of the stock market crash—it would top 30 percent on the Harbor by 1932—leading citizens chipped in $100 apiece to incorporate a two-year college. Otherwise, they feared, hundreds of Harbor-area young people would never have a chance at higher education."

Grays Harbor Junior College in 1940. *GHC Nautilus*

Laborers from the New Deal's Works Progress Administration completed some rudimentary renovation of the drafty old school. Grays Harbor Junior College opened its doors to 122 students in the fall of 1930. Its first dean was a resourceful educator named Lewis C. Tidball. In Wyoming, Tidball had been a teacher, principal, school superintendent and state commissioner of education before receiving a Ph.D. in political science from the University of Washington. His career in higher education started out on the lowest rung at the outset of the Great Depression. "Eco-

Dean Lewis Tidball, who gave Graham a scholarship to Grays Harbor Junior College. *GHC Nautilus*

nomic conditions bordered on the catastrophic," Tidball recalled.

At the college's 50th anniversary in 1980, it was written that "probably no institution—public, private or industrial—in Harbor history has had as much impact upon as many people as Grays Harbor College. ..." What was true then is even more so today, Bob Graham said. He believed the community college system had transformed the quality of life in Washington State by keeping academic and vocational training affordable.

Without Dean Tidball, however, Grays Harbor Junior College likely would have died aborning. In addition to teaching psychology, philosophy and political science, Tidball recruited talented young instructors who stayed the course even though they were often paid in vegetables, fish, clams and game "brought in by students in lieu of tuition." He raised scholarship money, schmoozed legislators and bummed firewood to feed a cranky old boiler. Somewhere on the sprawling modern campus that now overlooks Grays Harbor, Graham said, there ought to be a statue of Lewis C. Tidball, perhaps smoking his professorial briar pipe.

It was Lewis C. Tidball whom Eli T. Moawad took Bob Graham to see on May 17, 1939.

"I'm going to apply for a scholarship for you," Moawad revealed as they arrived at the school on the hill. On graduation day he and the other superintendents for miles around had received letters from Dean Tidball, announcing the availability of one $150, full-tuition scholarship.

Tidball welcomed them, settled back in his chair and listened intently as Moawad launched into his pitch about why it should go to Graham. "Eli, he was a car salesman! He really did a sales job," Graham said, smiling at the memory.

When Moawad stopped to catch his breath, Tidball said Bob seemed to be an exemplary boy, but if he got the scholarship it wouldn't be fair to the other superintendents who had yet to respond with applicants of their own. "I wrote to all of them," he said.

Moawad said he doubted any of them could come up with as fine a candidate as Graham. He was an honor roll student, student body president and tenacious athlete. He got up early to milk the cows and slop the pigs. He sang in the church choir. This boy, Moawad declared, could become someone special.

Graham sat up straighter. He felt like Huck Finn and Tom Sawyer eavesdropping from the church balcony at their own funeral.

Tidball sighed. "I'm going to give him the scholarship!" But there was a catch: he had to stoke the furnace at the crack of dawn. No problem, Graham said. He'd rent a room in Aberdeen so he could keep his end of the bargain. "Oh no. You're coming to live with us," said Tidball. After two months with the Tidballs, Graham protested that he was imposing. The dean hired a carpenter to enclose a space under the third-floor stairwell. It was

Graham, left, as student body president at Grays Harbor Junior College in 1941.
GHC Nautilus

big enough for a small bed, a wash bowl and a makeshift desk.

Graham plunged into everything. He was business manager of the school's *Nautilus* yearbook and a member of the college's debate team, which posted victories against the College of Puget Sound and other four-year schools. He was rushed by the Midshipmen, the school's self-proclaimed "live-wire" fraternity. With a flower in his lapel, Graham sported a striped tie and two-tone shoes as he posed with his frat brothers on the bow of a boat at Westport.

In the fall of 1940, Graham was resoundingly elected president of the associated students of Grays Harbor Junior College. Soon he was in the thick of a landmark battle to shore up the state's community colleges. State Rep. John Pearsall, a Grays Harbor Junior College alumnus elected to the Legislature in 1938 at the age of 25, had taken up the challenge of securing state aid for the two-year schools. Governor Clarence D. Martin, a frugal Democrat from Cheney, vetoed a $100,000 appropriation in 1937. Martin feared the mandate was unsustainable, a recession having stalled recovery from the Depression. Two years later, with an improving economy and the governor's support, Pearsall jawboned similar legislation through the House, only to see it die in conference committee. For the 1941 session, Pearsall and Dean Tidball mobilized junior college boosters from around the state and assembled the seven student body presidents for a strategy session. They chose Graham as their spokesman. The group made several trips to the capitol to lobby legislative committees. Graham, shrewdly, had also secured signed statements of support from both 1940 gubernatorial candidates, Seattle Mayor Arthur B. Langlie and former U.S. senator Clarence

State Rep. John Pearsall, D-Aberdeen, was the youngest member of the Legislature in 1939 when he first proposed state aid for the junior colleges. *GHC Nautilus*

Junior College Bill Becomes Law

Scene at Olympia as Governor Langlie signed Saturday the junior college aid bill, which is expected to double enrollment and expand educational services at Grays Harbor and other junior colleges in the state. Watching the ceremony are three legislators, Senators Harry Wall of Chelan and Shirley R. Marsh of Cowlitz, who introduced the measure in the senate, and Representative John Pearsall of Grays Harbor, who sponsored the measure in the house. *(Courtesy Longview Daily News)*

Gov. Arthur Langlie signs the junior college aid bill in 1941. Looking on at right is Rep. Pearsall. It was Graham who pinned down the candidates for governor. *Longview Daily News photo*

C. Dill. Pearsall's bill cleared both houses and was duly signed by Langlie, a good-government Republican who had won by a whisker in a Democratic year. The junior colleges were granted a total of $200,000 from the general fund, the equivalent of $6.1 million in 2015 dollars. The heady experience with lawmaking strengthened Graham's goal to study law or accounting and pursue a career in government.

Pearsall, an Irish Catholic wunderkind in his day, went on to become a longtime Grays Harbor County commissioner. He was a cross between Lyndon B. Johnson and Tip O'Neill, who famously posited that "all politics is local." Pearsall's statue should be next to Tidball's, Graham said. "The legislation John sponsored was a watershed. It led to our modern community college educational system in Washington State, which has improved hundreds of thousands of lives, including mine." Graham's yearbook staff voted to dedicate the 1941 annual to Pearsall, saying "what we owe to him can never be fully repaid."

The winter of 1941 otherwise was fraught with anxiety. President Roosevelt, struggling with the isolationists, hatched a plan to "lend" embattled Great Britain 50 old destroyers and vowed to make America "the arsenal of democracy." Imperial Japan, pursuing its own ruthless version of Manifest Destiny, had signed a Tripartite Pact with Hitler and Mussolini.

There were only a couple of a Japanese families on Grays Harbor, a province of working-class Scandinavians and Croatians." Yet many of the pages in the 1941 edition of the *Nautilus* yearbook feature Bob Graham's best friend at Grays Harbor Junior College. Perry Saito was a tall, handsome, impeccably dressed youth with jet-black, Brylcreemed hair. By year's end, Graham, Saito, their families and hundreds of friends on the Harbor would be caught up in a war that would claim 65 million lives.

Perry Saito's father was a Japanese immigrant who supplied ships calling on the Port of Grays Harbor. The Saitos also owned the Oriental Art Store, an import shop, in downtown Aberdeen. Like many *Nisei*—the second-generation, American-born children of Japanese immigrants—Lincoln, Perry, Morse and Dahlia Saito were steeped in patriotism. Ransaku Saito had named his sons after Commodore Perry, Abraham Lincoln and Samuel F.B. Morse, the pioneer telegrapher. The Saito children could recite the Declaration of Independence.

At Aberdeen High School and Grays Harbor Junior College, Perry Saito was a model student and active in Methodist youth groups. He was serious about his studies and his faith, yet the life of any

Perry Saito's sophomore portrait at Grays Harbor Junior College in 1940. *GHC Nautilus*

Perry Saito was a standout tennis player at the Junior College. *GHC Nautilus*

party. He played the clarinet, sang beautifully and was light on his feet. "All the girls loved to dance with him," Graham recalled. As if all that wasn't enough, Perry played tennis with flair and was a rangy right fielder. Graham savored the day he finally beat his friend at Ping Pong. Perry even learned Finnish from a friend's dad. ("What kind of town is Aberdeen that a Jap speaks Finnish?" a surprised listener declared when Perry was visiting a classmate studying at an Army language school in Minnesota during the war.) At the Junior College, Perry was sports editor of the yearbook, treasurer of the Men's Club and, together with Graham, a member of the debate team. He helped organize a "Jinx Dance" featuring black cats, broken mirrors and ladders. One gag photo in the yearbook shows Perry Saito and a classmate with their heads in stocks.

When the war hit home on Grays Harbor six months after their graduation, one of the strangest, bitterest ironies was, as Graham put it, "that a Jewish Army colonel who grew up in Aberdeen sent the Saitos to a concentration camp."

The tangled story of Karl Bendetsen, Perry Saito and the incarceration of Japanese Americans during World War II unfolds in *The Colonel and The Pacifist,* a book by Klancy Clark de Nevers of Salt Lake City. The award-winning author grew up on Grays Harbor.

When Imperial Japan attacked Pearl Harbor, 20-year-old Perry Saito, a fledgling pacifist, was a music major at Washington State College in Pullman. On December 9, 1941, his widowed mother, Natsu, was arrested by the FBI and accused of being a spy. Japanese seamen had frequented the store; she received mail from other Japanese in both America and Japan. Moreover, she owned a typewriter and rumors had circulated that the import shop was a front for subversive activities. The agents ransacked the shop and took Mrs. Saito to the Aberdeen City Jail for interrogation. "After a week she was taken to Seattle for detention. ... Her family still knew nothing of her whereabouts as Christmas approached." Syndicated columnist, Westbrook Pegler, appealing as usual to the worst instincts of his readers, declared, "... to hell with habeas corpus until the danger is over."

Karl Bendetsen, the son of a prosperous Aberdeen haberdasher, was 34 and just months away from becoming the youngest full colonel in the U.S. Army. The Stanford Law School graduate became the architect of the "military necessity" rationale behind Roosevelt's executive order mandating the evacuation and internment of 110,000 West Coast Americans of Japanese ancestry. Perry Saito, ironically, had been an after-school elevator operator in the Aberdeen office building where Bendetsen practiced law before going on active duty with the military. De Nevers writes:

> Like all the men of their generation, their lives were vastly changed by World War II but in very different ways. ...As head of the Aliens Division of the provost marshal general's office, [Bendetsen] was about to take charge of an operation that would totally disrupt the lives of the West Coast Japanese and Japanese Americans, including Saito. A year later, while Perry Saito struggled to free himself from the incarceration that Bendetsen had organized, Bendetsen received a Distinguished Service Medal for a job well done. The forced removal and incarceration of the West Coast Japanese and Japanese Americans had repercussions for both men throughout their lives.
>
> Perry Saito's story is that of a young Nisei whose country had turned against him.

Karl Bendetsen's story is that of an ambitious young man who hid and denied his Jewish roots (presumably to avoid discrimination) and used his education and talents to direct a program that trampled the rights and denied the humanity of another ethnic minority.

In 1980 and 1981, the Grahams followed with fascination the congressional inquiry into the Japanese internment and the debate over proposed reparations to surviving internees. Perry Saito was now the activist pastor of the largest Methodist congregation in Milwaukee, Wisconsin. He told of his family's incarceration on a desolate dry lakebed in a remote corner of California. Tule Lake was the most notorious of the internment camps. During the 1960s, Saito had been in the forefront of the Civil Rights and anti-war movements. He decried the "flagrant violations of human rights" during the internment. "If any American can be incarcerated without trial or even proper accusation," he told the congressmen, "then it becomes a mockery for us to declare ... 'All persons are created equal.' "

His old adversary, Karl Bendetsen, testified too. He had retired from a long and distinguished career that included a stint as undersecretary of the Army and chairman and CEO of Champion International, the forest products giant. Bendetsen testified that the proceedings were an exercise in politically correct hindsight. You had to be there then, he said, to fully understand the fallout from "the grim events of December 7, 1941, and the terrible months which followed." Bendetsen flatly refused to concede that the internment had been a mistake. And in practically the next breath denied what he had boasted of in his *Who's Who* entry—that he written the president's executive order and played a key role in its execution. Japanese Americans and their allies in Congress were intent on a "raid on the treasury," Bendetsen asserted, his disgust palpable.

Bob Graham was appalled by Bendetsen's duplicity. At the height of the war, when he was a young sergeant flying missions against a ruthless Imperial Japan, it was "horrifying" to him that his friend and 110,000 other Japanese and Japanese Americans were behind barbed wire back home. They weren't the enemy. "I thought, 'My God! This cannot be happening here in free America.'

"One of my laments is that over the years I never got to see Perry again," Graham said. "I deeply regret that. He died in 1985 after years of heart problems. He was only 64. That book is filled with the names of people we knew and lessons about what America should stand for. Everyone should read it."

Ronald Reagan signed into law the Civil Liberties Act of 1988, which authorized $1.25 billion in redress to the surviving Japanese-American internees.

GRAHAM MODESTLY EMPHASIZED that he never saw combat in the Pacific Theater. But he saw its wake on practically every trip: White crosses and Stars of David over fresh graves; stretcher after stretcher of hollow-eyed survivors being carried aboard C-54's. "No one was shooting at us on any of the missions I flew," Graham said. "In fact, I never fired a weapon during World War II." It was still risky business. The crews of the Air Transport Command flew hundreds of thousands of miles over undifferentiated ocean and bounced down roller-coaster runways that were often a crude approximation of tarmac. Landings, likewise, were "an ass-pucker every time," a top-turret gunner on a bomber crew recalled. After hopping 30,000 miles across the Pacific Theater to entertain the troops, Bob Hope said, "Everyone claims I'm a little more serious than I was. ... Those men, those soldiers, they're not just a bunch of crap-shooting, wolfing guys we like to joke about. These men are men, with the deepest emotions and the keenest feelings that men can have about everything life holds dear."

"A flight engineer had a lot to do," Graham remembered. "Most people didn't understand the responsibility we had, especially when we got to larger planes. The pilot was on the left, the co-pilot on the right. The flight engineer sat on a little jump-seat in the middle. I ran the throttles and 'gear up and gear down.' Fuel consumption was my total responsibility. If you had a major malfunction out there, it was a long swim home."

Graham's closest call came one day as they set down on Kwajalein in the Marshall Islands, some 2,000 miles southwest of Honolulu. The pilot came in too fast on a short runway. Bob yanked the equivalent of the emergency brakes "but we ripped the tires off the landing gear—blew out all the tires—and went right into the ocean. Not very far, but far enough" to be scared spitless. "Some of those islands were so small you could go over to look out at the ocean, stand there, then look back to see the waves coming ashore on the other side. They called them atolls—a coral reef that's not much of an island.

"The first leg of the shuttle would be from Travis Field in California to Hickam Field in Hawaii. When we got off the plane there, there'd be a crew standing by to fly the next leg, hauling cargo deeper into the Pacific. But on some missions, we'd refuel and keep going. We found out later that some of the stuff we were hauling out to Tinian and Saipan was part of the atomic bomb system. It was stockpiled there to assemble the bombs. ... There was hardly an island in the Pacific I wasn't on. After Hawaii, Eniwetok was one stop, then Kwajalein. Then Johnson Island. I had to haul rock in there so they could build that thing up to make an airstrip on it. ... We never stayed in one place very long. Sometimes we'd shuttle along one route to Wake; another time we'd go the other route to the Marshalls. ... By late '44 and '45 we were getting closer and closer to Japan."

GERMANY SURRENDERED in the spring of 1945. Now that the main islands were within range of U.S. heavy bombers, the Japanese were taking a pounding. Yet signs were that the fanatical militarists would defend the homeland until the last kamikaze crashed and old men and boys with sharpened bamboo sticks were mobilized to repel invaders on the beaches

Graham got a two-week furlough to come home. He arrived in Hoquiam just as the first atomic bomb was leveling Hiroshima. Still no surrender.

Bob and Lloydine had decided to wait until war's end to get married. However, after he'd been home for a couple of days, he held her tight and said, "It may be a long time before this darn war is over. Maybe we should get married."

"I think we should," she said.

"When?"

"Sunday."

The newlyweds depart the Hoquiam First Presbyterian Church on August 12, 1945. *Robert Graham collection*

That was three days away. "I found a dress I liked at a little shop in Aberdeen," Lloydine recalled. "When I hear about brides today taking months to arrange everything I think to myself, 'That's too much time!' Ours turned out fine."

There was a hitch. Bob's job was to secure the Presbyterian Church and its minister. Problem was, the pastor was on vacation. So Bob walked a few blocks to the Methodist Church and shared his dilemma with Pastor Howard P. Buck. If it was OK with the Presbyterians it was OK with him, Buck said.

It was OK with the Presbyterians. On August, 12, 1945, the Grahams were wed in a packed Presbyterian Church by a Methodist minister.

It would be hard to imagine a happier honeymoon. As they arrived in Seattle two days later in Bob's uncle's Chevrolet, Japan's unconditional surrender was being announced. "People were dancing in the streets, and all the girls were grabbing service men and giving them hugs and kisses," Lloydine said. Bob was wearing his uniform. She yanked his hand and said, "C'mon. We're going to a movie!" The Grahams joked ever since that their marriage caused the war to end.

When his leave was up, Bob still had to go back to his base in California. There was mopping up to do, and a points system was in place to regulate the discharge of service men and women.

That December, Bob missed the marriage of Lloydine's sister June to a fighter squadron guy she'd met at Washington State College. His name was Ted Reder. "All I knew was his name. I'd never even seen a picture of him."

On January 5, 1946, Bob's crew arrived in Atsugi, Japan. Most of the fellows were dead tired and hit the sack. But Bob and the radio operator wanted to go into the city and see what Japan was like. They were standing on a dock in a rice paddy when Bob declared:

"You know, I wouldn't trade this whole damn island for an acre in Washington!"

"Pardon me," said another GI. "Did you say 'Washington'?"

"I sure did."

"Where you from in Washington?"

"You know where Aberdeen is?"

"I sure do. I just married a girl from Hoquiam."

"Hold on. Your name can't be Ted Reder, can it?"

"It is! You're not Bob Graham are you?"

Out of hundreds of thousands of GI's deployed around the world, what are the odds of that? "Phenomenal," Graham said.

"On January 6, June's birthday, Ted and I got on a little narrow-gauge electric train and went to Atsugi. We found a telegraph office and send Lloydine's sister a telegram. That was the first time they knew where he was and that we were together."

"I still get quivers thinking about that telegram," Lloydine said.

A day or two later, as Graham was assisting with the preflight inspection for the first leg of the trip home, he glanced down at the tarmac when the fuel truck arrived. "It was my old gas man from Travis! I said, 'Hey, you got extra gas?' 'Sure thing.' So I got our pilot, co-pilot and navigator together and they figured that with the extra fuel we could fly over Hiroshima on the way to the Philippines."

Ground zero of the first atomic bomb dropped on humanity struck him as "surreal." Thousands of people had been vaporized. "I thought to myself, 'That's something pretty powerful. Something pretty terrible.' But if [Truman] hadn't dropped the bombs there would have been a heckuva lot more killed. It was a frightening thing, but I agreed with Truman."

GRAHAM HAD BEEN ACCEPTED for officer training school, but when his discharge came through on January 31, 1946, he happily headed home. Lloydine's uncle was a partner in the largest medical/dental laboratory in Los Angeles. Eyeing retirement, he offered Bob a chance to learn the ropes. After only six months, however, the Grahams grew homesick for the Northwest. Ever since his first trip to the capital as junior college student body president, Bob had dreamed of living in Olympia.

In 1947, he became a claims adjustor for the Department of Labor & Industries. He soon jumped to the Budget Office, with the promise of $25 more per month after three months. Three months came and went. Then four. Then five. Then six. Disgusted, Graham quit. A promise is a promise.

"I went back to my office, put all my private things in a cardboard box, walked out, stood on the back steps and looked over at the Capitol Building and thought, 'Boy, Graham, you're out of a job!' "

To think things over, he went to the cafeteria in the basement of the marble-lined Capitol and had a cup of five-cent coffee. Then, box in hand, he walked down the hall. "There was a sign on a door that said, 'State Auditor's Division of Municipal Corporations, Lawrence Hubble, chief examiner.' I thought, 'Well, Lloydine's folks knew a Lawrence Hubble in Hoquiam. My God, this is fate! So I walked in and told the secretary, 'I have no appointment, but I'd sure like to meet Mr. Hubble.' She said, 'He's right here, right now.' I told him the story about why I'd left Labor & Industries. I told him that working for the Auditor's Office was something I was really interested in. 'You're in luck, Bob,' he said. There was an opening. 'Let's go upstairs so you can meet Cliff Yelle,' the state auditor. It was this beautiful big office with tapestries, and I thought, 'My God, what am I doing here? I'm from Copalis Crossing!' Hubble told Cliff the story about me leaving Labor & Industries and my background in college and the service. Back then everything was political patronage. Cliff asked me a bunch of questions and talked about the role of the office. Finally, he looked at me with a squint in his eye and said, 'Bob, what kind of a Democrat are you?' I said, *"I'm a Cliff Yelle Democrat!"* The next words that came out of his mouth were 'Hire him, Lawrence!' "

Graham's laughter filled the room.

"I worked for Cliff for 17 years. He became my friend and mentor. When he told me in 1963 that he was going to retire as state auditor after 32 years, I'd held every major administrative post in the agency. I was chief examiner of the Division of Municipal Corporations. It was the major crossroads of my government career: whether I should remain on the staff and take my chances when a new man—or woman—came in after the election or run for the auditor's job myself. I chose to run. It was a hard-fought primary but I went on to win election with a 200,000-vote plurality in 1964. Over the years, I never lost an election—from president of the Newton Sunday School Choir, to student body president at Moclips and Grays Harbor Junior College and seven runs for state auditor. I also served three or four terms as elder of the Westminster Presbyterian Church here in Olympia. And I was Sunday School Superintendent for nine years."

Graham retired as auditor in 1993. His most memorable battle focused on his assertion that the Auditor's Office had the right and responsibility to conduct "performance audits" of state agencies. A fiscal audit focused only on whether appropriated funds were being spent in keeping with the law. The broader question, Graham said, "is what kind of a job are they doing with the taxpayers' money?" After considerable study and staff training, Graham's team began conducting performance audits in 1967, late in his first term. The move received national recognition. It also soon angered influential lawmakers in both parties when the Auditor's Office reported that junkets to Europe and Puerto Rico had been reimbursed on a per-mile basis rather than actual cost.

There was even talk of making the office appointive. Graham said the state auditor's job was to be an independent watchdog, without fear or favor. He recommended that the office be nonpartisan. "I ran and won seven times as a Democrat because it's a partisan office, but it shouldn't be. I was never a

'Democrat' auditor." He clashed on some occasions with three-term Governor Dan Evans, a Republican, who in 1971 signed with mixed emotions legislation prohibiting the state auditor from conducting performance audits. All things considered, "Dan Evans was probably my favorite politician," Graham said. "Very progressive and fair-minded.

"During my years we brought the office into the modern era, and I put together a great team. We were hardnosed about the law, but fair and honest. The auditor and the auditee are often pretty difficult to bring together. But invariably I was able to bring people to the point where they felt ... that they would be treated fairly. That's the thing I'm most proud of. We also had fraud investigation courses. We received national awards for our accounting department. I always said that we were the 'Largest CPA firm in the state.' The federal General Accounting Office said our agency was one of the top 10 government accounting offices in the United States."

GRAHAM KNEW AND ADMIRED one of the greatest of "The Greatest Generation"—the late Bob Bush, who grew up in Pacific County. Bush received the Medal of Honor for his heroism under fire as an 18-year-old Navy medical corpsman during the horrific battle for Okinawa in 1945. He went on to found the highly successful Bayview Lumber Company. General Jimmy Doolittle became one of his best friends after Bush was elected president of the Congressional Medal of Honor Society. Bush's life story is featured in Tom Brokaw's best-seller, *The Greatest Generation*. Is that sobriquet

Bob and Lloydine Graham in the 1980s when he was state auditor. *Robert Graham collection*

over-reaching, as some suggest?

"I hold Tom Brokaw way up there," Graham said. " 'Greatest Generation' is kind of flattery in a way. But I feel we really did something. Individually and collectively. We stepped up."

Mrs. Graham said, "We were all drawn close together by the war, culturally and emotionally. I think our kids today are having knowledge beyond what we had ever dreamed. But it's how that gets used that will matter."

Three of the Grahams' five children have key roles in state government. The other two are doing well in the private sector. There are 12 grandchildren and 15 great-grandchildren, all close by, "another blessing."

"It's their world now," Bob said.

***

When we asked the Grahams to recreate their wedding photo, Bob interrupted the photographer after the first flash, pointed to a vase on the coffee table and said, "Hand me those flowers."

Robert V. Graham died peacefully—at home in his own bed—on April 16, 2014, four days after his 93rd birthday and two weeks after our last interview.

John C. Hughes

STAN JONES

The Atomic Veteran

"This is no ordinary time," Eleanor Roosevelt said as Europe was being engulfed by war. Stanley Gale Jones, a true survivor, has lived no ordinary life. In 1943, when he was a 17-year-old drifter in his own village, Jones resolved to fight for his country and himself. He had wandered across the Tulalip Reservation for years, sleeping in one impoverished household after the other. Family had come and gone with each new roof; poverty had followed him like a faithful companion. Wearing government-surplus clothing and second-hand shoes lined with cardboard, he'd sifted worms from flour at the government commissary and gone hungry staring into barren cupboards. The Indian village still lacked running water and electricity, so he'd caught rainwater off the roof and used kerosene lamps. The reservation was only 30 miles north of Seattle, yet it seemed suspended in the 19th century.

When the surprise assault on Pearl Harbor propelled waves of new recruits into the military, the Indian teenager eventually felt a blend of hope and patriotism. Maybe he'd escape poverty and defend his country as a U.S. Marine.

Seventy years have passed since Jones and 44,000 other Native Americans risked their lives for democracy. The passage of time is etched in Jones' face. But he remains full of spirit—as proud of his military tour of duty as he is of his Indian blood. The veteran of the South Pacific can recite more Japanese than Lushootseed, the original language of the Salish tribes. His thick black hair is often tucked inside his Marine cap.

The war left emotional and physical scars. Frightening noises that pierced the humid darkness of the South Pacific stirred nightmares for years. Jones still sleeps with a knife and pistol. Occasionally, the memories rouse him from a deep slumber. "Everything comes back to me at night," Jones says. "I hear something and listen for the jungle noises. Then I wake up and realize I am at home."

Nagasaki, a city one eyewitness recounted frizzling like a baked apple after the atomic blast in 1945, rarely leaves Jones' mind. He saw something familiar in the dazed expressions of those orphans—the children mourning the abrupt loss of their parents and scavenging trash for scraps. The Japanese word for the A-bomb survivors is *Hibakusha*. For Jones, the kids' faces are indelible.

Jones' tour of duty took him from the jungles of Saipan to postwar Japan where he patrolled the ruins of Nagasaki in the aftermath of the bomb. *Stan Jones collection*

Jones couldn't believe what he found when he and 27,000 American troops occupied the devastated industrial city. They were there to defuse what was left of the Japanese war machine. A secret super bomb with unforgiving might had produced a massive fireball and black rain. In some cases, only the soot-like shadows of the victims remained. "We'd be walking around doing guard duty all through the area where the bomb was dropped," Jones remembers. "Then finally we heard, 'Get off the area! Get off the area!' We didn't understand why." Later he did. "The radiation from the atomic bomb eats your legs up. It's eaten my leg up." Jones lifts a pant leg to reveal an old battle scar. The skin is red, rippled with grafts, perpetually swollen. "It's still active," he says, referring to only one injury among a myriad of health problems he attributes to radiation exposure.

Jones first noticed the sore on his left leg after the war. While doctors diagnosed the wound as an amyloid tumor—hard masses or nodules beneath the skin—they never identified its cause. Jones filed a claim with the Department of Veterans Affairs. "I have had one large tumor removed and replaced with a muscle off my back," he wrote in his letter to the Board of Veterans' Appeals. "I am now three-quarters blind in one eye, hearing loss in both ears, and have tumors on my legs that will not heal. I do believe the tumors are attributed to the atomic radiation exposure." The board rejected Jones' claim in 2005. "I was pretty angry right off the bat," Jones concedes. "Why don't I get something for that? I was angry for a while. I might have broken some windows." His voice trails off. Jones remains disappointed, but at peace with the decision.

The Tulalip Indian moves his lean frame back in his easy chair in his home on the reservation, which has undergone something of a renaissance, thanks to a first-rate casino and discount shopping mall. He tosses a bone for his golden lab, Champ. All around are photos documenting a rare life remade by war.

STANLEY GALE JONES, "SCHO-HALLEM," was born on July 10, 1926, a descendant of the Snohomish, Snoqualmie, Squaxin, Skykomish, Clallam and Stoc-welee-jub tribes. He grew up as a timid child of the Depression. There was poverty, bullying and worse. His mother, Juanita Giddings Jones, a Klamath Indian from Monroe, died from a gall bladder infection in 1930. Stan was only 3. His father moved the children from Monroe to the Tulalip Indian Reservation to be near family. Jones spent the rest of his childhood missing the mother he barely knew.

His father remarried and fathered 14 additional children. Jones felt like a kind of misfit. He traveled from relative to rela-

Jones' parents, Juanita and George Jones. *Stan Jones collection*

George Jones Sr., a Tulalip tribal member, appears in full regalia in 1914, marking the opening of a longhouse. *Stan Jones collection*

tive on the reservation, constantly in fear of wearing out his welcome. "It was rough losing his mother at a young age like that," says JoAnn, Jones' longtime wife. "Then not knowing where he belonged afterward—[and moving] from pillar to post. Every time we'd go to a funeral, he'd get up and say, 'Well, I used to live with them.'"

Too proud to accept welfare, the senior Jones—a hardworking logger, fisherman and carpenter—took whatever jobs came his way.

Efforts to assimilate Native Americans into white culture threatened Jones' Indian identity. The Tulalip Indian School closed down in the 1930s, and Jones' presence in the Marysville public schools was unsettling to whites who didn't know what to make of a Native American.

When Jones was 9, he was taken to Cushman Indian Hospital in Tacoma. The tuberculosis sanitarium treated Native Americans in the West. "When the invaders came from the north, they gave us the gift of TB, tuberculosis," Jones says sardonically. "So many Indian people had TB and they were dying." After all he'd been through, Jones was lucky to be healthy. But his older brother, Norman, was gravely ill with TB, a disease that wreaks havoc

Decades before he would become a global ambassador for the Tulalip Tribes, Jones bounced from house to house on the Indian reservation. *Stan Jones collection*

Jones spent three difficult years in Tacoma at Cushman Indian Hospital, which included a tuberculosis sanitarium. *Tacoma Public Library*

on the body when bacteria are inhaled into the lungs.

The compound at Cushman doubled as a school because so many children were in the hospital's care. Jones says assimilation into white culture carried on there too. For speaking Lushootseed, he once had his mouth washed out with lye soap. His tongue cracked and bled. The punishments came often. During another episode, Stan was confined to a closet and overheard two nurses praying for a boy who'd just died. It was Norman, who was only 14. Stan wailed, but the nurses never heard. Norman's funeral brought Jones' only departure from Cushman Indian Hospital in three years.

A couple of years later, Bill Steve, a night watchman, returned the 12-year-old to the Tulalip Reservation. He'd been sent home for splashing water on another student. After several stops at households, Jones was finally heartily welcomed by an

How about this old time Jr. High football team? Left to right are Ralph Ebert, Ben Butters, Bud Quast, Clayton Jacobson, Bud Guetlin, George ? and Stan Jones in the line. Backfield was Paul Timm, Bubs Gross, Don Koplitz and flash George Herd the latter scoring 11 touchdowns to lead the team. They won all games and held the opposition scoreless. They were champions for three straight years back in the early 1940's.

Stan Jones collection

aunt and uncle. He spent his time hunting, fishing, swimming and playing sports. After the eighth grade, however, Jones quit school to work in the logging camps.

The attack at Pearl Harbor on December 7, 1941, the date "which will live in infamy," persuaded Jones to fight for his country. At 17, he lied about his age and joined the United States Marine Corps. He went active duty a year later.

He'd hoped to become a paratrooper, but the Marine Corps assigned him to a tank battalion because of his experience driving a caterpillar tractor at logging camps. In 1944, the recruit was at boot camp in San Diego, running until he couldn't take another step and tossing hand grenades until his arms went numb. "Your arms would be so sore," Jones remembers. "There was lots of hand-to-hand bayonet training—full packs and rifles—jumping 40 feet off a ship into the water. We trained day after day. It was really kind of a beating. It was good teaching, though."

Driving a Sherman tank was like driving a bulldozer for Jones. "I remember to this day how it works—setting the box, turning the dial until the gun quivers, then down a little while you're running over big bumps, the gun will hold the target and you shoot. We were in twin Chrysler Sherman tanks

The United States Marine Corps gave Jones a strong work ethic and self discipline, strengths he carried with him the rest of his life. *Stan Jones collection*

with smoke launchers and Thompson machine guns with a gyrostabilizer."

Jones soon found himself aboard a troop ship with 2,000 Marines, zigzagging across the sea.

DUBBED "JAPAN'S PEARL HARBOR," D-Day in the Pacific fell on June 15, 1944, among valleys of head-high sugarcane, deep swamps and jagged peaks. Saipan, one of 15 islands in the 400-mile Marianas chain, promised strategic airfields that would place B-29 bombers within striking distance of mainland Japan. Thousands of men stormed the beaches; guns fired from armored amphibian tractors and rockets launched from gunboats. The shells rained down with pinpoint accuracy, one Marine coming ashore recalled. "All around us was the chaotic debris of bitter combat: Jap and Marine bodies lying in mangled and grotesque positions; blasted and burnt-out pillboxes; the burning wrecks of LVTs that had been knocked out by Jap high-velocity fire; the acrid smell of high explosives; the shattered trees, and the churned-up sand littered with discarded equipment. Then the shells really began to pour down on us: ahead, behind, on both sides, and right in our midst. They would come rocketing down with a freight-train roar and then explode with a deafening cataclysm that is beyond description."

Troops established a beachhead and moved inland. In the jungles, Jones drove *Aloha*, his Sherman tank, and hunted for Japanese stragglers. "It reminded me of hunting deer back home," he says. "We had to walk silently—tiptoeing through the jungle and trying to catch them. Usually we would go in three-man patrols, but sometimes it was just the two of us."

"Every day was scary. A lot of the time, we were in tanks. But some of the time we were on foot searching for Japanese soldiers in caves. We got to be an expert in searching the caves and the jungle at Saipan. We never thought we were coming back. We were willing to give up our lives."

When the afternoon light faded, Jones patrolled the jungle to guard the ammunition tent or attempted sleep with a knife and pistol under his pillow. "Was I scared? *Yes*. [The jungle was literally alive] with noises, such as birds and other animals moving, and you never knew who or what was out there. The enemy is all through the area. You'd hear a noise and it would get you alert. Sometimes, you'd have to shoot around the area to find out what it was. Then you'll see somebody else there. They'd come out. But if it was the enemy they'd take off. "I was the only one that had to do guard duty alone. I know they were prejudiced against me because I'm Native American, and my papers said 'Indian.' So, I had my own big tent. There were bunks in that tent, but you wouldn't sleep in the bunk. You'd put something in the bunk that looks like somebody was there, then you'd sleep back on the ground and have your submachine gun and listen for the noise."

Savage fighting erupted around Mount Tapotchau. Eventually, the Japanese were trapped in the northern part of the island. In a final suicidal "banzai" charge, the largest of the war, 3,000 Japanese troops perished. The battle also killed more than 3,000 American troops, but the Japanese fared worse. Of 30,000 troops, only 1,000 survived when the island was secured on July 9. Japanese civilian deaths, the result of mass suicides, were deemed heroic by the Japanese government. General Saito, who died after the battle by ritual suicide, had labeled the Japanese civilians martyrs: "There is no longer any distinction between civilians and troops. It would be better for them to join in the attack with bamboo spears than be captured."

The 2nd Marine Division with a captured Japanese tank in Saipan, 1944. The battle for Saipan in World War II was dubbed "Japan's Pearl Harbor." *U.S. Marine Corps*

In the summer of 1945, as Jones was preparing to invade Japan, he heard the big news: an atomic bomb had detonated over a tennis court in Nagasaki—the second blow to the country in three days. "When they told us Japan had surrendered, and two atomic bombs leveled two cities of Hiroshima and Nagasaki, we felt relief. We were going to make it back home. I felt elated."

Some of the Japanese were unaware that the war had ended and hid in caves. "When another Marine and I were doing guard duty at night, we were by a river and my partner lit a match for his cigarette," Jones remembers. "Shots rang out across the water, bouncing next to us. We learned our lesson. I never smoked and if he lit up I stood far away from him."

THE B-29 SUPERFORTRESS *BOCKSCAR* flew over Nagasaki, its second target, on August 9, 1945. At 11:02 a.m., it let loose a massive hurricane of melted glass, fire and debris. The nuclear blast pulverized buildings, incinerated people and reduced nearly three square miles to ashes. An estimated 76,000 people were killed or injured.

More powerful than *Little Boy*, the atomic bomb dropped on Hiroshima, *Fat Man* was filled with plutonium-239. The to-

The plutonium-filled weapon known as "Fat Man" detonated over Nagasaki at 11:02 a.m. on August 9, 1945, killing an estimated 60,000 people. This picture of Ground Zero captures the aftermath of the blast. *Joe O'Donnell*

pography of Nagasaki lessened its impact, but the horrors were unimaginable just the same.

When the 2nd Marine Division arrived at the industrial center in September, the port city was in rubble. Roughly 70 percent of Nagasaki had been destroyed. Streets were filled with remains of the dead; the dazed wounded walked the rubble in shredded clothing. City hospitals, a skeleton of what they once were, offered no place to die with dignity. Thirty-two first aid stations and 18 of the city hospitals were destroyed in the nuclear blast. Ninety percent of the doctors in Nagasaki were injured or killed. In one of the few remaining hospitals, eight physicians and eight nurses treated more than 10,000 patients. "The people there were no longer the enemy, they were people in need of help, desperate, starving, suffering and dying," Jones says. "It was like a living hell. We could see the Mitsubishi factory, which was one of the targets. All the steel frames were bent in one direction, with all metal coverings blown away. I saw older people and children with scarred faces and pieces of hair hanging on their heads. Many of the people that I talked to probably died within a year or two."

Jones arrived in Nagasaki in September 1945. "The people there were no longer the enemy. They were people in need of help—desperate, starving, suffering and dying." Joe O'Donnell

Fearful Japanese fled to the hills amid rumors they would be brutalized or killed. "The men were mainly hiding out in the woods. They were really afraid. So, we more or less came in and took over the area. I always said, [speaking in Japanese] 'I'm Mr. Jones. I'm from the 2nd Marine Division. Don't be afraid. You will not be hurt. Surrender.'"

The atomic bomb orphans—their lives forever changed—wandered the rubble in uncounted numbers. Burned and disfigured, they scavenged trash cans for food and slept in the open.

Jones was so haunted by the young survivors that he began delivering his rations to them with any leftovers he could smuggle from the officers' quarters as a military cook. "We'd see a lot of food, dump it into our big sack and go visit the areas. We would give them food like that because they didn't have any. And they were happy. We made a lot of friends."

Yet hostility remained in postwar Nagasaki. One day as Jones returned to the barracks, Japanese civilians clubbed him. The assault left the young Marine with a broken upper jawbone and partial hearing loss in one ear.

After nine months, Jones' tour of duty came to an end. It was the summer of 1946. Jones boarded the troop ship holding a bouquet of flowers, a gift from the Japanese people.

STANLEY JONES RETURNED FROM THE WAR wiser and matured. He'd lost part of his youth, but developed a work ethic that would serve him well the rest of his life. Jones wore his Marine dress blues when he arrived in Marysville by train. He was unsure where to go. Eventually, Jones settled on his father's house and knocked on the front door. "Stanley!" his stepmother cried.

In 1948, JoAnn Barrie, 15, a student at Seattle's Cleveland High School, "handpicked" Stan after admiring his picture in a friend's wallet. Their 65-year union has produced four children, and a bevy of grandchildren, great-grandchildren and great-great-grandchildren. Humor is always present in the household.

Jones is perhaps best known for his indelible mark on Indian Country. Prompted by Harriette Shelton Dover, the second woman to

JoAnn and Stan at their wedding in 1950. The bride turned 17 the day after the ceremony. *Stan Jones collection*

Jones, longest-serving board member of the Tulalip Tribes, poses with the late Billy Frank Jr., chairman of the Northwest Indian Fisheries Commission, and Glen Gobin, vice chairman of the Tulalip Tribes. *Stan Jones collection*

serve on the Tulalip board of directors, Jones ran for a position in 1966. Over the course of 44 years, he made history as the longest-serving board member. He spent 26 of those years as a chairman known for his disarming and persuasive leadership style. He became a global ambassador for the Tulalip Tribes, a visionary behind the lucrative Quil Ceda Village retail center in Marysville, a preservationist of Native culture, a crucial activist in the fight for Indian fishing rights and a friend of some of the most notable leaders of our time. He's met Bill Gates, Donald Trump and U.S. presidents. Framed photos of Jones with Jesse Jackson and Bill Clinton hang on the walls of his Tulalip home.

And in the summer of 2015, the proud U.S. Marine prepares to pose for another photograph. He flashes a smile and slips on one

Known for his disarming leadership style, Jones has met some of the most prominent leaders in American politics. The Tulalip notes that he once sat in President Clinton's chair at the White House and felt at ease. *Stan Jones collection*

Jones remains as proud of his tour of duty as he is his Indian heritage. Above, the tribal leader holds a paddle, quipping that it resembled one used by tribal canoeists in the "very first navy" at Everett. *Mate 2nd Class Eli J. Medellin/U.S. Navy*

of his most treasured possessions—a black leather vest with the words *Atomic Veteran* stitched in yellow.

Trova Heffernan

BIBLIOGRAPHY

FRED SHIOSAKI

Allerfeldt, Kristofer, *Race, Radicalism, Religion, and Restriction: Immigration in the Pacific Northwest*, 1890-1924, Praeger Publishers, Westport, Conn., 2003

Ambrose, Stephen E., *The Victors*, Simon & Schuster, New York, 1998

Asahina, Robert, *Just Americans, How Japanese Americans Won a War at Home and Abroad*, Gotham Books, New York, 2006

Atkinson, Rick, *The Guns at Last Light, The War in Western Europe, 1944-1945*, Henry Holt & Co., New York, 2013

Crost, Lyn, *Honor by Fire, Japanese Americans at War in Europe and the Pacific*, Presidio Press, Novato, Calif., 1994

De Nevers, Klancy Clark, *The Colonel and The Pacifist*, University of Utah Press, Salt Lake City, 2004

Dickerson, James L., *Inside America's Concentration Camps*, Lawrence Hill Books, Chicago, 2010

Duffy, Peter, *Double Agent*, , N.Y., 2014

Grizzle, Charles R., *Riding the Bomb*, Plateau Publications, Spokane, 1994

Jordan, Jonathan W., *American Warlords*, NAL Caliber, New York, 2015

Kaufman, Robert G., *Henry M. Jackson, A Life in Politics*, University of Washington Press, Seattle, 2000

Kent, Deborah, *The Tragic History of the Japanese-American Internment Camps*, Enslow Publishers Inc., Berkeley Heights, New Jersey, 2008

McCaffrey, James M., *Going for Broke, Japanese American Soldiers in the War Against Nazi Germany*, University of Oklahoma Press, Norman, 2013

Newton, Jim, *Justice for All, Earl Warren and the Nation He Made*, Riverhead Books, New York, 2006

Okihiro, Gary Y., and Myers, Joan, *Whispered Silences, Japanese Americans and World War II*, University of Washington Press, Seattle, 1996

Reeves, Richard, *Infamy, the Shocking Story of the Japanese American Internment in World War II*, Henry Holt & Co., New York, 2015

Robinson, Greg, *By Order of the President, FDR and the Internment of Japanese Americans*, Harvard University Press, Cambridge, 2001

Russell, Jan Jarboe, *The Train to Crystal City*, Scribner, New York, 2015

Shimabukuro, Robert Sadamu, *Born in Seattle, The Campaign for Japanese American Redress*, University of Washington Press, Seattle, 2001

Smith, C. Mark, *Raising Cain, The Life and Politics of Senator Harry P. Cain*, Book Publishers Network, Bothell, Wash., 2011

Stanley, Jerry, *I am an American*, Crown Publishers Inc., New York, 1994

Steidl, Franz, *Lost Battalions, Going for Broke in the Vosages Autumn 1944*, Presidio Press, Novato, Calif., 1997

Ward, Geoffrey C., *The War*, Alfred A. Knopf, New York, 2007

Weglyn, Michi Nishiura, *Years of Infamy, The Untold Story of America's Concentration Camps*, University of Washington Press, Seattle, 1996

Yenne, Bill, *Rising Sons, The Japanese American GIs Who Fought for the United States in World War II*, Thomas Dunne Books, St. Martin's Press, New York, 2007

Other key Sources:

Densho, The Japanese American Legacy Project: www.densho.org

Densho Encyclopedia, A free on-line resource about the history of the Japanese American WWII exclusion and incarceration experience: encyclopedia.densho.org

Densho oral history clips:

Deciding to Volunteer for the Army - Masao Watanabe: Masao was born in

Seattle and was working in the Pike Place Market when the war started. He talks about his decision to volunteer for the Army while he and his family were incarcerated at the Minidoka, Idaho camp. www.youtube.com/watch?v=ZsZ2Ev9uBEI&list=PL_txUBUpMcH58AjpXD6xN9nEGolH5hırl&index=3

The Rescue of the "Lost Battalion" - Fred Shiosaki: Fred describes his personal involvement when the 442nd fought to rescue the Lost Battalion. www.youtube.com/watch?v=Oi6Yosy4Fw8&list=PL_txUBUpMcH58AjpXD6xN9nEGolH5hırl&index=7

442nd Regimental Combat Team Ordered to Pass in Review - Rudy Tokiwa: Rudy describes the aftermath of rescue when only about 800 men (out of a regiment of 3,800) were able to parade in front of the commanding general. www.youtube.com/watch?v=4AZmEfzdqTM&list=PL_txUBUpMcH58AjpXD6xN9nEGolH5hırl&index=1

Meeting a Member of the "Lost Battalion" After the War - Fred Shiosaki: Fred describes his angry response when he meets one of the men he helped save. www.youtube.com/watch?v=XWpH_Skg9yE&list=PL_txUBUpMcH58AjpXD6xN9nEGolH5hırl&index=8

Go For Broke National Education Center: www.goforbroke.org/about_us/about_us_educational.php

442nd Regimental Combat Team Historical Society Website: www.the442.org

HistoryLink.org, *The Free Online Encyclopedia of Washington State History,* www.historylink.org

Four-Four-Two, F Company at War, a compelling documentary on the 442nd Regimental Combat Team: vimeo.com/128020556

Regina Tollfedlt

Baime, A.J., *The Arsenal of Democracy,* Houghton Mifflin Harcourt, Boston/New York, 2014

Bowden, Ray, *Plane Names & Bloody Noses,* Volume 2, Design Oracle Partnership, Dorset, England, 2000

Bowman, Martin, *B-17 Combat Missions*, Barnes & Noble, New York, 2007

Case, Betsy, *Trailblazers, The Women of the Boeing Company*, Boeing, Seattle, 2014

Freeman, Roger A., *The Mighty Eighth*, Cassell & Co., London, 2000

Grimm, Jacob L., *Heroes of the 483rd*, 483rd Bombardment Group Association, 1997

Jablonski, Edward, *Flying Fortress*, Doubleday & Co., New York, 1965

Jackson, Robert, *The B-17 Flying Fortress*, MBI Publishing Co., Osceola, WI, 2001

Kaplan, Philip, *Bombers, The Aircrew Experience*, Barnes & Noble Books, New York, 2000

Le Strange, Richard, *Century Bombers*, 100th Bomb Group Memorial Museum, Great Britain, 1989

Miller, Donald L., *Masters of the Air*, Simon & Schuster, New York, 2006

Moorhouse, Roger, *The Devils' Alliance, Hitler's Pact with Stalin, 1939-1941*, Basic Books, New York, 2014

Myers, Polly Reed, *Boeing Aircraft Company's Manpower Campaign during World War II*, Pacific Northwest Quarterly, Vol. 98, No. 4, Fall 2007

Perret, Geoffrey, *Winged Victory*, Random House, New York, 1993

Warren, James R., *The War Years, A Chronicle of Washington State in World War II*, University of Washington Press, Seattle, 2000

YouTube videos:

"Battle Stations B-17" www.youtube.com/watch?v=0Mj3W5vjNiw

War Department film of the famous *Memphis Belle*:
www.youtube.com/watch?v=9LZP5R109yo

Boeing's camouflaged Plant No. 2 in Seattle:
www.youtube.com/watch?v=NA5JIrLep6k

Restored footage of the first B-17 mission over Europe:
www.youtube.com/watch?v=OoIZoKehoBw

B-17s in combat: www.youtube.com/watch?v=gpXMeVD6CpI

Official USAAF training film of B-17s over Germany:
www.youtube.com/watch?v=HwlVH5KcWSs&list=PL74EED5B008FBC47E

"Living Legends": A simulated B-17 flight:
www.youtube.com/watch?v=nsPjn1Loelw

Jay Leno gets a B-17 tour from a tail gunner:
www.youtube.com/watch?v=OjRQXjcY6uo

Startup and takeoff of the restored *Sentimental Journey*:
www.youtube.com/watch?v=2GlJvFLo59w

Loading bombs on a B-17:
www.youtube.com/watch?v=nQhUhoOYqrs

Restored B-17 at an air show:
www.youtube.com/watch?v=LFRJutxsbYg

"Bombing up" at the Museum of Flight:
www.youtube.com/watch?v=RvOWH-YZtKk

Bob Hart

Ambrose, Stephen E., *Band of Brothers*, Simon & Schuster, New York, 2001

Citizen Soldiers, The U.S. Army from the Normandy Beaches to the Bulge to the Surrender of Germany, Simon & Schuster, New York, 1997

Archer, Clark L., *Paratroopers' Odyssey, A History of the 517th Parachute Combat Team*, 517 Parachute Regimental Combat Team Association, Hudson, Fla., 1985

Astor, Gerald, *Battling Buzzards, The Odyssey of the 517th Parachute Regimental Combat Team 1943-1945*, Donald I. Fine Inc., New York, 1993

A Blood-Dimmed Tide, The Battle of the Bulge by the Men Who Fought It, Donald I. Fine Inc., New York, 1992

Churchill, Winston, *Triumph and Tragedy,* Houghton Mifflin Co., Boston, 1953

517th Parachute Infantry Regiment Unit History, 13th Airborne Web page, www.ww2-airborne.us/units/517/517.html, condensed from *Paratroopers' Odyssey*

517 Parachute Combat Team souvenir booklet, Attack, 1945, Washington State Archives and Robert D. Hart collection

Graves, Rupert D., *The History of the 517th Parachute Infantry Regiment,* 517prct.org/documents/13th_airborne/13th_airborne_book.htm

Kagan, Neil, and Hyslop, Stephen G., *Eyewitness to World War II,* National Geographic Society, Washington, D.C., 2012

MacDonald, John, *Great Battles of World War II,* Chartwell Books, New York, 2014

Miller, Donald L., (revising original text by **Commager, Henry Steele**), *The Story of World War II,* Simon & Schuster, New York, 2001

O'Donnell, Patrick K., *Beyond Valor, World War II's Ranger and Airborne Veterans Reveal the Heart of Combat,* The Free Press, New York, 2001

Stolley, Richard B. (editor), *Life: World War 2,* A Bullfinch Press Book, Little Brown and Co., New York, 2001

Zaloga, Steven J., *Operation Dragoon 1944: France's Other D-Day,* Osprey Publishing, New York, 2009

YouTube videos:

www.youtube.com/watch?v=EzOdPPAkhWo
www.youtube.com/watch?v=P_Iu0Vu9Reo
www.youtube.com/watch?v=DWTE8nYarUM
www.youtube.com/watch?v=8a8fqGpHgsk
www.youtube.com/watch?v=guJE71blP1o

Arnold Samuels

Aly, Gotz, *Why the Germans? Why the Jews: Envy, Race Hatred and the Prehistory of the Holocaust*, Metropolitan Books, New York, 2011

Baker, Nicholson, *Human Smoke: The Beginnings of World War II, the End of Civilization*, Simon & Schuster, New York, 2014

Breitman, Richard, and Lichtman, Allan J., *FDR and the Jews*, the Belknap Press of Harvard University Press, Cambridge, 2013

Dunn, Susan, *1940: FDR, Willkie, Lindbergh, Hitler—the Election amid the Storm*, Yale University Press, New Haven, 2013

Ferguson, Niall, *Kissinger, Volume I, 1923-1968: The Idealist*, Penguin Press, New York, 2015

Goldsmith, Martin, *Alex's Wake*, Da Capo Press, Philadelphia, 2014

Isaacson, Walter, *Kissinger: A Biography*, Simon & Schuster, New York, 1992

Kaye, Harvey J., *The Fight for The Four Freedoms*, Simon & Schuster, New York, 2014

Kershaw, Alex, *The Liberator*, Crown Publishers, New York, 2012

Larson, Erik, *In the Garden of Beasts*, Crown, New York, 2011

Lower, Wendy, *Hitler's Furies: German Women in the Killing Fields*, Houghton Mifflin Harcourt, Boston/New York, 2013

Manning, Molly Guptill, *When Books Went to War: The Stories that Helped us Win World War II*, Houghton Mifflin Harcourt, Boston/New York, 2014

McMillan, Dan, *How Could This Happen: Explaining the Holocaust*, Basic Books, New York, 2014

Moore, Deborah Dash, *GI Jews: How World War II Changed a Generation*, The Belknap Press, Cambridge, Mass., 2006

Rosen, Robert N., *Saving the Jews, Franklin D. Roosevelt and the Holocaust*, Thunder's Mouth Press, New York, 2006

Sacco, Jack, *Where the Birds Never Sing: The True Story of the 92nd Signal Battalion and the Liberation of Dachau*, Regan Books, New York, 2003

Schruers, Fred, *Billy Joel: The Definitive Biography*, Crown Archetype, New York, 2014

Shirer, William L., *20th Century Journey, Volume II, The Nightmare Years, 1930-1940*, Little, Brown & Company, Boston, 1984

Townsend, Tim, *Mission at Nuremberg*, William Morrow, New York, 2014

Wheeler, Leigh Ann, *How Sex Became a Civil Liberty*, Oxford University Press, 2013

Morris Troper and the Passengers of the *St. Louis*:
www.youtube.com/watch?v=ROTmhh6C8Ng

Documentary on the Nazis rise to power and the concentration camp at Dachau (Warning: some footage is horrifying):
www.youtube.com/watch?v=DXMqEpp3gSQ

SOURCE NOTES

FRED SHIOSAKI

"You fought not only the enemy," Truman addressing the 442nd, NBC Learn, archives.nbclearn.com/portal/site/k-12/flatview?cuecard=1356

Spokane 99.1% white, 1940 U.S. Census, *Characteristics of Spokane Population*, p. 408

"patriotic ties to Japan," *Colonel and the Pacifist*, p. 148

"A Jap's a Jap," quoted in *The Perilous Fight*, www.pbs.org/perilousfight/social/asian_americans

"Chills went up our spines," quoted in *Infamy*, p. 230

average height was 5-3, Ibid., p. 222

"the preservation of civil liberties," FDR, 1941 State of the Union Address ("The Four Freedoms") 1-6-1941, voicesofdemocracy.umd.edu/fdr-the-four-freedoms-speech-text

"fancy-named concentration camps," *Years of Infamy*, p. 218

Spokane and state census statistics, 1940 U.S. Census data, p. 408, 304, 346

"Fully 90 percent of the vegetables," *The Internment Camps, Dateline: Northwest*, A Living Textbook Supplement, Seattle Post-Intelligencer, 1976, Washington State Library

Nearly 26,000 Japanese came to Washington, *Race, Radicalism*, p. 160

Kisaburo Shiosaki's path to Spokane, Patricia Bayonne-Johnson, *Northwest Railroad Pioneer Kisaburo Shiosaki*, 4comculture.com, 4comculture.com/other-cultures/northwest-railroad-pioneer-kisaburo-shiosaki

Hillyard neighborhood, Jim Kershner, *Spokane Neighborhoods: Hillyard*, HistoryLink.org Essay 8406: www.historylink.org/index.cfm?DisplayPage=output.cfm&file_id=8406

"George set a bad example!" Floyd Shiosaki to author, 6-18-2015

"didn't really grasp," Ibid.

"My friends were still my friends," also described in Fred Shiosaki Interview Segment 12, Densho, 2006, archive.densho.org/main.aspx, and Jim Kershner, *An American Story*, Spokesman-Review, 4-15-2001

"I'm just too busy," the 2015 version of this story told to the author for Legacy Washington was related largely the same as in Fred Shiosaki Interview Segment 1, 2003, Densho, archive.densho.org/main.aspx; Fred Shiosaki Interview Seqment 11, Densho, 2006, archive.densho.org/main.aspx; and in Kershner, *An American Story*, Spokesman-Review, 4-15-2001. In the Kershner interview, however, Shiosaki says his father replied, "By god, I'm just too busy."

"Seattle Japs Who Disobeyed Orders," AP Wirephoto caption in Spokesman-Review, 12-11-41

"I am Chinese," Julie Sullivan, *Freedom Fighters*, Spokesman-Review, 8-13-95

"great body" of U.S.-born Japanese, *An Important Precaution*, Spokesman-Review, 12-9-41, p. 4

"nothing could be more unjust, *Let Us Do No Shameful Wrong*, Spokesman-Review, 12-11-41, p. 4

"Mad Brute" gorillas and "Huns," Samuel Walker, *In Defense of American Liberties: A History of the ACLU*, p. 15

"every dirty yellow tooth," Stirlings office supply ad, Grays Harbor Washingtonian, page H-3, 5-8-1945

"just a bunch of opera singers," quoted in Tom Santopietro, *The Godfather Effect*, p. 60

Our Enemy: The Japanese, U.S. Office of War Information, archive.org/details/OurEnemy1943

"from which any or all," quoted in *By Order of the President*, p. 108

"Executive Order 9066 was unprecedented," Ibid.

"farcical and fantastic stuff," quoted in *Infamy*, p. 24

"a substantial majority," Ibid., p. 45

"one of the gross absurdities," *Years of Infamy*, p. 42

"Be as reasonable as you can," quoted in *American Warlords*, p. 147

"I am determined," quoted in Ibid., p. 77

"I can't believe that any informed," Magnuson quoted in *The Internment Camps, Dateline: Northwest*, A Living Textbook Supplement, Seattle Post-Intelligencer, 1976, Washington State Library

"plans to make Spokane a dumping ground," Carl Quackenbush quoted in Ibid.

4,500 Japanese moved to Spokane County, Kershner, *An American Story*, Spokesman-Review, 4-15-2001

"Are we drawing attention," Ibid.

"rolling through" and "Hey, you Japs!" quoted in *Infamy*, p. 70

"We might as well be honest," Ibid., p. 20

"It was a terrible scene," Fred Shiosaki Interview Segment 17, Densho, 2006, archive.densho.org/main.aspx

"Purple Heart Battalion," Rudi Williams, American Forces Press Service, *The "Go for Broke" Regiment: Lives Duty, Honor, Country*, DoD News, 5-25-2000, www.defense.gov/news/newsarticle.aspx?id=45180

"Exempt from conscription" and "boys as young as 15," *Conscription*, The Pacific War Online Encyclopedia, pwencycl.kgbudge.com/C/o/Conscription.htm

"I thought that I would be exempt," Mutsuo (George) Shiosaki letter to Congressman Walt Horan, R-Wash., 5-19-1958, Washington State University Libraries Collection number: Cage 192, Box number: 388, Folder number: 7570

"boldly facing murderous fire," quoted in *Rising Sons*, Appendix 3

Rome to Arno casualties, 442nd Historical Society, *Facts about the 442nd,* www.the442.org/442ndfacts.html

14,000 men had served in the 442nd, Ibid.

"Steep, wooded and nearly trackless," *The War,* p. 276

"sense of nightmare," quoted in Ibid., p. 278

"Humorless, blunt, and given to brooding," *Guns at Last Light,* pp. 209-210

"desk-jockey" general, Jim Saito, Los Angeles, Letter to the Editor, Vox Populi, NCRR Nikkei for Civil Rights and Redress 9/15/06

"violated every principal of leadership and tactics," Colonel Young O. Kim, (U.S. Army Ret.), quoted in 100th *Bn. Losses attributed to poor leadership,* The Hawaii Herald, 7-16-1982

"a bunch of damn liars," quoted in *The War,* p. 278

"a gantlet of machine guns," *Stand Where They Fought,* standwheretheyfought.jimdo.com/the-vosges-2009-battle-of-bruy%C3%A8res-and-the-relief-of-the-lost-battalion-by-the-442nd-rct-then-and-now

"strips of toilet paper," *Honor by Fire,* p. 185

"that seemed interminable," "someone would fall down," "We cannot move," includes elements from Densho, Interview Segment 8, 2003-2004, archive.densho.org/main.aspx

Outnumbered at least four to one," *Rising Sons,* p. 166

"Order your men to fix bayonets," quoted in *Honor by Fire,* p. 191

"Those are my boys," Ibid.

Grabbing the general by his lapels, *Riding the Bomb,* p. 144

Close call with artillery, *Honor by Fire,* p. 191

Caught him in his arms, *Going for Broke,* p. 266

"It astounds me," quoted in *Just Americans,* p. 190

Franz Steidl's view of Dahlquist, *Lost Battalions*, p. 146

"narrow forested ridge," *The War*, p. 286

using his body to protect a wounded soldier, *Just Americans*, p. 170

"We didn't care anymore," quoted in *Infamy*, p. 229

With "fearless courage," quoted in *Just Americans*, p. 200

"Patrol from 442nd here," quoted in *Lost Battalions*, p. 95

"It was the happiest day of my life," quoted in *Going for Broke*, p. 270

"It was really ironical, Ibid.

"the first time he'd seen the colonel cry," Densho oral history interview with Rudy Tokiwa, 4/9/2015, archive.densho.org/main.aspx

"Dahlqust called out the ravaged 442nd ...," *Honor by Fire*, p. 199

"Let bygones be bygones," *The War*, p. 289; *Honor by Fire*, p. 202

Nisei vet rebuffed by Spokane VFW, Julie Sullivan, *Freedom Fighters*, Spokesman-Review, 8-13-95, p. E1

"shoddy new government facilities," *Infamy*, p. 273

"It was quite a shock," Floyd Shiosaki to author, 6-18-2015

"a bunch of Japs," Densho Interview Segment 43, 2006, archive.densho.org/main.aspx

"so rummy," Ibid.

"screaming again," Ibid.

"part of your psyche," Ibid.

Shiosaki attends opening of Go For Broke!, Jim Camden, *For Fred Shiosaki, 'War' is personal*, Spokesman-Review, 9-29-07, p. 1

"My mother was just hilarious," Shiosaki to Ikeda, Densho Segment 45, 2006, archive.densho.org/main.aspx

"By god, you had a piece of this one," Ibid.

"I have always felt America is my country," Mutsuo (George) Shiosaki letter to Congressman Walt Horan, R-Wash., 5-19-1958, Washington State University Libraries Collection number: Cage 192, Box number: 388, Folder number: 7570

State Department reversal, Ibid., U.S. Department of Justice letter to Emanuel Celler, chairman, House Judiciary Committee, 12-30-1958; also: *Unwilling Fighter Keeps Citizenship*, Spokane Daily Chronicle, 12-15-1958

"felt it necessary to assure," Jim Kershner, *Spokane's Japanese Community*, HistoryLink File No. 8048

Details of 1988 redress legislation, Sharon Yamato, *Civil Liberties Act of 1988*, Densho Encyclopedia, encyclopedia.densho.org/Civil_Liberties_Act_of_1988/

"They risked their lives," quoted in *Just Americans*, p. 8

"People forget," quoted in "In Time of War," Stories & Quotes, Whitworth Today magazine, www.whitworth.edu/Library/Archives/CurrentProjects/TimeofWar/Index.htm

Clayton Pitre

Interview, Clayton Pitre, Montford Point Marine, 2015

Montford Point Marine Association, www.montfordpointmarines.com/History.html

Bernard C. Nalty, *The Right To Fight: African-American Marines In World War II*, 2013

Interview, Joseph Geeter, past president, Montford Point Marine Association, 2015

100 Milestone Documents, National Archives, www.ourdocuments.gov

Interview, James Averhart, president, Montford Point Marine Association, 2015

Dr. Charles P. Neimeyer, *Giants Among the Marine Corps,* Fortitudine, Vol. 37, Number 2, 2012

James H. Dormon, *Creoles of Color of the Gulf South,* 1996

Sybil Klein, *Creole, The History and Legacy of Louisiana's Free People of Color,* 2000

United States Federal Censuses—1870, 1880, 1900, 1910, 1920, Ancestry.com

Lemelle Birth & Marriage Records, Opelousas, St. Landry, Louisiana, Ancestry.com

Carl A. Brasseaux, Claude F. Oubre, *Creoles of Color in the Bayou Country,* 1994

The Historic New Orleans Collection—Williams Research Center

The City of Opelousas, History, www.cityofopelousas.com

Dr. Melton A. McLaurin, *The Marines of Montford Point: America's First Black Marines,* 2009

Battle of Okinawa, The History Channel, www.history.com

Walter Hazen, *American Black History,* 2004

Montford Point Marines (1942-1949), www.blackpast.org

Cheryl Devall, Daily World, *Opelousas' Black History, Written and Lived,* February 26, 2015

Henry I. Shaw, Jr., Ralph W. Donnelly, *Blacks in the Marine Corps,* U.S. Marine Corps, 1975

Morris J. MacGregor, Jr., *Integration of the Armed Forces 1940-1965,* 2012

Jeanette Steele, *For first black Marines, Finally a Medal,* 2012

Montford Point Marines, San Diego State University Library, 2013

Regina Tollfeldt

"Four million were young," Kevin Starr, *Embattled Dreams: California in War and Peace, 1940–1950*. Oxford University Press 2003, p. 129.

"15,000 women" at Boeing, Myers, *Boeing Aircraft Company's Manpower Campaign*, p. 192

"A dozen a day," Betsy Case, *Trailblazers, The Women of the Boeing Company*, p. 18

J. Neils Lumber Company during the Depression, Patricia Neils, *Julius Neils: Lumber Baron*, The Pacific Northwest Forum, Vol. 5, No. 3, Summer 1980, www.narhist.ewu.edu/pnf/articles/s1/v-3/Julius%20Neils/juliusneils.html

"eight branch plants in Western Washington," Myers, *Boeing Aircraft Company's Manpower Campaign*, p. 183

"elegance and impression of power," Jackson, *The B-17 Flying Fortress*, p. 12

The Girl Mechanic's Manual, Julie McDonald Zander, *Chehalis*, Images of America Series, Arcadia Publishing, Charleston, S.C., 2011, pp. 104-107

"The Flying Fortress," Bill Yenne, *Hap Arnold*, Regnery History, 2013, p. 64

"The Navy jealously maintained," Jackson, *The B-17*, p. 17

Haggling over price, Jablonski, *Flying Fortress*, p. 25

Cost of B-2 bomber, Kris Osborn, *B-2 Bomber set to receive massive upgrade*, DoD Buzz, Military.com, 6-25-2014

"Boeing had used its own funds," Jablonski, *Flying Fortress*, p. 16

"behind Portugal and only slightly ahead of Bulgaria," W. Gardner Selby, *U.S. Army was smaller*, Austin-American-Statesman, 6-13-2014

"the great arsenal of democracy," FDR, Fireside Chat transcript, 12-29-1940, The American Presidency Project, www.presidency.ucsb.edu/ws/?pid=15917

Boeing worker totals, "peaked at 31,750" and "amidst the growth," Myers, *Boeing Aircraft Company's Manpower Campaign*, pp. 183-184

44 percent of the workforce, Ibid., p. 185

Boeing help wanted ad, reproduced in Ibid., p. 189

"Women were considered too stupid," quoted in Ibid., p. 184

"I had to work with a man ...who hated me," Ibid.

38 died in accidents, WASP Facts, wingsacrossamerica.us/wasp/facts.htm

"finally lifted the ban," Myers, *Boeing Aircraft Company's Manpower Campaign*, p. 187

"system of work permits," Ibid.

"although racial tensions," Ibid., p. 191

"The wing, in fact, was exactly the same," Jablonski, *Flying Fortress*, p. 312

When the censors cracked down, Bowden, *Plane Names and Bloody Noses*, p. 11

"The fighters are our salvation," Winston Churchill, 1940, inscription on Bomber Command Memorial, London

"It came with a high tingle factor," Geoffrey Perret, *Winged Victory*, p. 27

"The best combat plane ever built," quoted in Kaplan, *Bombers*, pp. 66-67

"Meyer's trumpets," Joe Guttman, *Why did Goering say 'You can call me Meyer'?* Historynet, www.historynet.com/why-did-goering-say-you-can-call-me-meyer.htm

A new aircraft every five minutes, Baime, *The Arsenal of Democracy*, p. 252

"Of the 416,800 American battle deaths," Ibid., p. 288

Bob Hart

"Only about 20 percent landed within the drop zone," 517th Unit History, www.ww2-airborne.us/units/517/517.html

"into a state of chaos," Col. Rupert D. Graves, *517th Parachute Infantry History, Book VII*, 517prct.org/documents/13th_airborne/13th_airborne_book.htm

Each group "was met at the station," 517th Unit History

"used whistles to form them up," *Battling Buzzards*, p. 53

C-47 would drop 50,000 paratroops, Len Cacutt, *The World's Greatest Aircraft*, Exeter Books, New York, NY, 1988

"stuffed their M-1s in the golf bags," *Battling Buzzards*, p. 78

"shivering and knee-deep in mud," 517th Unit History

"despite desperate attempts," *Attack*, p. 5

"But you are foolhardy," quoted in Ibid.

"escape kits" and last-minute preparations, Ibid., p. 8

"scattered as far as 44 kilometers," Ibid. and *Operation Dragoon*, www.517prct.org/documents/airborne_invasion/airborne_invasion_history.htm

"Instead of a bitter battle" and casualty numbers, *Operation Dragoon 1944*, introduction and p. 6

"Yet he was still capable," *Eyewitness to World War II*, p. 282

"I have just made a momentous decision," Ibid.

"Eisenhower suspected something was afoot," *Triumph and Tragedy*, pp. 272-273

Eisenhower's bet with Montgomery, *The Story of World War II*, p. 337

"broke down into an every man for himself," *A Blood-Dimmed Tide*, p. xi

Some as young as 15, *The Story of World War II*, p. 338

Casualty figures, *Band of Brothers*, p. 173

Winter boots in short supply, *The Story of World War II*, p. 351

"amputation preferable to gangrene," Edward Watson, *A Rifleman in World War II*, p. 15

"Russians love watches," Kevin Conley Ruffner, *The Black Market in Postwar Berlin*, Prologue Magazine, Fall 2002, Vol. 34, No. 3

"the snap of hot lead," *Attack*, p. 3

ARNOLD SAMUELS

"thousands of students," Manning, *When Books Went to War*, p. 6

"Jewish intellectualism is dead!" Ibid.

a "bibliocaust," Ibid.

"We couldn't go anywhere," Isaacson, *Kissinger*, p. 27

"Aryan" racial purity, *The Nuremberg Laws*, American-Israeli Virtual Library, www.jewishvirtuallibrary.org/jsource/Holocaust/nurlaws.html; also The Nuremberg Race Laws, U.S. Holocaust Memorial Museum, http://www.ushmm.org/outreach/en/article.php?ModuleId=10007695

"Nazism was propelled," Aly, *Why the Germans? Why the Jews?*, p. 2, 5

Ernst's background, "Morris Ernst, 'Ulysses' Case Lawyer, Dies," New York Times, 5-23-1976; Wheeler, How Sex Became a Civil Liberty, pp. 41-42, 62

Family connection to Arnold Samuels, John F. Samuels to author, 2-18-15

"in the name of preserving," Schruers, *Billy Joel*, p. 14

"likely to become a public charge" clause, Larson, *In the Garden of Beasts*, p. 31

"Jewish activists charged," Ibid.

"I know some of you think," Baker, *Human Smoke*, p. 68

"guinea pigs in an experiment," Eyewitness to History, *The Bombing of Guernica*, www.eyewitnesstohistory.com/guernica.htm

"many Cubans resented," U.S. Holocaust Memorial Museum, *Voyage of the St. Louis*, www.ushmm.org/wlc/en/article.php?ModuleId=10005267

"too much power," Larson, *Garden of Beasts*, p. 41

SOURCE NOTES 251

"Sailing so close," U.S. Holocaust Memorial Museum, *Voyage of the St. Louis*, www.ushmm.org/wlc/en/article.php?ModuleId=10005267

"hanging between hope and despair," telegram from passengers, U.S. Holocaust Memorial Museum, digitalassets.ushmm.org/photoarchives/detail.aspx?id=1127120

"I was lucky," Schruers, *Billy Joel*, p.13

part of Patton's Third Army, Ibid.

Minorities served in higher percentages, Kaye, *Four Freedoms*, p. 107

"stereotypes portrayed Brooklyn Jews," Moore, *GI Jews*, p. 32

Samuels arrived at Marseille, *Narrative History*, 70th Infantry Division Association, www.trailblazersww2.org/pdf/70thnarrativetoJan3145.pdf

crack SS mountain troops, Ibid.

the Nazis held on, *The Capture of Saarbrücken*, 70th Infantry Division Association, www.trailblazersww2.org/history_capturesaarbrucken.htm

their colonel rushed over, Kershaw, *The Liberator*, pp. 285-288

had castrated a prisoner, Ibid., p. 283

"I said farewell to my youth," Isaacson, *Kissinger*, p. 51

His goal had been to murder, McMillan, *How Could This Happen*, p. 1

"the universal poisoner of all peoples, *Hitler's Political Testament*, ihr.org/other/hitlertestament.html

discovered by another German-born, *German-born U.S. soldier*, Washington Post, 2-10-2010, www.washingtonpost.com/wp-dyn/content/article/2010/12/09/AR2010120906180.html

By the fall of 1945, Townsend, *Mission at Nuremberg*, pp. 113-116

"Suddenly the Army needed men," Ferguson, *Kissinger*, p. 159

"We know you're not important," Isaacson, *Kissinger*, p. 49

Samuels "lost no time," Ferguson, *Kissinger*, p. 191

Pew Center study on anti-Semitism, Emma Green, *The Increasing Harassment of Jews Around the World*, The Atlantic, 2-26-2015, www.theatlantic.com/international/archive/2015/02/the-world-is-becoming-more-hostile-toward-jews/386165/

I Am War, thedailyworld.com/opinion/columnist/i-am-war-forget-me-not

A day in the life of an infantryman, from *Up Front*, Bill Mauldin, Henry Holt & Co. New York., 1945, pp. 19-20; also quoted in *A Life Up Front*, Todd DePastino, W.W. Norton & Co., 2008, pp. 143-144

Stan Jones

Interview, Stan Jones, U.S. Marine Corps, June 2015

Stanley G. Jones, *"Our Way" Hoy yud dud*, 2010

America Goes To War, National World War II Museum, New Orleans

Sherry Guydelkon, 2005 *Directory of Tulalip Veterans*

George Weller, *First Into Nagasaki*, 2006

Hiroshima and Nagasaki Occupational Forces, Defense Threat Reduction Agency

Letter to Board of Veterans Appeals, Department of Veterans Affairs, 12/27/2005

Cushman Indian Hospital, Image Archives, Tacoma Public Library

40 Years After Pacific D-Day, No Crowds And No Parades, The New York Times, 1984

John C. Chapin, *Breaching the Marianas*: The Battle for Saipan, 1994

James Lewis, *World War Two: Pacific War*

Japan Under American Occupation, youtu.be/AuPYzWnT1aA

Radiation Dose Reconstruction, U.S. Occupation Forces in Hiroshima and Nagasaki, Japan, 1945-1946, Science Applications, Inc. for the Defense Nuclear Agency

Discharge Papers, Stanley G. Jones, U.S. Marine Corps, 1946

Turner Publishing Company, *Heritage Years: Second Marine Division 1940-1999,* 1999

VA Programs For Veterans Exposed To Radiation, Department of Veterans Affairs, 2002

The Atomic Bombings of Hiroshima and Nagasaki, atomicarchive.com

Joe O'Donnell, *Japan 1945, A U.S. Marine's Photographs from Ground Zero,* 2005

Claim Letter, Department of Veterans Affairs, December 27, 2005

Fact Sheet, Department of Veterans Affairs, September 2002

Harriette Shelton Dover, *Tulalip From My Heart,* 2013

INDEX

- Symbols -

2nd Marine Division 228
2nd Parachute Brigade, British 123
3rd Army 139
3rd Infantry Division 176
VIII Bomber Command 80
8th Air Force 80, 128
9th Air Force 141
36th "Texas" Division,
 U.S. Seventh Army 25
42nd Infantry Division 178
45th Infantry Division 178
70th Infantry Division 157, 174-176
82nd Airborne Division 99, 121
84th Infantry Division 182
94th Division 138, 139
100th Infantry Battalion 20
101st Airborne Division 99, 121, 127, 128
429th Fighter Squadron 141
442nd Regimental Combat Team 1, 3, 20-26, 28- 33, 35, 113
517th Parachute Regimental Combat Team ("Battling Buzzards") 108, 109, 110, 115, 117, 120-125, 127-129, 131, 134, 135

- A -

Aberdeen, Wash. 16, 66, 67, 70- 72, 74, 80, 83, 187, 190, 199, 201, 203, 204, 206- 208, 212, 213
Aberdeen Daily World, The 190
Aberdeen High School 201, 206
Action Comics 13
Aeronautical Mechanics Union, Local 751 78
Air Transport Command 195, 210
Alaska Airlines 133
Alsace-Lorraine 25, 176
Aly, Götz 164
American Civil Liberties Union 166
American Lake Veterans Hospital 134
Amundson, Les 86, 87
Ancestry.com 111
Antwerp, Belgium 126, 169, 170
Anzio, Italy 23, 111, 124

Ardennes, Belgium 126, 127
Army Specialized Training Program, ASTP 23, 175
Arno River, Italy 24
Aryan "racial purity" laws 164
Astor, Gerald 128
Atlanta, Georgia 175
Atomic bombs 34, 55, 58, 82, 195, 211, 213, 220, 221, 227, 228
Atsugi, Japan 213
Auschwitz 169, 171
Autobahn 184
Austro-Hungarian Empire 65, 66
Averhart, James 41, 42, 44
Axis 74, 166
"Axis Sally" 122

- B -

B-17 "Flying Fortress" 64, 71, 76, 77, 80-82, 87, 113, 128, 149
B-24 "Liberator" 80, 81
B-29 "Superfortress" 73, 81, 82, 225, 227
Bad Königshofen im Grabfeld, Germany 159, 165
Bad Muskau, Germany 152
Baime, A.J. 82
Baldwin, Stanley 167
Barkdoll, Inez 111
Bastogne, Belgium 127, 128
Battle of the Bulge 110, 111, 116, 125, 127, 128, 130, 135, 139, 196
Battle of Dunkirk 94
Battle of Monmouth 91
Bavaria 157, 159, 160, 164
Bayou Country 41, 47, 59
Bayou Courtableau 46
Bayview Lumber Company 216
Bellingham, Wash. 31, 71
Belorussia 92
Bendetsen, Karl 4, 15, 16, 19, 207-209
Bensheim, Germany 182-184
Berle, Milton 185
Berlin, Germany 86, 87, 123, 131, 132, 151, 162, 167, 177, 180
Billings, Montana 111

Black Market 132
"Bockscar" (B-29) 227
Boeing Company 64, 71-82
Boeing Company Plant No. 2 64
Bonner, John 117, 120, 135
Brandenburg Gate 132
Brandeis, Louis 166
Broadway-Edison Tech 59
Brokaw, Tom 216, 217
Brooklyn, N.Y. 167, 171
Browning machine gun 119
Browns Point, Wash. 134
Bruyères, France 25
Buchenwald 145-151, 155, 168
Buck, the Rev. Howard P. 212
Budd Inlet 105
Bund Deutscher Mädel, (BDM) the league of German girls 162
Burns, Ken 25
Bush, Bob 216

- C -
C-47 107, 118, 123
C-54 195, 210
Cain, Harry P. 17
Calamity Jane 111
Campbell, Bill 199
Camp Beauregard, Louisiana 50
Camp Croft, Spartanburg, S.C. 174, 175
Camp 5, Glenwood, Wash. 68-70
Camp 7, Glenwood, Wash. 69
Camp Lejeune, N.C. 51
Camp Mackall, N.C. 118, 119
Camp Polk, Louisiana 50
Camp Shelby, Mississippi 20,
Camp Toccoa, Georgia 114-116
Cavett, Dick 134
Central Area Motivation Program 60
"Champagne Campaign" 33, 124
Chehalis, Wash. 67, 71
Cheney, Wash. 204
Cherbourg, France 100, 102, 126, 130
Champion International 209
Choir of the West, Pacific Lutheran University 83
Churchill, Winston 80, 93, 94, 99, 122, 127, 157, 188
City College, N.Y. 175

Civil Liberties Act of 1988 210
Civitavecchia, Italy 24, 121
Clallam Tribe 221
Clinton, Bill 38, 230
Clover Park Vocational-Technical Institute 133
Cochran, Eddie 97, 99, 102
Columbia Union High School 70
Columbia University 173
Communist Party 146, 161, 185
Congressional Gold Medal 39, 42, 59
Consolidated Aircraft Corp. 80
Cotentin Peninsula, France 99
Copalis Crossing, Wash. 195, 198, 199, 214
Copalis River 198
Côte d'Azur 108, 122
Coughlin, Father Charles 168
Counter Intelligence Corps, CIC 181-184
Cuba 158, 168, 171
Cushman Indian Hospital 223

- D -
D-Day 24, 89, 94, 100, 102,104, 105, 107, 121, 124, 225
de Nevers, Klancy Clark 207, 208
D&R Theater, Aberdeen, Wash. 83
Dahlquist, Major General John E. 25-27, 29, 30, 32, 33
Dachau, Germany 157, 158, 161, 171, 178 180, 183, 188
Dafter, Michigan 198
Darmstadt, Germany 182
Davenport Hotel, Spokane 6
Davion, Marie-Jeanne 64
De Gaulle, Charles 110
Densho 36
Detroit, Mich. 31, 68
DeWitt, General John 15
Dill, Clarence C. 205
Dole, Elizabeth 104
Doolittle, General Jimmy 216
Dover, Harriette Shelton 229
Dreeszen, Doug 199, 200
Dreux, France 141, 144
Dutch Resistance 87
Duwamish Waterway 71

- E -
Eaker, Brigadier General Ira 80
Elks Club 189
English Channel 89, 98, 99, 101
Eniwetok 211
Eisenhower, General Dwight D. "Ike"
    93, 99, 122, 127
Erasmus Hall High School 172
Ernst, Morris L. 166, 167
Ettersberg, Germany 145
European Theater Intelligence School,
    Oberammergau, Germany 183
Evans, Gov. Dan 216
Everett, Wash. 16, 60, 71, 133, 231
Executive Order 8802 42, 43
Executive Order 9066 15

- F -
Fat Man (atomic bomb) 227
FBI 2, 4, 11, 13, 14, 21, 207
Ferdinand, Archduke Franz 65
Ferguson, Niall 182, 184
Ferndale, Wash. 142, 155
Fife, Wash. 113
Flatbush Jewish Center 173
Florence, Italy 24
Ford Motor Company 68
Fort Benning 117
Fort Bragg, N.C. 33, 119
Fort Douglas, Utah 21
Fort Leonard Wood, Missouri 175
Fort Lewis, Wash. 105, 108, 113, 133
Fortune magazine 169
Frank, Billy Jr. 230
Fresnes Prison 145
"40 et 8" French railcars 124, 125
4-H Club 200
Foubert, Ed 35
Frascati, Italy 122, 123
Freehold, N.J. 92
French Foreign Legion 136
French Legion of Honor 104, 110, 134
French Riviera 123
Friedman, Henry 192, 193
Furth, Germany 163

- G -
Gates, Bill 230

Geeter, Joe 45, 52
Geneva Convention 147
Georgia Tech 175
General Accounting Office 216
Gestapo 86, 145, 162, 165, 168, 177, 182,
    192
GI Bill 34, 60, 133, 185
GI insurance 114
Gifford Pinchot National Forest 68
Go For Broke! (film) 35
Goebbels, Joseph 162
Gobin, Glen 230
Goldsmith Bros. 174
Göring, Hermann 81
Gonzaga University 8, 20, 34, 35, 39
Graham, Hazel Smith 198
Graham, Lloydine Ryan 195, 198, 200,
    211-214, 216
Graham, Ralph "Moonie" 196
Graham, Ralph V. 198
Graham, Robert V. 195-217
Grasse, France 124
Grays Harbor, Wash. 2, 4, 66, 67, 70,
    71, 186, 195, 197, 198, 200-207, 215
Grays Harbor Junior College 197, 201,
    204, 206, 215
Great Depression 92, 168, 201
Great Escape, The (film) 151
"Greatest Generation, The" 135, 195,
    216, 217
Guam 44
Guernica, Spain 168
Gulf War 64
Gustav Line 22

- H -
Halifax, Nova Scotia 96
Hamburg, Germany 165, 167, 168
Hammelburg, Germany 160, 161, 163
    165, 177, 178, 183, 187
Hart, Bob 106-136
Hart, Frances 111
Hart, Karl 134
Hart, Kathleen Williams 109, 110, 133, 134
Havana, Cuba 168
Hayes, Floyd 55
Hawaii National Guardsmen 20-22, 33
Hebrew Tech 172

Heidelberg, Germany 181, 182
Heller, Heinz ("Henry") 165, 184, 167
Heller, Joseph 107
Hess, Rudolf 159
Hibakusha (A-bomb survivors) 220
Hicks, George 99
Hickam Field 211
Hillyard Laundry 6, 9, 10
Himmler, Heinrich 150
Hindenburg airship 91
Hiroshima, Japan 34, 58, 211, 213, 227
Hitler, Adolf 13, 24, 25, 44, 60, 64, 72, 81, 91, 96, 110, 113, 122, 126, 131, 145, 157, 159, 161-168, 171, 180, 181, 188, 206
Hitlerjugend (Hitler Youth) 162
Hofstetter, Markus 161, 178, 186
Holcomb, Major General Thomas 44
Holocaust 157, 158, 162, 169, 170, 188, 192, 193
Holocaust Center for Humanity, Seattle 193
Holland 87, 165
Honolulu, Hawaii 186, 211
Hood River, Ore. 34
Hoover, J. Edgar 4, 166
Hope, Bob 210
Hoquiam, Wash. 13, 67, 70, 71, 195, 197-200, 211-214
Hoquiam High School 199
Horan, Walt 37
Hubble, Lawrence 214
Humptulips 195, 198
Hyslop, Stephen G. 126
Ickes, Harold 4

- I -

Indian Guides 134
International Association of Machinists 78
Ikeda, Tom 36
Inouye, Daniel 25, 38
Iron Curtain 185
Iwo Jima 44

- J -

J. Neils Lumber Company 68, 69
Jackson, Gene "Cubby" 200

Jackson, Henry M. "Scoop" 16
Jackson, Jesse 230
Jacksonville, N.C. 41, 50
Jehovah's Witnesses 146
Jersey Central Power Company 92
"Jim Crow" laws 4, 47
Joel, Billy 158, 171
Joel, Gunter 168, 170, 171
Joel, Helmut (later Howard) 168, 171
Joel, Johanna 158, 168, 169, 170, 171
Joel, Karl 168
Joel, Leon 158, 168, 169, 170, 171
Joel, Meta 162, 168
Johnson Island 211
Johnson, Lyndon B. 205
Jones, George Sr. 221, 222
Jones, JoAnn Barrie 222, 229
Jones, Juanita Giddings 221
Jones, Norman 222, 223
Jones, Stanley G., "Scho-Hallem" 218-231

- K -

Kagan, Neil 126
Kamikaze suicide bombers 53, 54, 57, 103, 211
Kesselring, Albert 22
King Roller Rink, Tacoma 113
Kissinger, Henry (originally Heinz) 163, 175, 180-184
Klamath Tribe 221
Klickitat County, Wash. 68, 69, 80
Königshofen, Germany 159, 165
Krefeld, Germany 182
Kristallnacht 146, 165
Kwajalein 53, 210, 211

- L -

Labbe, Charlotte 46
Lakehurst, N.J. 91
Lake Limerick 110
Lakewood High School 92
Lamason, Phil 150
Langlie, Gov. Arthur B. 16, 204, 205
LaRiviere, John Robert 138, 139
Larson, Erik 167
Lemelle, Francois 45-47
Lewis, Sinclair 30
Lewis, Wells 30

Les Arcs, France 109, 124
Libby, Montana 66-68
Lichtenstaedter, Siegfried 164
Lincoln High School, Tacoma 112
Lindbergh, Charles 72
Little Bighorn 111
Little Boy (atomic bomb) 227
Little League baseball 134
Locke, Gov. Gary 37
Low Countries 126
Los Angeles, Calif. 16, 18, 214
"Lost Battalion" 3, 27, 29, 30
LSTs (Landing Ship Tank) 93-99, 102, 103, 105
Luce, Henry 166
Luftwaffe 72, 94, 143, 168
USS LST-501 93, 96, 102
Lushootseed 219

- M -
M-1 rifle 108, 119, 146
Macy's 185
McQueen, Steve 151
MacArthur, General Douglas 34
Magnuson, Warren G. 16, 17
Malmedy Massacre 127
Manalapan, New Jersey 91, 92
Maritime Alps 33, 109, 125
Marseille, France 24, 102, 103, 122, 125, 126, 175
Marshall Islands 72, 122, 210, 211
Martin, Gov. Clarence D. 204
Marysville, Wash. 222, 229, 230
Mason County, Wash. 110, 135
Marshall, General George C. 122
Marx, Groucho 166
Mauldin, Bill 35, 191
McChord Field 105
McDade, Charles 116, 135
Medal of Honor 38, 216
Mediterranean 24, 103, 107, 122
Mein Kampf 63, 91, 159
Meingasner, Edward 117, 120, 135
Memphis Belle (B-17) 80
Mencken, H.L. 166
Mercedes-Benz 159, 160, 164, 171, 183, 184
Methodist Japanese Mission 7
Miami, Florida 169

Midland, Wash. 111, 112
Mitchell, Jimmy 176, 177
Mitsubishi aircraft factory 228
Moawad, Eli T. 200-203
Moclips High School 197, 199, 200, 215
Moclips, Wash. 198, 199, 200, 215
Montford Point Marines 5, 41, 42, 44, 45, 49-53, 55, 57, 59, 60
Montford Point Marine Association 42, 45, 44, 52
Montgomery, Field Marshal Bernard 127
Monroe, Wash. 221
Moore, Deborah Dash 175
Moosburg, Germany 153
Moser, Mary 141, 143
Moser, Joseph Jr. 140-155
Moser, Joseph Sr. 142
Mount Currahee 115, 134
Mount Tapotchau 226
Munro, Ralph 197
Munich, Germany 158
M.S. St. Louis 169
Mussolini, Benito 64, 92, 122, 166, 206
Myers, Polly Reed 73, 78

- N -
Nagasaki, Japan 34, 58, 220, 227-229
Naples, Italy 22, 120, 132,
Napoleon 104, 110
Narozonick, George 88-105
Narozonick, Stanley 91, 92
Narozonick, Vila Hanaford 104, 105
National Bank of Commerce 66
Netherlands, The 87, 170
New York Daily Mirror 170
New Yorker magazine 166
New York University 185
Newton School 198, 199
Newton Sunday School Choir 215
New Zealand 142, 150
Nooksack River 142
Normandy Invasion 90, 99, 102, 104, 118, 121, 122, 123, 139
North Coast News 187
Northern Pacific Railway 198
Northwest Indian Fisheries Commission 230

Nuremberg, Germany 153, 164, 180, 181, 183

- O -
Ocean Shores, Wash. 71, 157, 159, 186-189
O'Neill, Thomas P., "Tip" 205
Okubo, Jim 31, 38
Okinawa 21, 53-58, 103, 216
Oldsmobile 112, 113
Olympic Games (Berlin 1936) 165
Omaha Beach 99, 100
Ontario, Canada 198
Opelousas, Louisiana 45, 46, 49
Operation Anvil 102
Operation Dragoon 102, 103, 107, 122, 123
Operation Neptune 98
Operation Overlord 100
Operation Revival 87
Oriental Trading Company 5
Oriental Art Store 206

- P -
Pacific Beach, Wash. 71
Pacific Northern Railroad 134
Pacific Theater 52, 210
Paine Field, Everett 133
Panama Canal 53
Patton, George S. Jr. 29, 127, 131, 138, 139, 171, 177, 178
P-38 141, 143, 144, 148, 155
Pearl Harbor 1, 2, 8, 13, 15, 19, 50, 53, 71, 73, 113, 143, 174, 207, 219, 224-226
Pearsall, John 204-206
Pegler, Westbrook 208
Peleliu 44, 45
Perret, Geoffrey 80
Pew Research Center 188
Philippines 185, 186, 213
Pike Place Market 75
Pitre, Clayton 40-61
Pitre, Edgar 48
Pitre, Emmett 48
Pitre, Eugenie 48, 49
Pitre, Gilbert 48, 49
Pitre, Gilda 48
Pitre, Gloria 59, 60
Pitre, John 48
Pitre, Wilfred 48

Pitre, Willie 48
Pisa, Italy 24
Poland 64-66, 73, 91, 151, 153, 167, 193
Port of Grays Harbor 206
PTSD 136
Puget Sound 5, 75, 105, 204
Pullman, Wash. 3, 5, 20, 200, 207
Purple Heart 3, 23, 110
Pursall, Lt. Col. Alfred 28, 29, 31, 33
Puyallup, Wash. 111, 198

- Q -
Quackenbush, Carl 17
Queen Anne Hill 75
Quinault Nation 200
Quil Ceda Village 230

- R -
Rayonier Inc. 70
RCA Institute School of Radio Technology 173, 174
Reagan, Ronald 38, 210
Red Cross 151
Reder, Ted 213
Remagen, Germany 177
Renton, Wash. 73
Rhine River, Germany 25, 177, 182
Rhone Valley 25, 124
Riverside Dairy 198
Robinson, Greg 15
Rockwell, Norman 63
Rogers High School, Spokane 7, 14, 37
Roma (Gypsies) 146
Rome, Italy 22-24, 120-122, 134
Rosenthal, Lieutenant Robert "Rosie" 81
Rosie the Riveter (song) 63
Roosevelt, Eleanor 219
Roosevelt, Franklin D. 1, 4, 13, 15-20, 42, 72, 100, 143, 153, 166, 169, 170, 206, 208
Ross and Cromarty County, Scotland 197
Ruffner, Kevin Conley 132
Ryan, June 213
Ryukyus Islands 53

- S -
SA "Brownshirts" 159, 164
Saarbrücken, Germany 177

Saar River 177
Saint-Dié, France 25, 28
Salvation Army 187
Skykomish Tribe 221
Snohomish Tribe 221
Snoqualmie Tribe 221
Squaxin Tribe 221
Stoc-welee-jub Tribe 221
S.S. Manhattan 167
St. Landry Parish 46
St. Michael's Church, Olympia 104
Saints' Pantry Food Bank 110, 134, 135
Saipan 53, 211, 220, 225, 226
Saito, Dahlia 206
Saito, Lincoln 206
Saito, Morse 206
Saito, Natsu 2, 207
Saito, Perry 2, 197, 206-210
Saito, Ransaku 206
Saito, General 226
Salerno, Italy 22
Samuel, Blanka Sichel (later Samuels) 160, 162, 163, 168
Samuel, Emanuel 166, 167
Samuel, Max 167
Samuel Sichel Platz 187
Samuel, Wilhelm "Willi" (later Samuels) 159
Samuels, Arnold (originally Kurt Daniel Samuel) 156-190
Samuels, Frank L. 167
Samuels, Jerry (originally Gerhard Samuel) 174
Samuels, Margaret Ernst 166, 167
Samuels, Phyllis Krasner 173, 177, 184-187
San Diego, Calif. 17, 18, 55, 56, 224
Sanford, Terry 135
Sarajevo, Yugoslavia 65
Siegfried Line 139, 164, 176
Saturday Evening Post 19, 63
Savina, Frank 66, 70
Savina, Tony 66
Sawina, Gizela Stor 66-68
Sawina, John 65
Sawina, Valentine (later Walenty) 65-67
Sawina, Viola 70, 71, 73, 74, 75, 81, 83
Sampson Naval Training Station,

Seneca, New York 92
Scheldt Estuary, Belgium 126
Scotland 197, 198
Sears & Roebuck 185
Seattle Post-Intelligencer 5
Seattle Parks and Recreation 39
Seattle Seahawks 154
Seattle Times, The 72
Seattle University 59
Shelton, Wash. 110, 134, 135
Sherman Tank 94, 95, 224, 225
Shipton, Elmer 113
Shiosaki, Blanche 6-9, 37
Shiosaki, Floyd 6-9, 34
Shiosaki, Fred 1-39
Shiosaki, George 2, 6-9, 19, 23, 34, 37
Shiosaki, Kisaburo 2, 5-8, 36
Shiosaki, Lily Nakai 33, 35-37, 39
Shiosaki, Michael 37-39
Shiosaki, Nancy 37, 39
Shiosaki, Roy 6-9, 19, 23, 35, 36
Shiosaki, Tori 2, 6-9, 36
Sichel, Fanny 160, 162, 165
Sichel, Rosa 162
Sichel, Samuel 160, 187
Sinti (Gypsies) 146
Slovenia 64-66
Smith, L.T. 198
Snohomish County, Wash. 134
Soissons, France 125
Sospel, France 124, 125
South Pacific 105, 131, 174, 196, 219
Spanish Civil War 150
Sperry Flour Company 133
Spokane Air Pollution Control Authority 37
Spokane Health Department 35
Spokane Valley 38
Spokane VFW Post 33
Spokesman-Review, The 10, 12
Spremberg, Germany 153
SS (Schutzstaffel) 145
SS Totenkopfverband 179
Stalag Luft I 87
Stalag Luft III 151
Stalag VII/A 153
Stalin, Joseph 73, 112
Stanford Law School 15, 208

Starkey, Lt. Carl 108, 116, 124, 129
Stars and Stripes 191
Statue of Liberty 168, 170
Steve, Bill 223
Stuhler, Alfred 186
Stumpf, Herr 164
Stuyvesant High School 172-174
Superman 13
Symchuck, Julia 192
Switzerland 142, 171

- T -
Tacoma, Wash. 5, 17, 71, 108, 112, 113, 133, 134, 154, 222, 223
Terrace Heights School 201
Trautloft, Hannes 150, 155
Temple Beth Israel 16, 187
Thalmann, Ernst 145, 146
The Girl Mechanic's Manual 71
Third Reich 23, 72, 80, 157, 167, 168, 197
Tidball, Lewis C. 201-205
Tientsin, China 58
Time magazine 162
Tinian 211
Todd Pacific Shipyards, Tacoma 113
Todd Shipyard, Seattle 59
Tollfeldt, Regina Sawina 62-85
Tollfeldt, Roy 66, 83, 85
Tomiko, Higa 58
Tokyo, Japan 2, 37
Torquay, England 98
Toulon, France 102, 103, 122
Travis Field 211
Treaty of Versailles 161
Tremont Temple, Bronx, N.Y. 165
Troper, Ethel 169
Troper, Morris 169
Truman, Harry S. 1, 33, 55, 214
Tulalip Indian School 222
Tulalip Reservation 219, 223
Tuskegee Airmen 5
Twibell, Charles 117
Twelve O'Clock High (B-17) 80

- U -
Ulysses (novel) 166
University of Washington 35

U.S. Air Force 80, 86, 113, 128, 142, 143, 149, 186, 195
U.S. Army Strategic Communications Command 186
U.S. Holocaust Memorial Museum 169
U.S. Marine Corps 2, 5, 41, 42, 44, 45, 50-55, 57-60, 225
U.S. Navy 20, 50, 59, 60, 72, 75, 89, 92, 97, 100, 103, 104, 216
U.S. Office of Military Government, OMGUS 181
U.S. Office of War Information 13
U.S. State Department 20, 37, 167, 169, 170
U.S. War Department 72
USS Ancon 99
USS Bladen 53
USS LST-282 103
Utah Beach 90, 99, 100

- V -
V-2 rocket 149
Van Syckle, Edwin 190
Vatican 122
Veterans Administration ("VA") 110
Voice of America 185
Yale University 167
Yelle, Cliff 214, 215
Yelm, Wash. 112
Vietnam 119, 135, 136
VFW 33, 187, 188
Vosges Mountains 3, 25, 27, 29, 35

- W -
Waffen SS 24, 127
Wagner, Joseph (Arnold Samuels' wartime alias) 177
Wake Island 186
Walla Walla, Wash. 80, 87
Wallgren, Mon 16
Ward, Geoffrey C. 25
War Manpower Commission 73
Weimar Republic 146, 157, 159
Weiss, Arnold 181
Warren, Earl 4, 16, 19
Washington State Auditor's Office 195, 214-216
Washington State Budget Office 214

Washington State Department of Labor
& Industries 214
Washington Division of Municipal
Corporations 214, 215
Washington Fish and Wildlife
Commission 37
Washington Fish and Wildlife
Department 38
Washington State Ecological
Commission 37
Washington State College 200, 207, 213
Washington State Board for Vocational
Education 82
Washington State Division of
Vocational Rehabilitation 64, 83
Washington Water Power Company 37
Wellesley College 166
Western Airlines 134
Westinghouse Corp. 173
Westminster Presbyterian Church 215
White, E.B. 166
Whitefish, Montana 8
White Salmon, Wash. 68-70
Whitworth College 20
Winchell, Walter 166
"Willie and Joe" 191
Williams, Richard 72
Wilson, Woodrow 65
Women in Black 64
Wood, R.J. 44
Works Progress Administration
("WPA") 112, 201
World's Fair, New York (1939) 173
World War I 12, 50, 66, 125, 159, 161,
165, 188
Wounded Warriors 136
Würzburg, Germany 165, 188
Wyman, Kim 105

- Y -
Yontan Airfield 57
Yugoslavians 65

- Z -
Zaloga, Steven J. 124

*With gratitude to generous donors of the
Washington State Heritage Center Trust
who made the publication of this book possible.*

Gerry Alexander	Loralee Koetje
Jan Ames	Robert Lovely
Dave Ammons	Patricia Mack
Jean Brechan	Laurie Maricle
Jim Bricker	Alex McGregor
Norwood Brooks	C. Louise Miller
Marty Brown	Laura Mott
Norm and Suzanne Dicks	Ralph Munro
Lori Drummond	Vila Narozonick
Pat and Susan Dunn	Mark Neary
Wayne Ehlers	Sally Paxton
Candace Espeseth	Frances Pettit
Dan and Nancy Evans	Clayton Pitre
Slade Gorton	Paul Razore
Daniel Grimm	Samuel and Patricia Smith
Charles Hansen	Edwin Sterner
Bob Hart	Elizabeth Stricklin
J. Robin Hunt	Bette Snyder
Robert J. Doran	Regina Tollfeldt
Donna Kaminski	Betty Utter
Philip Kerrigan	Jan Walsh

Arnold Samuels with his biographer, John Hughes, before Arnold departed for a trip to Washington, D.C., to view battlefield monuments and visit the National Holocaust Memorial Museum. *Angelo Bruscas/North Coast News*

John C. Hughes is chief historian for Legacy Washington. He retired as editor and publisher of *The Daily World* in Aberdeen in 2008 after a 42-year career in journalism that saw him win awards for reporting, photography, historical features, editorials and columns. An alumnus of the University of Puget Sound and the University of Maryland, he is a trustee of the Washington State Historical Society. He is the author of seven books on Northwest history, including "Un-sold," a new biography of former congresswoman Jolene Unsoeld.

Trova Heffernan and Clayton Pitre in the Washington State Capitol. On Veterans Day in 2015 Pitre raised the 12th Man Flag for the Seattle Seahawks. *Washington Secretary of State's Office*

Trova Heffernan is director of Legacy Washington. Over a 25-year career in media and communications, Heffernan oversaw public affairs for the Secretary of State during the battle over the state primary and one of the closest governor's races in U.S. history. The former television journalist covered major breaking stories in the Pacific Northwest including the arrest of a serial murderer in Spokane and a shooting spree at a high school in Oregon. She is a graduate of the Edward R. Murrow College of Communication at Washington State University. Heffernan has authored numerous historical works on American politicians, citizen newsmakers and world renowned indigenous leaders. Her book *Where the Salmon Run, the Life and Legacy of Billy Frank Jr.* is in its third printing.